This book is a gift to

_____

From

_____

Date

_____

LIVING IN THE
POWER OF GOD

366 Devotions for a powerful life in Christ

CHRISTIAN ART
PUBLISHERS

Published by Christian Art Publishers
PO Box 1599, Vereeniging, 1930, RSA

© 2012
First edition 2012

Compiled by Sonja Oosthuizen from the following
devotionals by Solly Ozrovech:
The Voice Behind You
New Beginnings
Intimate Moments with God
The Glory of God's Grace

Cover designed by Christian Art Publishers

Set in 12 on 15 pt Palatino LT Std by Christian Art Publishers

Printed in China

ISBN 978-1-4321-0481-8

13 14 15 16 17 18 19 20 21 22 – 11 10 9 8 7 6 5 4 3 2

"My grace is sufficient for you, for My power is made perfect in weakness."

~ 2 Corinthians 12:9

This I Know

Devote yourselves to prayer, being watchful and thankful.

~ COLOSSIANS 4:2

There are many people whose lives are ruled by anxiety, worry and fear. They may be concerned about themselves or about others. They may worry about their own future or that of their country or the world.

In many cases, violence, crime, civil unrest, terrorism, or political and economic instability, are the cause of their fears and anxieties. How does one handle a situation like this?

It seems as if the apostle Paul provides the answers to these questions when he says, "Do not be anxious about anything, but in everything, by prayer and petition, with thanksgiving, present your requests to God. And the peace of God, which transcends all understanding, will guard your hearts and your minds in Christ Jesus" (Phil. 4:6-7).

Especially in circumstances of adversity, there is absolutely nothing that you can do in your own strength to solve your problem. Jesus said that without Him we can do nothing, but He also said that in God, all things are possible.

Regardless of how difficult, or how bleak the future may seem, your peace of mind is assured if you seek Jesus in quiet prayer. Prayer and meditation, accompanied by praise and thanksgiving, is the only infallible method to ensure that you will be able to confront and handle life. Do not deny yourself the opportunity to find peace in Jesus, your Savior.

How wonderful, Lord, that I may come to You for peace of mind. Thank You for hearing my prayers with love. *Amen.*

Confidence in Christ

The way of the LORD is a refuge for the righteous.

~ PROVERBS 10:29

To be forewarned should mean to be equipped to cope with every life situation. Unfortunately, many people disregard warnings and then they are surprised and hurt when they have to bear the consequences of their actions.

The Bible is full of warnings. Some have already been fulfilled, but others refer to prophecies that have not yet been fulfilled. It would seem as if current world events are inevitably moving towards a climax. The times in which we live are unparalleled in human history, and intelligent people justifiably wonder what the future holds.

People who live within God's will because they are faithful, and who believe that mankind is not controlled by fate but by a loving Creator, draw comfort from the knowledge that, despite appearances to the contrary, there is a divine plan at work in our lives.

This faith creates trust and provides hope; it conquers fear and gives the Christian disciple the ability to step into the future with confidence and with the certainty that God is still in control.

To possess this kind of faith God must stand at the center of your life. If this is the case, you will see world events in the light of the eternal design of God and you will be equipped to meet the future with confidence.

Almighty God, I believe with conviction that You are still completely in control of Your Creation as well as of the world events of our time. Once more I place my trust fully in You. *Amen.*

Be Positive

Do everything without complaining or arguing, so that you may become blameless and pure, children of God without fault in a crooked and depraved generation.

~ PHILIPPIANS 2:14-15

Circumstances in large parts of the world leave much to be desired. There are wars and rumors of wars, bitterness, poverty, famine and disasters, corruption and scandals.

If one takes stock of the situation, one can't help but feel that the world has veered far from what God meant for it to be, and that humans are abusing that which God entrusted to their care.

Consequently humankind has become unhappy, discontented and unsafe. People have developed the tendency to assume a critical and pessimistic attitude towards life in general.

Even if we accept that there is much that is wrong in the world, the fact remains that we as Christians are Christ's ambassadors, with the duty and the privilege to preserve the Christian faith in even the most negative and difficult circumstances.

If you open your life to the influence of the Holy Spirit and allow Him to strengthen your faith so that your life may bear witness to the power and glory of God's love, you cannot be anything but positive. In doing so you will uplift the spirits of those around you and once again find meaning and significance in life.

Lord, You have always been the mighty Redeemer. Use me through Your Holy Spirit to be Your witness in a negative world. *Amen.*

Life Is an Open Door

"See, I have set before you an open door, and no one can shut it."
~ Revelation 3:8 (NKJV)

There are people who complain that life is empty and meaningless. For them life is one dreary hour after the next, one uninteresting day after the other, and time drags by while they lead a useless existence. It doesn't take them long to wilt intellectually and to develop a negative, narrow-minded attitude towards life.

It is totally unnecessary for such a situation to develop in your life because Jesus Christ has given to you the promise of an abundant life – and the opportunity to experience it to the full (see John 10:10). Scripture, history and your personal experience offer ample testimony to this fact. It testifies that an ordinary, dull life is transformed by the power of the living Christ and through His Holy Spirit.

Through the wonder of God's grace, sadness is transformed into joy, defeat into victory; fear disappears; hate changes into love and despair into hope – even death becomes life. The moment you accept Christ into your life as Redeemer and Savior, everything in life gets new meaning and purpose. You enter through the door of redemption into a new world. Paul says, "Therefore, if anyone is in Christ, he is a new creation; old things have passed away; behold, all things have become new" (2 Cor. 5:17 NKJV).

This new life of abundance which Christ offers you, is yours for the taking. If you only exist, without really living, turn to Christ and He will open the door for you to a new, meaningful life.

Lord Jesus, thank You that the open door of Your grace leads me into a world where old things pass away. *Amen.*

Say Yes to Life

So we are always confident. For we walk by faith, not by sight.
~ 2 CORINTHIANS 5:6, 7 (NKJV)

Meditate on your faith for a while. When you are battling with difficulties or disappointments, or when you have to make extremely important decisions, do you trust God sufficiently to place yourself and your future unconditionally in His hands; and do you believe that, regardless of what He brings across your path, it will always work together for your good? Or do you try to struggle through the problems in your own strength?

Jesus came to confirm that God loves you unconditionally. You are precious in His sight. He died on Golgotha for you. And if that is certain, then it is equally true that Christ will not allow anything that will cause you irreparable loss. He wants what is best for you. With this assurance, you can trust God unconditionally in everything you undertake.

To ensure peace and tranquility of mind, place yourself, your plans and your problems in the hands of your Savior. Take your problems and secret fears to Him in prayer. Remember you are talking to someone who, by grace, calls you His friend.

In this way you will experience the living presence of Christ in every situation of life. He will guide you through His Spirit and accompany you to the place where you experience peace and tranquility of mind. Even though you cannot see the complete road ahead, faith will carry you through.

Lord, accompany me to the place where I can experience peace. Help me to have faith in You in every situation. *Amen.*

Jesus Is Alive Today!

He is not here; He has risen, just as He said.

~ MATTHEW 28:6

Early on the Sunday morning following the crucifixion, the women arrived at the grave of Jesus, but were met with an empty tomb. There was no sign of death, only of pulsating life. Then a messenger spoke to them, "Why do you look for the living among the dead?" (Luke 24:5). Our religion is not a death cult. Our Lord lives.

It was an extraordinary moment in the history of the world. We are elevated from mortality to true "life". He that died for our sins is not dead. He lives! We do not talk about Him in the past tense, but in the present tense. He was not, He is! He did not live, He lives! We know where He is: in the heaven of His glory where we will live with Him forever. Through His Spirit, He resides in the blessed gospel that brings hope to our despondent hearts. He is here on earth, to strengthen us, to guide us, to govern us and to inspire us to new life. Through His Spirit, He resides in the hearts that He made alive.

In conclusion, the heavenly messenger says to the women, "Then go quickly and tell His disciples: 'He has risen from the dead'" (Matt. 28:7). That is our calling and duty as His disciples: to spread the word of a living Savior. Carry the living Christ's gospel of resurrection in your heart and mouth! Its aroma should spread through the entire world to give new courage to the broken-hearted and the dying: A fragrance of life to life!

Lord, thank You that You died on the cross for me. I know that there is new life in You. Thank You that I may place my hope in You. *Amen.*

Seize the Day!

"At the time of my favor I heard you, and in the day of salvation I helped you."

~ 2 Corinthians 6:2

When you look back on the life that you have lived, you can easily point out the highlights – those special moments you will remember forever.

How wonderful it would be if every day could be lived on a high spiritual and inspirational level. The truth is that every day could be a "great" day in your life if only you appreciated and exploited the present and passing moment. Every day is a new birth with new prospects and opportunities that fall to you from the loving hand of God so that you can *live*. We must say *Yes!* to life in totality. Jesus says in John 10:10, "I have come that they may have life, and have it to the full." Accept every moment of every day as a gift of grace from the hand of God and utilize it fully. Then every day will be a "great" day.

Cherish your memories, but appreciate the importance and wonderful possibilities of "today". Your attitude towards today will influence all your tomorrows, therefore "today" could be the greatest and most creative moment of your whole life. Do not regard it as less important, but thank God for the opportunities it presents. Today you can draw on the memories of yesteryear; today you can receive forgiveness from God; today you can erase the sins and failures of the past; today you can create the foundations for an even greater tomorrow!

When I am confused and surrounded by darkness, I know that You will deliver me. Thank You for Your constant presence. *Amen.*

Christ Will Protect You

The Lord is faithful, who will establish you and guard you from the Evil One.

~ 2 THESSALONIANS 3:3 (NKJV)

There comes a time in every person's life – and especially in a Christian's life – when one falls into temptation. This doesn't necessarily mean that you are seduced into committing terrible crimes. Temptation has many faces but they all result in undermining your faith one way or another.

When facing temptation the average person will always conclude that it is impossible to resist it. In general this is true, because there is very little you can do in your own strength to overcome it. It has been proven time and time again that people are weak and easily influenced by the circumstances of the moment.

The living Christ has come to say to us that without God we can do nothing, but that with God all things are possible. This is where the tremendous message of hope and encouragement is to be found for all Christians: when all else has failed, God is still there and He is in control.

In order for you to be a stronger person, it is important that you should be able to handle your problems. You will have to overcome all those temptations that descend upon your life like a plague. That is why it is important that you should allow the Spirit of the living God to enter into your life and control it. Then you will receive the assurance and trust that Jesus Christ is with you in every temptation and every difficult situation.

Lord, with You in control of my life I can do all things. I know You will give me the strength to resist temptation. *Amen.*

God's Peace Is Unfailing

For who is God, except the LORD? And who is a rock, except our God?

~ 2 SAMUEL 22:32 (NKJV)

Every time people have a need or a problem, they turn to someone or something for help or advice. They may look for advice or tangible help from a friend, or they may look for relief in the form of some medicine or drug. Regardless of what the problem may be, they do require help in some form or another.

If you perhaps find yourself in a situation like this, you must never underestimate the omnipotence and love of God. In your efforts to handle your problems and relieve your difficulties, you should never forget the fact that the only true and effective remedy is to be found in the encompassing love and tender care that Jesus Christ bestows on all who turn to Him.

Regardless of the good intentions of every human effort it always falls short in supplying the complete healing which flows from an absolute and unconditional trust in, and surrender to, the living Christ. It doesn't matter what your problem is, the only lasting solution is to be found in the unfathomable love which God, through Jesus Christ, bestowed upon mankind.

Under no circumstances should you underestimate this glorious gift of grace. Never be too proud or too afraid to turn to Jesus. Lay all your problems at His feet. He gave His life for you and wishes to grant you the healing balm of His peace.

I want to hold on to You, Lord, help me not to turn to other things in times of need. You are my provider for everything. Thank You Father. *Amen.*

Fly with the Wings of an Eagle

Those who wait on the LORD shall renew their strength; they shall mount up with wings like eagles.

~ Isaiah 40:31 (NKJV)

Life carries a heavy burden of human pettiness. Some issues are of little importance, but others are molehills which were allowed to become mountains. An insignificant thing that is blown out of proportion; an unwatched word which causes pain that was never intended. We so easily get bogged down by things that don't really matter. The vision of what you can be is easily dimmed by a narrow-minded view and petty spirit.

A positive Christian has the ability to rise above irritations by trusting in the Lord under all circumstances and by remaining conscious of His living presence. It is impossible to be petty and narrow-minded when the love of Christ fills your heart and mind. Spreading His love by the power of the Holy Spirit means to rise above petty narrow-mindedness and to reach those heights which the God of love desires all His children to live at.

Regardless of the circumstances that you live in, you must never allow them to claim your attention to the extent that you lose sight of spiritual realities. These are the very things that add depth, purpose, meaning and direction to your existence. By developing a consciousness of the presence of the living God and by always trusting in Him, you will be able to fly like the eagles, and see things in their right perspective.

Holy Spirit, fill me with Your love so that I may be ever conscious of Your presence. *Amen.*

Blessed Assurance

Commit your works to the LORD, and your thoughts will be established.

~ PROVERBS 16:3 (NKJV)

Planning is an important aspect in every area of life. You plan for the future, for your marriage, for your money matters and for retirement. Often, the amount of time spent planning is the same amount of time it takes to execute that plan. It would be interesting to calculate how much time and energy we waste on useless planning.

There is however a method to prevent this waste of energy and to ensure that your planning will definitely be successful. It requires strict spiritual discipline to make it effective and it must be undertaken in true honesty. It also requires real faith and trust in God and in His promises.

Whatever your concern might be, lay it before God in prayer, trusting in Him completely. Talk to Him, submitting all the details concerned, tell Him about your expectations and fears, seek His all-wise guidance and ask Him for clarity and the gift of discernment and wisdom, to know and to understand when He gives you the answer.

Then you have to trust Him steadfastly, leaving the matter in His hands. In His own perfect time and way, He will show you the path. And when the Master does that, you need to move ahead obediently and gratefully, bearing in mind the glorious knowledge that He is with you every step of the way.

Dear Guide, lead me in all Your ways. Help me to follow You in obedience and thank You that You are always with me. *Amen.*

Grace and Peace

I lay down and slept; I awoke, for the Lord sustained me.

~ Psalm 3:5 (nkjv)

Insecurity leads to uneasiness and confusion. If you are insecure about your future, if you are not sure at all about the next move of your competitor in the business world, if you are all alone in the dark of night, imagining that you've heard footsteps: all these experiences lead to the uneasy combination of anxiety, concern and confusion.

Foremost in your mind is the importance of preparation and self-defence. How do you prepare yourself to handle any situation that could arise, so that you may be relatively sure of a peaceful and safe life?

Right through history it is apparent that those people who had an intimate walk with God, were exactly those who found hidden resources of power to overcome their setbacks. Those who have an unflinching faith in the living Christ will not waver or break under attacks. Those who put their trust in the all-surrounding love of Christ will not give in to the icy touch of fear.

There is no magical power in these statements. The same Christ who hushed the wind and stilled the storm at sea when the disciples were panic-stricken, is calling out to you today, "Be strong and courageous; do not be afraid!" Put your trust in Him and experience for yourself how His love and grace cause the storms in your life to subside.

O Lord, Thank You that I do not need to be insecure about anything because I am Your child and I need not fear anything. *Amen.*

When Doubt Eats at Your Heart

Woe to you who are at ease in Zion, and trust in Mount Samaria.
~ Amos 6:1 (NKJV)

Those who are too much at ease are usually woken up with a shock. History is full of many such examples. This is what led to the devastating fall of the once mighty Roman Empire. This kind of indulgent apathy has brought about the failure of business concerns. Families and marriages have been torn apart as a result of this kind of indifference. There can be no doubt in any mind that anything that is worth having is also worth nurturing. As soon as you take something of great value for granted, you are in danger of losing it.

And the Christian's faith is no exception. What in the whole world could be more precious than the church of Jesus Christ? Christ's concern for it was so great that He was willing to lay down His life for His people. The apostle of love writes that there is no greater love than this.

A great responsibility rests on you as a Christian never to take your faith for granted or to regard the church of Christ with little concern. More than anything else of great value, your faith needs to be protected and offered in service to glorify Christ.

This requires an act of total commitment to the Master from you personally. He was willing to give His life for you. What value is there for you to nurture your faith?

Faithful Guide, keep me from being too at ease in my walk of faith. Help me to strengthen and protect my faith so I can use it in Your service. *Amen.*

Trust God

I heard, but I did not understand. So I asked, "My lord, what will the outcome of all this be?"

~ DANIEL 12:8

People often find it difficult to understand God's purpose and will for their lives. They are perplexed by things that happen to them and to others around them. They try to discover a cause and reason for what happens, especially when they suffer misfortune. In their confusion they have no clear outlook on the future and as their faith diminishes, many try to place the blame on God.

The core of a strong faith is your ability to trust God completely, whatever happens. It is one thing to say that you have faith while the sun is shining and everything in your life is running smoothly. But the true test of faith comes when things turn against you; when you are tempted to question God; when you, in your despair, see no purpose or reason for your grievous circumstances.

When you study the life of Jesus Christ, you will be deeply impressed by His unshakable and unconditional trust in God. Even in the darkest moments His faith was strong enough to enable Him to carry out the will of His Father.

If you walk with God on your path of life, and if you draw your strength from Him, you will develop the ability to trust God in all circumstances. The grace of God will always be sufficient to enable you to deal with every situation in life, in the knowledge that Christ knows and cares for you and that He will do everything for your good.

Lamb of God, I look up to You to strengthen my faith through the work of Your Holy Spirit in my life. *Amen.*

God's Perfect Will

"Yet not My will, but Yours be done."

~ LUKE 22:42

It is a privilege and an untold blessing to be able to say like our Master, "Yet not My will, but Yours be done." There are so many things that happen in life; however, we must confront and handle them all.

The Lord's love for us is endlessly tender and positive. His caring for us never ends. He assures us, "Never will I leave you; never will I forsake you" (Heb. 13:5). His thoughts for us are always to our ultimate benefit. He wants us to trust where we cannot see. It is not a reckless leap in the dark, but sincere trust and faith that says, "I know for certain that God's will is best for me." This kind of faith leaves the choice up to God, with the words that His Son taught us, "Your will be done!" Then we will experience the blessed reality of His peace flowing through us and touching our innermost being, so that we will spread joy around us and to others.

Our faithful prayer every day must simply be, "Your will be done!" This is the only way in which we can get to know His peace here on earth. We must trust in Him through grace, until we meet Him face to face. Then we will understand how His perfect will functions: always for our own good and to our benefit, even though it does not immediately appear so. It is a wonderful privilege to be able to testify that our will is voluntarily subject to God's perfect will.

Eternal God and Father, thank You for sending Your Son to come and teach me what it means to let Your will be done in my life. *Amen.*

On the Way with Jesus

"I have told you these things, so that in Me you may have peace. In this world you will have trouble. But take heart! I have overcome the world."

~ John 16:33

You dare not enter the new year with your own insights or in your own strength. You need a companion and a mentor who will show you the way and guide you with wisdom. The prospect of a new year can be simultaneously exciting and upsetting: exciting because it is filled with unknown opportunities, yet upsetting because you anxiously stare into the unknown.

It is a common mistake to allow the past to cloud your view when you consider the future. Crises, financial setbacks, droughts, floods and personal disappointments tend to determine the pattern of your life. As a result you may find yourself at the gateway to the new year, full of anxiety, worry and fear about the way ahead.

More than any other time of the year, you need to make a decision to put all your trust in the triune God. He loves you and cares about you. He wants to be your companion, but the choice is yours. Steadfastly believe Jesus' promise that He has already overcome the world.

Enter into the new year holding His loving hand. He will lead you through the maze because He knows what is best for you. Your duty is to obey Him; then your fear and anxiety will be replaced by an increasing assurance that the Lord loves you. And you will become a partaker of His peace.

Savior, I thank You that You are my companion and that I can walk into this new year fully relying on You. *Amen.*

Holy and Omniscient

The Lord has established His throne in heaven, and His kingdom rules over all.

~ Psalm 103:19

In adverse circumstances, people often experience a decline in their perception of God's power and majesty. When devastated by trouble or when they experience problems, when tragedy strikes or when they encounter hardships, their faith often wanes and the obstacles of life cause them to stumble. This kind of experience is not unusual and even some of God's most devout children fall prey to it. A study of Scripture will indicate exactly how many of the well-known biblical characters fell prey to the affliction of despondency and depression.

When you find yourself in the midst of such circumstances, it is important that you should hold on to your faith and put all your trust in the victorious Christ. Meditate on Scripture and the history of the human race during times when it seemed as if evil had gained the upper hand – then pay attention to what happened when God stepped into the situation. In all the millennia since Creation, there is not one instance when the righteousness of God did not triumph over evil.

This same God wants to be your companion this year. Let your faith be powerful in all situations, believe fearlessly in the omnipotence of the living Christ and that He reigns supremely over everything and everyone. Let this be your strength and power in the new year with all its problems and demands.

Father, I find my strength and inspiration in knowing that You always triumph over evil. You have overcome the world. *Amen.*

Shield and Stronghold

The LORD is my rock and my fortress and my deliverer; my God, my strength, in whom I will trust; my shield and the horn of my salvation, my stronghold.

~ PSALM 18:2 (NKJV)

Regardless of who you are or what your circumstances may be, there comes a time in your life when you need someone you can fully trust. You might need advice, assistance or encouragement and you look for someone you can trust to assist you in your particular situation.

The problem is that people are often fickle and not to be trusted. Sometimes those you approach for help are so engrossed in their own problems that they have very little time to assist you, thus causing you to become disappointed and vulnerable.

The joy of Christianity is the fact that God is only a prayer away. Whatever your problem or need, whenever it may occur, the Lord is waiting for you to turn to Him. Submit your problems to Him as He accompanies you on the journey He has laid out for your life. Because He is omniscient, omnipotent and all-seeing, you can rest assured that His way will eventually be to your benefit.

The absolute trustworthiness of the risen Christ, who is the same yesterday, today and forever more, is your guarantee that God's way is the best for you. This fact has been proven over and over again through the years. Therefore, when you are in need, turn to Him and allow Christ to enfold you with His love and to protect and encourage you.

Lord, You are my rock and my fortress. You will deliver me from anything if I just turn to You. *Amen.*

More Than a Conqueror

Yet in all these things we are more than conquerors through Him who loved us.

~ Romans 8:37 (NKJV)

Things might seem worse to you now than they have done for many years. There might be many reasons to be discouraged. You may be asking yourself, "Is it worth the trouble to slave away like this, without attaining anything? I might as well give up."

Remember, you are never defeated until you admit defeat. Unfortunately life is full of people who have accepted defeat as a fact, and whose pessimism has influenced others very negatively. It is so easy to become one of the crowd and become a victim of self-pity.

There are many inspirational stories about people who, when faced with defeat, eventually managed to gain victory in spite of tremendous odds against them. People who are dispirited by looming defeat would be wise to read these inspirational stories.

Before you give up in total despair, first ask yourself the following questions: Whom do I submit myself to in my despair? Will life be easier once I have admitted defeat? Will I be able to escape from moral responsibilities and obligations because I feel that I cannot cope any longer?

To answer the first question: You submit to your fear and unless you resist and overcome fear through the power of the triumphant Christ, you will certainly go under. It is through faith in Jesus Christ that you obtain victory.

Christ, I praise You because I am triumphant in every situation through You. Because of You I am more than a conqueror! *Amen.*

Plan with God

Your faith should not be in the wisdom of men but in the power of God.

~ 1 Corinthians 2:5 (NKJV)

How often have you, or others that you know and love, experienced the disappointment of unfulfilled dreams, watched them disintegrate and feel your hope collapse like a house of cards? It leaves you with a feeling of complete dejection. Many people who experience such a stroke of ill fate, never recover. They are therefore not willing to take upon themselves the risk of another disaster, and thus a tremendous amount of talent lies wasted and unused.

There are those who will mock the idea that you need to call in God's help to realize your plans. These people promote the idea of self-sufficiency in everything they undertake and they trust completely in their own ability. That is why, when success has been achieved, they also take all the praise for themselves. It is all very well as long as their plans are successful, but if they fail they experience the destructive results of failure.

When you trust completely in God for everything you do, if you want to follow His will and obey Him, you might feel that things are moving too slowly for you. However, be patient and steadfastly put your trust in God. Then you will have peace of mind, knowing that God is in control and that the fulfillment of your plans will be to your lasting benefit. Trust God's protective love when planning your life and your work.

Lord, I know that You have a plan for my life. Help me to trust You steadfastly always. *Amen.*

God Remains in Control

He is before all things, and in Him all things hold together.

~ COLOSSIANS 1:17

In matters of state, a business undertaking, in the workplace and in your private life, there comes a time when it seems as though everything is going wrong. The future seems uncertain and the present leaves much to be desired. Under such circumstances, the temptation arises to look back at the past in nostalgia and to yearn for "the good old days".

Regardless of what problems might be upsetting your personal life or the world around you, look back over history. You will discover that nations and individuals have struggled through difficult times that can be compared with what we are experiencing in our times. Disasters, hardships and dangers existed in the past. People were confronted with sorrow and adversity, just as we are today. And yet the world has remained standing.

Before giving in to despondency, first acknowledge the greatness, glory and constancy of God. He called the world into existence, He created man, He has kept watch over His creation and cared for us through the ages and sheltered us in every disaster. He is the Creator God who shall never abandon His workmanship. In His unfathomable love, He gave His Son to this world, so that whoever believes in Him shall not perish but have everlasting life (see John 3:16). Therefore, hold on to His promises; place your entire trust and faith in the living Christ. Through Him you will survive all dangers and adversities, to His greater glory.

You are eternal, Lord, and the workmanship of Your creation bears testimony to Your greater glory. *Amen.*

Under God's Protection

Blessed is the man who trusts in the LORD, and whose hope is the LORD.

~ JEREMIAH 17:7 (NKJV)

The whole world is experiencing ominous times. From every corner of the earth comes the news of famines, droughts, financial crises, violence, earthquakes, hurricanes, floods and many more destructive happenings. The result is that people are restless, insecure and afraid. They don't know who to turn to or what to do for protection.

In order for you to maintain peace of mind, it is imperative that you place your faith and trust totally in God. He who has promised to be with you till the end of time is there with you in every situation. He will protect you and will safely lead you from the darkness into His marvelous light. If your life is Christ-centered and if you acknowledge Him in everything that you do, He will protect you and lead you safely.

Regardless of how hopeless things might seem, never lose your faith in Christ's ability. Make Him your constant, inseparable companion. While you walk with Him, He will give you the strength to handle any imaginable situation; and also to overcome every disappointment and stroke of bad luck. Without His protection you are exposed to every possible danger and attacks from the Evil One. You need not continue living like that while the glorious alternative is available to you: to live under the protection of the Most High.

With my trust in You, O Lord, I experience peace and security even in the midst of chaos. You protect me from all dangers. *Amen.*

Safe in God's Hand

We are not of those who draw back to perdition, but of those who believe to the saving of the soul.

~ HEBREWS 10:39 (NKJV)

It is very interesting to study people's reactions to the circumstances they find themselves in. In most cases, their attitude is determined by what's going on around them.

If the country experiences an economic slump, they immediately feel depressed; crime and unrest paralyze them with fear; personal setbacks create a feeling of hopelessness; sorrow drives them to despair. The end result in many cases is that they simply give up. Suddenly life loses its meaning, its purpose and its joy. They are like people who stumble along in darkness.

The one very important fact which we have to cling to in the midst of setbacks, is that Christ, through the Holy Spirit, is always with us and that He is holding us in the hollow of His hand. Indeed He is the One who came to give us life in abundance (see John 10:10). This implies that He wants what is best for you under all circumstances. In order for you to obtain that, Jesus has made the utmost sacrifice. And through that act He has overcome evil for time and eternity.

When circumstances seem dark and ominous to you, remember that you are a child of God, He loves you and cares for you; He wants to, and can, protect you from all evil. Believe His promise that He will never leave you nor forsake you. Put your trust totally in Him and He will lift you from your depression and fear.

Loving Savior, grant me the peace that comes only from security in You. Thank You that You are always with me. *Amen.*

Trust in God

Though an army besiege me, my heart will not fear; though war break out against me, even then will I be confident.

~ PSALM 27:3

This trust in God can only be possible if we can also make this foregoing pronouncement: "The LORD is my light and my salvation – whom shall I fear? The LORD is the stronghold of my life – of whom shall I be afraid?" (Ps. 27:1).

In times like these, where people are fearful about the future it is essential that they have a spiritual foundation on which to base their hope and expectations. Faith in God must be intimate and personal if it is to contribute to hope for the future. The omnipotent Creator God has not surrendered this world to its fate, despite the fact that the contrary appears to be true. His master plan for humankind will still be carried out.

In an ever darkening world, He proclaims, "But take heart! I have overcome the world" (John 16:33).

If you put all your trust in Him, you will be able to meet the future with an internal peace and calmness, and this will also inspire trust in those who surround you.

A Christian who is permeated by the Holy Spirit will have a stabilizing effect on his society, since he knows irrefutably that the future is in God's almighty hand.

Savior and Lord, I live from day to day in the undeniable reality of Your presence and omnipotence in this world. Therefore, I do not fear, since You are my refuge. *Amen.*

Unshakable Trust

Be joyful in hope, patient in affliction.

When everything seems to be going wrong, people either collapse under their problems or try to solve them in their own strength.

In both cases you have little chance of coming out unharmed. The Lord has promised never to forsake or leave you. The Scriptures tell time and again of how God kept His promises. It is therefore imperative that you trust Him completely.

Nevertheless, you must have patience, because you cannot hurry God or prescribe to Him. He has His good time and method. His timing is always perfect. Even if you find it difficult to understand in your present confusion, you must accept that God sees the overall picture of your life. He is all-knowing and all-seeing. Your faith in Him must be of such a quality that you will unwaveringly trust His promises and abide obediently by His judgment.

When dark days and difficulties cross your path, place your burdens in His care and keep on trusting. Seek the guidance of the Holy Spirit to teach you to wait patiently on the Lord. Ask Him for the discernment to see His answers to your prayers.

Having done that, you can, with childlike faith, leave everything in God's hands and believe that He will provide. He wants you to experience only the best and the most beneficial, and if this takes place in strange and roundabout ways, you should continue believing and steadfastly trusting. They who stand steadfast in affliction, receive God's most precious gifts from His treasury.

Lord and Father, I find peace of mind in trusting You. *Amen.*

Not Now ... Later!

Jesus replied, "You do not realize now what I am doing, but later you will understand."

~ JOHN 13:7

Sometimes confusing things happen in life and we find them so hard to believe that we want to blame God in our ignorance and confusion.

From the cradle to the grave, we are engaged in a struggle. However, what often worsens the situation is the fact that we sometimes do not understand what is happening to us at all. This is what happened to Peter.

Peter could not and did not want to understand: "No, You shall never wash my feet" (John 13:8). He had to realize that he had to share in the cleansing grace of the Redeemer, Jesus Christ. He also had to learn the lesson of absolute humility. It was necessary to prepare him for the great task that he had to perform.

God can make every misfortune and puzzling situation in your life work out for your benefit. Paul states it strikingly, "No discipline seems pleasant at the time, but painful. Later on, however, it produces a harvest of righteousness and peace for those who have been trained by it"(Heb. 12:11).

Perhaps something occurred in your life that left you bewildered. The Master has something to tell you, "If you do not understand now, believe and trust to the end. Do not fear, only believe. Later you will understand everything."

Your ways are so different from our ways, Lord Jesus. I do not always understand You, but I want to follow You in faith and truth. *Amen.*

The Christian's Self-Image

Though an army besiege me, my heart will not fear.

~ PSALM 27:3

Nurturing feelings of inferiority and incompetence can paralyze you spiritually. You know that these negative feelings are contrary to the wishes of the indwelling Spirit of God for your life, but you feel incompetent to do anything about them. The only antidote for a poor self-image, insecurity and feeling inferior, is a positive attitude towards God.

To achieve and maintain religious confidence, you must allow Christ into your life and dedicate yourself to Him completely. Then He will live in you and His power will be expressed through you. Prayer and meditation will strengthen your self-confidence and your faith in God.

God works in you through Christ, enabling you to lead a life of faith, trust and victory. The more you cultivate an awareness of the presence and omnipotence of Christ in your life, the stronger your faith and trust in Him will become.

Through this, you will conquer your feelings of insecurity and inferiority, and you will be able to lead a fruitful and satisfying life. Nothing is impossible if we are anchored in the power of Jesus Christ: "If you remain in Me and My words remain in you, ask whatever you wish, and it will be given you" (John 15:7).

The treasury of God is wide open to those who want to enter into a life of fruitfulness and victory through Jesus Christ.

Eternal God and Father, dwell in me through Your Holy Spirit so that I will never be saddled with feelings of insecurity and inferiority. I praise You that I can do all things through Your strength. *Amen.*

When Dark Clouds Gather

How great is God – beyond our understanding! The number of His years is past finding out.

~ JOB 36:26

One of the biggest stumbling blocks in spiritual development is having a limited perception of God. When adversity strikes you do not call upon His wisdom, serenity, omnipotence and power, even though He has placed these qualities at your disposal.

Unless you remind yourself constantly of the unlimited resources that God has placed at your disposal, and unless you make regular use of them in times of need and distress, you will discover that your trials and tribulations are always greater than your God.

Be determined to grow in your perception of the greatness of God, as well as of all the means of grace that He has placed at your disposal through which you can get to know Him more intimately. Then, when the storms of life erupt, which will happen without a doubt, you will have a spiritual reserve, enabling you to keep your footing – regardless of how difficult the moment may be.

When you have been united with the Great God, you will find that in times of temptation He will give you strength; that your faith is not merely a question of emotion, but seeing the power of God. He assures you of His presence, even in your times of indifference. Know that God is great, and you will have great faith.

Lord, I am speechless when I behold the wonders of Your creation. You are miraculous in Your greatness and I want to sing Your praises all my life. *Amen.*

Jesus, You Lead the Way

He restores my soul. He guides me in paths of righteousness for His name's sake.

~ Psalm 23:3

Are you perhaps one of those people who is afraid of the future? Fear of what the future holds can sometimes totally paralyze your mind and your spirit.

If this is true in your life, it is true because you allow it to be. It is not at all the Lord's will for you to be robbed of all power and beauty because of the awful presence of fear. His desire is for you to be totally free from debilitating fear.

This is only possible if your trust in God exceeds your faith in fear. Accept the glorious fact that God is omniscient and that He presides over the past, the present and the future and that He desires only the very best for your life. This will bring such balance into your everyday life that no amount of fear will be able to upset you. Because God is also omnipresent, you need to realize that He is always with you.

Never forget that while you are moving into the future, God is already there waiting. He knows the future and He knows the right road to follow. You can put all your trust in Him. If you truly and totally trust Him, such profound peace will descend upon your life that, even if storms of fear and insecurity rage around you, they will never be able to paralyze or destroy you.

Jesus, lead me into Your light, and into Your way. You know my future and I can trust You to lead me on the right path. *Amen.*

Depend on God

"When they deliver you up, do not worry about how or what you should speak. For it will be given to you in that hour what you should speak; for it is not you who speak, but the Spirit of your Father who speaks in you."

~ MATTHEW 10:19, 20 (NKJV)

We are inclined to read many Scripture passages within a historical context only. We then often have difficulty relating them to ourselves or the circumstances of our lives. In some parts of the world those who follow Jesus are experiencing persecution and adversity that is very real. When living in a Christian society, we find it very hard to think that it is possible to be imprisoned because you are a Christian, to be challenged to defend your faith, and sometimes even your life.

Nowadays it is more likely that you will be tested in your daily activities. Your test will come when you have to comfort someone who has experienced a tragic loss, to express words of hope to someone who threatens to commit suicide, or to reassure the invalid, who suffers constant pain, that God loves him.

Then it is important that you, as well as the one that you are ministering to, should depend totally on the grace of Jesus Christ. Open up your life completely to receive His Spirit and He will inspire you with the words you need to say.

Holy Spirit, what a wonderful comfort You are in every situation. Flow through me so I too can be a comfort to those in need. *Amen.*

God Goes before You

And the LORD, He is the One who goes before you. He will not leave you nor forsake you.

~ DEUTERONOMY 31:8 (NKJV)

Many people are afraid to fulfill their plans because they fear the unknown which lies ahead. This was especially true of some spiritual giants in the Old Testament. One cannot help but wonder what course humanity would have taken had they been daunted by the challenges that were set before them. However, they moved forward in faith and did their part in executing God's great plan with humanity.

It was of the utmost importance that God's hand should be stretched out in protection over every person that He sent out in His name. As a result of this, and because of the steadfast faith of the biblical heroes, much has been achieved for the kingdom of God. The most important fact is that they believed in the Lord. His view is perfect and eternal and He will never place you in a situation that will be harmful to you. He will be with you to protect you at all times, and to support and guide you.

Before putting your plans into action you need to lay them before God first and submit them to His will. Wait on His Holy Spirit to guide you. Walk intimately with Christ in prayer, meditation and Bible study and move ahead when and as He guides you. He knows what is best for you. Trust Him completely and never doubt the fact that He will keep you safe. He will grant you the fulfillment of your plans.

Lord Jesus, with Your guidance I will move in the direction You want me to go, because You always have my best interests at heart. *Amen.*

February

The Cornerstone of Your Faith

And now abide faith, hope, love, these three; but the greatest of these is love.

~ 1 CORINTHIANS 13:13 (NKJV)

The Christian faith has many facets. People regard and interpret the teachings of Christ according to their own frame of reference, traditions and personality. Disaster enters your spiritual life when you deny the fact that another person's viewpoint could be correct, even though it differs from yours. Such a denial is the result of fanaticism and pettiness.

The real test of your faith is the amount of love you have towards others, especially those whose beliefs differ radically from yours. Such a faith can only have its roots in a way of life that stays so close to Christ that His love starts flowing through you to others. Your love for Christ includes all people who love Him, even though you may not be able to agree with them on an intellectual level about matters such as dogma and church government.

Love should be predominant in your spiritual life. This love doesn't always mean peacefulness. There are times when it challenges and reprimands; it makes you feel humble in order that you may be carried to great spiritual heights; it empties you of yourself, of covetousness and pride, in order that you may be filled with the love of God. If you love God and His love finds expression in you, you will find that that love extends to your fellow man.

Lord, I pray that love will flow through me in abundance. Increase my love for others so that people will be able to see You in me. *Amen.*

When God's Love Possesses You

Having predestined us to adoption as sons by Jesus Christ to Himself, according to the good pleasure of His will.

~ EPHESIANS 1:5 (NKJV)

It is impossible to compare the existence of the holy God with your own unimportant, insignificant and incomplete life. He is perfect while you are not, and therefore it seems as if there is no shared common ground between God and you. This would have been true if the name and character of God, as revealed to us through Jesus Christ, had not been love. But because He is love, He calls you to Him and if you react to this love-call, your life will be changed miraculously.

As the love of God becomes a reality to you, it controls your spirit and you become aware of your unity with the Father. It stimulates and inspires you. Yet the love of God which is at work in you is not an entirely emotional experience, it is a way of life. The wonder of grace is that God gives Himself to you! As you open yourself up to His life and influence, the Holy Spirit will enable you to live as He intended you to live: in His strength and in the consciousness of His living presence.

When the love of God fills your life and you become thoroughly aware of His divine presence, you experience a feeling of unity with Him. This is something that every person desires. This unity isn't something that you can earn through your own efforts. It is a gift from God. However, it only becomes yours when you appropriate it for yourself in faith and with gratitude.

Eternal God, Your unfathomable love astounds me. Let it fill my life so that I can be more aware of Your divine presence. *Amen.*

Love Brings Life

We know that we have passed from death to life, because we love the brethren.

~ 1 JOHN. 3:14

In the teachings of Jesus Christ, love is all-powerful. Everything He was, everything He taught and did were manifestations of love. He made it a condition for discipleship and stated very clearly that man cannot serve or glorify God without love.

People who are not in harmony with God's teachings simply cannot understand such a strong accent on love. Their concept of love is that it is an emotion which operates in response to every passing mood. They just don't understand that the power of love overcomes hate, that love can offer years of service without counting the cost. Love is a God-like characteristic that enriches everyone who allows God to reveal it in their lives.

It is possible to have a first-hand experience of the love of God and to allow your life to become a channel of God's love. This is the wisest way of life there is for man. The opposite of loving is to hate. This path will lead to bitterness, conflict and broken relationships.

When the love of God is a powerful influence in your life and His love reaches out to others through you, your personal life is enriched in a way you never dreamt possible. It is impossible to love without being enriched in your mind and spirit.

Lord God, through Your Holy Spirit please do the impossible in my life. Let Your love flow through me and become a powerful influence in my life. *Amen.*

Love One Another

Follow the way of love.

~ 1 CORINTHIANS 14:1

All around the world people are seeking greater knowledge and awareness of our Lord, Jesus Christ. As the Holy Spirit awakens them, people are striving to meet the Master in prayer, worship, communion and study. It is probably true to say that the enthusiasm which people have displayed in this quest is as great now as it has ever been throughout history.

While this diligent approach to one's faith is commendable and should be encouraged, one has to remember not to lose sight of the foundation of the Christian faith in one's eagerness to get to know Jesus better. The birth, death and resurrection of Jesus demonstrate God's unfathomable love for His people. Through Jesus Christ, He has made it abundantly clear that out of all the things that He has commanded you to do, the willingness to show love stands out from everything else.

Knowledge of the Master and the blessing of spiritual gifts are much sought after attributes among His modern disciples, but regardless of how scripturally knowledgeable you are or how much you know of God, there is nothing that manifests the glory of God more than the love of Jesus Christ. Concentrate your pilgrimage on continually getting to know Him better. Don't merely learn about Him. Allow His love to fill your being so that you may reflect it in your everyday life.

Jesus, loving Master, let my daily life be an expression of Your love so that I may be a witness for You. *Amen.*

True Love

Love must be sincere.

~ ROMANS 12:9

The word "love" is probably the most used and least understood word in any language. Through the years it has been used to express people's feelings towards art, food, leisure and relaxation. On a personal level it is used to express one's feelings of affection. It is even used in connection with clothes and other material possessions.

When you are professing your love towards people, it would be beneficial to take a moment to consider the actual depth of your love. To what lengths would you go and what sacrifices would you be willing to make for the sake of love?

Jesus Christ came to demonstrate to us the meaning of true love when He willingly gave His life for you and for all of humanity. To redeem mankind of its sin, He was willing to die for all of us and to take our punishment upon Him. As Jesus said, "Greater love has no one than this, that he lay down his life for his friends" (John 15:13).

True love involves making sacrifices for the sake of another. It is tolerant, patient and understanding, even in the most trying circumstances. It encompasses forgiveness and a giving of yourself for the benefit of others. It means to love others as Jesus loves you.

Loving Lord Jesus, help me to distribute Your love in the world around me. *Amen.*

Let Your Love Be Practical

Dear children, let us not love with words or tongue but with actions and in truth.

~ 1 John 3:18

True love is not something that can be fathomed by the human mind. It cannot be sufficiently explained, and yet it is the most important and dynamic human emotion.

Because of the unique quality of love, words remain incapable of explaining it. Compassion, goodness, tenderness and many other beautiful and highly emotive words cannot fully describe the strength and power of love. However, there is an unfortunate tendency to equate love with sentimentality which reduces this dynamic force to something weak and ineffectual.

The foundation of true love is complete identification with the beloved. The same joys, sorrows, temptations and failures are experienced. True love entails sacrifice and often includes sadness. The quality of love transcends sympathy and comes to expression in loyalty and faithfulness, even if the whole world should turn against the beloved.

Love in action is more than just the performance of good deeds. True love is deep and unselfish and encompasses qualities such as faithfulness, trust, noble principles and many other similar values that enrich the mind and spirit. It cannot be bought, and it is precisely for this reason that love is so precious.

Eternal God of love, help me to love without calculating the cost; help me to love faithfully and unselfishly so that I may love others with a true heart. *Amen.*

The Litmus Test of Faith

"My command is this: Love each other as I have loved you."
~ JOHN 15:12

Fanaticism is a common sin among spiritually attuned people. They have fought their way through many problems to reach a state of faith, and then they suddenly believe that they are the only ones to have found the full truth.

Their faith is the product of their personal thinking and possibly also of their individual experiences. However, when they claim to be the only ones to possess true faith and knowledge, while denying other people the same privilege, their lives are no longer receptive to God's love. Their fanaticism and narrow-mindedness prevent the love of God from spreading to their neighbors.

It is vital to know exactly what you believe in. But it is even more important that your love for your neighbor transcends any dogmatic differences. For the Spirit of the living Christ to live in you and for you to realize that He can also live in those who differ from you, love has to be the dominant emotion in your spiritual experience: "By this all men will know that you are My disciples, if you love one another" (John 13:35).

Unless we have become a channel for Christ's love and unless we possess the ability to embrace people who differ from us, love has not yet been perfected in us. Love that is manifested in service and in caring for others is the divine test for those who want to be His disciples.

God of love, Your Holy Spirit teaches us that love is the key to each problem and each human heart. Let Your love fill my life. *Amen.*

Love: Absolutely Essential!

If I give all I possess to the poor but have not love, I gain nothing.

~ 1 Corinthians 13:3

There is no substitute for love – nothing can take its place. That is why the question that Jesus asked Peter in John 21:16 is so meaningful, "Do you truly love Me?"

This question reaches down to the roots of our relationship with Christ and touches on the quality of our fellowship.

Jesus doesn't ask, "Do you believe in Me?"; "Do you understand My teaching?"; "Do you confess My name?"; "Are you obedient in your service to Me?" or "Do you love My Word?" Although these are all important questions, they are secondary. The primary question is, "Do you truly love Me?" Only if your reply is positive can you approach the future fearlessly and with spiritual security.

It is fair to ask this because Jesus had invested a lot in Peter. For three years Peter had the wonderful privilege of attending the "School of Christ". Even when Peter did not live up to the expectations that Jesus had for him, He did not leave him to himself. Jesus also prayed for Peter (see Luke 22:30) and – as He did for us all – Jesus died for Peter too. "Greater love has no one than this, that he lay down his life for his friends" (John 15:13).

Considering the trouble Jesus takes with us in all areas of our lives, it is only fair for Him to ask about our love for Him. It is also fair then that He should receive the reply, "Lord, You know all things; You know that I love You" (John 21:17).

I dearly love You, Lord. Thank You for Your loving involvement in my life. Please help me to reveal this love to others. *Amen.*

Faithful to Love

"If you love Me, you will obey what I command."

~ JOHN 14:15

Discipline is not a very popular concept and is therefore often ignored. This can create a negative attitude that spoils the work you are doing and prevents you from excelling. The person that truly enjoys his work is the one who loves it and finds joy in doing it. Such a person is always on the lookout for new methods to become increasingly productive.

This is the attitude God requires from those who serve Him. Many people think that because they are serving the Lord, they are entitled to VIP treatment or special rewards. It is, however, true to God's character that He experiences great pleasure in His children who serve Him with gladness and joy.

The Christian's faith must be founded on love and not on fear. It is impossible to enjoy life if you are fearful of God. The driving force behind a true Christian life and service to God is His love for you and your love for Him. When the quality of your service is determined by your love for Him, it becomes inspired and filled with gladness. Nothing you do is a burden and no sacrifice is too great if you possess His love and are possessed by it.

If your faith and service to God have become a burden and you regard everything you do as a sacrifice, it is time to flame God-given love into your life again. Service is love in action.

Lord, nothing You want me to do can ever be a burden because I truly love You. *Amen.*

The Holy Spirit Cultivates Love

God has poured out His love into our hearts by the Holy Spirit,
whom He has given us.

~ Romans 5:5

The certain knowledge that Christ lives in you can bring about a spiritual revival in your life. It inspires your thoughts, enriches you, generates new trust, creates enthusiasm and gives purpose and meaning to your everyday existence. It is the work of the Holy Spirit alone that assures you of your unity with the Source of perfect love.

No matter how powerful and inspiring you might find this mutual love between you and God, it must be firmly founded on reality and practical faith. To declare that you love Christ, yet refuse to lift the burden of another is a blatant denial of that love.

If you love Christ through the Holy Spirit, you become painfully aware of the needs of others and you will have an uncontrollable desire to do something about it.

If you proclaim that the love of God is in your heart, it will be revealed in your words, attitudes and willingness to serve others. God is expressed in your life through the love of His Holy Spirit and as a result you accept the full responsibility of your faith in love.

This love enables you to want only what is best for your fellow man, in spite of insults, pain or humiliation. It is a conscious effort to seek nothing but the best for others. The basis of this love is God Himself, and has been demonstrated to us through Jesus Christ and revealed in our hearts through the Holy Spirit.

O Holy Spirit, enlighten me and make Your love burn brightly in me. I pray this in the name of Jesus Christ, my Lord. *Amen.*

The Safe Haven of Jesus' Love

"Since you have asked for this and not for long life or wealth for yourself, nor have asked for the death of your enemies but for discernment in administering justice, I will do what you have asked. I will give you a wise and discerning heart, so that there will never have been anyone like you, nor will there ever be. Moreover, I will give you what you have not asked for – both riches and honor."

~ 1 KINGS: 3:11-13

In a Christian's prayer life there is a strong temptation to focus on the "self". Many people have the tendency to go before God with lists of requests. The serious danger of this approach is that your prayers soon become self-centered and the praise and gratitude to God, as well as the interests of others, take a back seat when you pray.

Every prayer to God must repeat the immortal words of the living Christ, "Yet not as I will, but as You will" (Matt. 26:39). This is the highest practice in faith: complete surrender of your prayers to the Lord, while you subject yourself to His will and devote yourself to Him. In this way you acknowledge His sovereignty over your life and all your circumstances – as well as over the lives of those on whose behalf you intercede.

When you succeed in committing your prayers completely to God, while trusting Him absolutely with your welfare and future, an untold feeling of peace will descend on your life. You will come to the realization that Christ has laid His hands on you and that the Holy Spirit has guided you onto the perfect path.

Lord, You guide me when words fail me in prayer. Your mercy intervenes and gives me peace. Guide my prayers now and always. *Amen.*

Enveloped by His Love

Afterwards Jesus appeared in a different form to two of them while they were walking in the country.

~ MARK 16:12

It is possible that you are one of those people who is jealous of others who have had a dramatic and personal encounter with Jesus Christ. They could have been converted or received the baptism of the Holy Spirit during a prayer meeting or a gospel campaign.

Regardless of how it took place, it was without a doubt with great joy. Now you are wondering why it did not happen to you!

Never allow this to dampen your spirit or affect your relationship with Christ. Always bear in mind that Christ has made us unique creations, and that not all Christians have an encounter with Jesus that is as dramatic as Paul's.

Jesus knows every one of His disciples personally – including you – better than you know yourself. He is fully aware of your nature, how you react; your ability to handle emotions. As the psalmist writes, "O LORD, You have searched me and You know me. Search me, O God, and know my heart; test me and know my anxious thoughts" (Ps. 139:1, 23).

Do not brood on this issue, but persevere in prayer and meditation and wait on the Lord. The living Christ will appear to you in a manner which *He* will choose, as He has always done in the lives of those who love Him dearly.

Come, O Holy Spirit, and visit my soul and innermost being and fill it with Your precious fire. *Amen.*

Love Is Complete and Perfect

A man's own folly ruins his life, yet his heart rages against the
LORD.

~ PROVERBS 19:3

G od is often accused of things for which He is not responsible.
It is His desire that everybody should live in harmony and
have a peaceful and productive life. He wants us to submit our
will to His will. Regardless of this truth, however, there are many
people who blame God for their wretched state.

But the irrefutable truth is that people are responsible for their
own actions. This should have an enormous influence on each of
us. It is a constant law of nature, and of spiritual life, that man
reaps exactly what he sows.

If you are unhappy in an uncomfortable situation and display
an aggressive disposition towards God and life, be sensible. Come
to peace with your disappointment, frustration and bitterness,
and ask yourself where you have gone wrong. Cooperate with life
instead of rebelling and kicking against it. Acknowledge the
sovereignty of Christ over your life by cooperating with Him and
allowing yourself to be guided by Him. Those who share in His
life have been invited by Him to enter into a new dimension of life.

They will approach their problems from a new perspective, the
true values of life will find their rightful place and life will become
meaningful because you will view it from Christ's perspective.

Lord, Your kindness is everlasting! Even when afflicted by sin, You will
not forsake me. I want to sing Your praises and I beseech You to lead
me in Your truth. *Amen.*

To Love ... in Spite Of

God created man in His own image, in the image of God He created him.

~ GENESIS 1:27

Some people radiate sparkling sunshine. Other people just cause problems and frustration. In His wisdom, God did not create any two people alike: He made no duplicates. This causes human relationships to be challenging.

In your life you will get to know people who are difficult to understand. Regardless of how you approach them, you never experience harmony in your relationship with them. As time passes and no mutual understanding develops, you become impatient. A complete break in the relationship may seem unavoidable.

We have all been created in the image of God. God is Spirit and man was created as a spiritual being. Deep in the spirit of even the most depraved person there is a trace of the Divine which can never be extinguished.

"Come unto Me, ye weary, And I will give you rest!"
O blessed voice of Jesus, which comes to hearts oppressed.
It tells of benediction, of pardon, grace and peace,
Of joy that hath no ending, of love that cannot cease.

The realization of this truth enables us to love the innermost being of a fallen person; that part of him which reacts to the divine love of Jesus Christ.

Teach me every day, loving Master, to love even the most difficult people I meet. *Amen.*

I Truly Love You, O Lord!

"Yes, Lord," he said, "You know that I love You."

~ JOHN 21:15

It is foolish to accept certain things as a matter of course, like the love and regard your family has for you. Too many people think they deserve the love and respect of all their family members just because they are part of the family. Being born into that family does not give you the right to demand their love. It is something that has to be earned. Parents should give love to their children in order to receive love and vice versa.

A huge weakness in many marriages is that love is never expressed. The parties accept one another as a matter of course, as if they are part of the furniture in the house. Something very precious is lost in that marriage. Saying to your partner, "I love you" and showing this through your deeds, strengthens the marriage bond in a special way.

In the spiritual sphere of life, the expression of love and appreciation has enormous power and value. When last did you tell the Lord that you love Him? You may argue like Peter, "Lord, You know all things; You know that I love You."

Not only does it gladden your Father's heart to hear you confirm your love for Him, but it also strengthens your spirit and your inner joy and peace. Tell God in your quiet time that you love Him. You will feel how strength and inspiration fill your spirit when He responds to the declaration of your love.

Lord Jesus, I love You with all my heart, my mind and all my strength. I rejoice in our growing relationship of love. *Amen.*

Love Does not Have a Price Tag

Live a life of love, just as Christ loved us and gave Himself up for us as a fragrant offering and sacrifice to God.

~ EPHESIANS 5:2

A sensitive awareness of the distress and suffering of others brings its own pain. But it is another command of God that we must obey.

Many people think sensitivity is a sign of weakness. However, it is sensitive people in particular who serve their fellow man best, and who bring light to lives where darkness has descended. Sensitivity for the distress of others is the base of true Christian service.

Unfortunately, it is a fact that this sensitivity often causes us pain. When this happens, you should thank Christ that you can identify with Him in this special way. His sensitive Spirit knows the pain and grief that follow when those you love pursue the path of self-destruction. Furthermore, He took our sickness and grief upon Himself. Will He not therefore understand?

The more you become aware of the living presence of Christ in your life, the more you become aware of the distress of others. This is the price of love; and we, who follow His Holy example, should be willing to pay the price. In this way, we can make this broken world a better place to live in, as Christ did. In addition, our lives will become acceptable to God.

O Jesus, Man of grief, help me to develop a sensitive spirit and to care for the distress of others. Give me the will to bring sunshine where dark shadows threaten. *Amen.*

Love Overrides Theology

Be completely humble and gentle; be patient, bearing with one another in love.

~ EPHESIANS 4:2

Slowly but surely the gap between Christian churches is being narrowed. Old issues and disputes are seen for what they really are – instruments of Satan to divide the body of Christ. Yet there are important differences and they will continue to exist for many years. Disputes may be justified when deep-rooted convictions cannot allow you to accept contentious theological principles.

When two opposing theological viewpoints are maintained by people who are equally convinced of their beliefs, the final test is whether love can rise above the differences.

There are cases where spiritual consensus can be achieved, even if there are intellectual differences. The conviction that Christ is gloriously and triumphantly alive and should be praised, is a binding truth of Christianity. Ways of worshiping may differ, but love can rise above variety. Love should be the binding force that finds expression in service.

One of the reasons why churches are moving closer together is because of the urgent need to save a world that is rapidly declining and falling apart. God's children realize that division is futile and that it is a sin to allow intellectual differences to suppress the Spirit of God.

Where there is Christian love, there is a spirit of underlying unity, despite diverse theological viewpoints.

Holy Shepherd, save me from a heart that refuses to love. *Amen.*

Love and Growth

Therefore, if anyone is in Christ, he is a new creation; the old has gone, the new has come! All this is from God, who reconciled us to Himself through Christ and gave us the ministry of reconciliation.
~ 2 CORINTHIANS 5:17-18

For this month may God open your heart to His love; your mind to His wonders; your ears to His voice and your entire life to His holy and loving presence.

May you receive from His hand His peace for your unease, His forgiveness for your guilt, His presence in your loneliness, His light when your way becomes dark, His guidance on your pilgrimage and His love for every day. Many people wish that they could start over with their lives. They are tortured by feelings of guilt from the past, or by failures and missed opportunities. They want to erase these and other negative things.

The living Christ offers you such an opportunity! Despite what you are or what you have done, He asks you to allow Him to come into your life and to take control of your life. He does not break down doors – He waits for you to open them (see Rev. 3:20).

Ask God to take control of your life and to fill it with His Holy Spirit. Surrender your life unconditionally and confess to Him everything that depresses you and causes you sorrow. Then accept the "new life" in faith. He erases the past completely and never thinks of it again. Follow Him while He guides you out into the light of a new life of love and spiritual growth.

Holy Lord Jesus, I open my life to Your Holy Spirit. I thank You that my life has found new purpose, sense and meaning. *Amen.*

Love Transforms

Dear children, let us not love with words or tongue but with actions and in truth.

~ 1 JOHN 3:18

So many people think love is only an emotion that changes according to the circumstances we find ourselves in. The popular song, "I'm in the mood for love", expresses people's tendency to regard love as a fleeting emotion.

Love is far more than a theory or passing emotion. It is the expression of the character of God and should never be taken for granted. It surrounds you; it is the way in which God revealed Himself to mankind. God is love. Divine love should first be accepted intellectually before it can become visible in man's life. It can never be taken for granted, but has to be accepted consciously. When this happens, it transforms your character and your personality. You are in a completely new relationship with God.

The knowledge that God loves you makes you humble, but at the same time gives you self-confidence. You are humbled because He calls you His child, despite your failings. You develop self-confidence because you can live victoriously through the spiritual strength that He gives you.

When you start experiencing His love in your daily life, you will find that you do not have a vague, pious desire to do good. It means carrying His love into every aspect of your life. It is often difficult and demanding. It is only when you allow God to love you that such a love is possible.

God of love, when I find it difficult to love, I plead with You to continue Your love in my life, despite myself. *Amen.*

The Wonder of Love

Love is patient, love is kind. It does not envy, it does not boast, it is not proud. It is not rude, it is not self-seeking, it is not easily angered, it keeps no record of wrongs. Love does not delight in evil but rejoices with the truth.

– 1 CORINTHIANS 13:4-6

In everyday language this means: when I felt weak and worthless, you had time to listen to me and your love picked me up again. When I could not pray, you prayed with me. When I was afraid, you were tender with me; your love was patient and kind. When I searched for the will of God, you searched with me.

When I was successful, you also rejoiced. When you knew that I was hurt, you came and said, "I am sorry!" When I spoke, you gave me your undivided attention.

I made mistakes and failed, but you accepted me. When I hurt you, you forgave me. When I was eager to accept responsibility, you did not remind me of my previous mistakes.

When I was envious of other people's gifts, you taught me to appreciate my own. When I saw only the negative, you pointed out the positive. When I was lonely, when I doubted and strayed, your faith supported me. When I took life too seriously, you taught me to laugh. Due to your presence in my life, I grew in my commitment to and love for Christ. In this your love has become immortal.

I thank You, Lord God, for people who love me and make me understand something of Your unfathomable love for me. *Amen.*

The Song of Love

If I speak in the tongues of men and of angels, but have not love, I am only a resounding gong or a clanging cymbal.

~ 1 Corinthians 13:1

This chapter unlocks all the noble qualities of love. In the preceding chapter, Paul spoke about spiritual gifts, but now he points to an even more excellent path: the path of love.

He begins by saying that one can possess any spiritual gift, but if it does not bear the stamp of love, it is useless. Even the sought-after speaking in tongues was as useless as the noise of resounding gongs and clanging cymbals when unaccompanied by love. The gift of prophecy or preaching has two kinds of practitioners. There are those who attempt to save souls through hell-fire and damnation. They preach as if they would rejoice as much in the redemption as in the damnation of the sinner. Then there are those who attempt to save sinners for eternity with love and tact.

If love is not a part of miracles, of sacrifice, or of our spoken and intellectual gifts, then they are useless.

The gift of intellectual excellence, without love, leads to intellectual arrogance. Knowledge lit by the fire of love is the only kind of knowledge that can save people. Even faith without love can become a heartless and cruel thing that cuts people up and hurts them. None of these, including the gift to perform miracles, or to live a moderate life, is worth anything if it does not go hand-in-hand with true love. There is virtually no section of the Bible that requires so much introspection as this chapter.

Lord, my God and Father, I thank You that all the love in my life is mere stepping stones to You. *Amen.*

Love Forgets about Self-Love

Knowledge puffs up, but love builds up.

~ 1 Corinthians 8:1

Paul accuses the Corinthians of following one specific teacher and then boasting about it. Time and again Paul reminds them that their knowledge drives them to boasting. That is a negative form of love which we call self-love.

True love is selfless. It would rather confess unworthiness than boast of its own achievements. Some people give their love as if they were bestowing an honor on the receiver. That is not love; that is conceit. The one who truly loves, cannot stop marveling at the fact that there is someone who loves him. Love is kept humble in the knowledge that it could never make a sufficiently worthy sacrifice for the one he loves.

This also applies to our spiritual lives. We dare not accept God's love as a matter of course as though we deserved it. Such pride robs us of the blessing and spiritual growth that God has in mind for us. If people's knowledge of the Scriptures drives them to arrogance, then they are studying the Bible in vain. If we pray to be seen and heard by people, the petticoat of our arrogance is showing. If we go to church for any other personal motive than to glorify God, our church-attendance will bring us no blessing.

False modesty is another form of boasting. Langenhoven justifiably said, "I am so modest that I have become arrogant about my modesty."

Spirit of Love, keep me humble in my love, so that it does not become the cause of pride and arrogance. *Amen.*

Self-Interest versus Christian Love

"Whoever finds his life will lose it, and whoever loses his life for My sake will find it."

~ MATTHEW 10:39

True and sincere Christian love does not insist on its rights. In the final analysis, there are only two kinds of people in this world: those who lay claim to their rights and those who think about their duties; those who always lay claim to their privileges and those who always think about their responsibilities; those who think that life owes them something and those who think that they owe life something.

People can be divided into "grabbers" and "givers". The grabbers are those who, with clenched fists and white knuckles, constantly cling to what they regard as theirs. They are dirt poor, bankrupt in love. Mercifully, we also get the givers. Those who are like the myrtle-tree on the plains that gives its lovely fragrance to the heavens, without expecting something in return.

If people were to think less about their rights and more about their obligations, it would serve as a remedy for much of the evil in this world. Every time I think about my own interests, I drift further away from Christian love. To work behind the scenes without receiving acknowledgement for what you do, is a revelation of true Christian love.

Holy Spirit of God, help me never to show love out of own interest or selfishness, but in the way Christ practiced it. *Amen.*

Demonstrate Love

Now about brotherly love we do not need to write to you, for you yourselves have been taught by God to love each other.

~ 1 Thessalonians 4:9

There are many people who are reluctant to reveal their deepest feelings. They appear to be cold and introverted. They are afraid of being misunderstood and revealing an aspect of their nature that they would rather keep hidden. This is sad because so many unexpressed emotions – that could have enriched the world – remain slumbering in their personalities.

The greatest constructive emotion is love, but it is often hidden in the human heart. There are many married couples who, since their days of courting, have never affirmed their love for one another. There are more broken and aching hearts than we realize because the short phrase, "I love you," is never or seldom expressed.

One of the characteristics of true love is expressing appreciation through your love. It takes so little to say it out loud, and yet, it brings so much joy to both giver and receiver. Love can be demonstrated in a variety of practical ways. It can rise above mere sentimental emotion and enable you to make a way of life out of it, that can enrich the lives of your loved ones.

It is the experience of many people that a life that is filled with declared love can be fulfilling and practical. Why don't you start today?

Holy God, I thank You that You have taught me what love is. Help me to demonstrate it every day of my life. *Amen.*

The Challenge of Christianity

In all my prayers for all of you, I always pray with joy.
~ PHILIPPIANS 1:4

People react to your personality and the attitude you have towards life. You cannot live in a society without people reacting to who and what you are.

What you need to realize is that fundamentally, people accept you for who you are. The way they feel about you is therefore your responsibility. If you don't like people, you must not be surprised if they in turn, don't like you. If you hate people, you can never live constructively.

The practical foundation of Christ's teachings becomes clearer when you realize this truth. He taught that love is always stronger than hate, that eventually love will triumph over all negative and evil forces. Jesus did not simply utter pious phrases that are remote from practical reality when He commanded us in Matthew 5:44, saying, "Love your enemies, bless those who curse you, and pray for those who persecute you."

When you start loving people and praying for them, a transformation occurs in human relationships. Gradually your enemies will become friends. It is difficult to be antagonistic towards someone who loves you and prays for you. This is one of the biggest challenges of Christianity.

As John, the apostle of love says, "If we love one another, God abides in us, and His love has been perfected in us" (1 John 4:12 NKJV).

Lord and Guide, grant me the courage to love my enemies. Give me the strength to pray for them, even when they persecute me. *Amen.*

Love One Another

Open your hearts to us.

~ 2 CORINTHIANS 7:2 (NKJV)

Feelings of loneliness, rejection and isolation could have a destructive effect on a person's spiritual and emotional well-being. Only those who have experienced it can fully comprehend and understand the depths of depression that utter loneliness can drive one to.

The core of the Christian faith is founded on the love of God. It was His love for the world that urged Him to send His Son, Jesus Christ, to the world to die for our transgressions and sins. Christ's whole life was the epitome of love. He fulfilled the words: "Greater love has no one than this, that he lay down his life for his friends." The Son of God died for us out of love. It was Jesus who reiterated that the greatest of all commands was to love God and our fellow man with all our heart.

If you are obedient to the commands of the Master, He will reveal His love through you. His Holy Spirit will urge you to seek out those who are alone in this world and to bring them comfort in the name of the great merciful God. Allow Christ into your life and let His love urge you to serve those who are lonely in this world. People will then be able to see the Lord in you and in your actions.

Love is the cornerstone of your faith. Build upon it diligently and bring comfort and encouragement to others. By doing that you will honor and glorify God.

Lord, may Your Holy Spirit move me to love. Increase my love so that through it I will bring You honor. *Amen.*

Speaking the Truth in Love

The lips of the righteous know what is acceptable, but the mouth of the wicked what is perverse.

~ PROVERBS 10:32 (NKJV)

Some people are very careless with regard to what they say. They don't care if what they say is appropriate or whether it hurts the person they are talking to. They take pride in the fact that they are straightforward people who honestly say what they think. However, it is nothing less than impertinence. They tread on the feelings of others with spikes on their feet. These people normally live a very lonely life because others steer clear of them as much as they possibly can.

People who are aware of the powerful impact words have, use them to help, encourage and heal. Unpleasant truths sometimes have to be expressed, but then one must do so with firmness and tenderness which will alleviate the pain that necessarily follows. When, as a Christian, you are required to speak frankly, it would be wise to spend time in quiet meditation with God first.

Pray for the guidance of the Holy Spirit in order that you may receive the grace to handle an unpleasant task with sympathy, dignity and love. As a "righteous" person, willing to say the "right thing" in a difficult situation, you can trust the Holy Spirit to assist you in your task of love.

Lord, guide me to tactfully express things that may not be easy to hear. Help me to handle the situation with firmness and tenderness. *Amen.*

The Joy of Grateful Service

For though I am free from all men, I have made myself a servant to all, that I might win the more.

~ 1 Corinthians 9:19 (NKJV)

Most of us strive to achieve independence. Children dream about the day when they will be adults, employees yearn to start their own companies in order to answer to themselves only.

Even though it is self-evident that the ordinary Christian will never consider being separated from the authority of Christ, we must watch against the danger of submitting ourselves totally to the will of another person. In order to serve God as we should, we need to be able to act independently of human pressure and influence, as long as it is not contrary to the will of God.

Nevertheless, if you want to witness effectively for Christ, it is important to willingly make yourself available to your fellow man so that you can lead him as the Holy Spirit leads you. Even though it is not comfortable for you, you must at all times give yourself as a sacrifice in order to be an instrument for God's peace and a channel of Christ's love and compassion.

Undoubtedly it will encroach upon your time and in certain situations it can be extremely frustrating. But the joy of winning souls for Christ through grateful service will more than compensate for anything you may suffer. Put this to the test and discover the truth for yourself.

Master, I am willing to sacrifice myself in order to be an instrument for You. Thank You that You will help me do this with a joyful heart. *Amen.*

Allow Your Enemies to Help You Grow Spiritually

"I tell you: Love your enemies and pray for those who persecute you."

~ MATTHEW 5:44

Blessed is the person who has no enemies! Even though the disciples spread God's love, they still had enemies. It was precisely their testimony to Christ that caused such intense hostility.

Man has a tendency to dislike those who dislike you. But if you do this, you cause a vicious circle that can only be broken by forgiveness and love.

If you have an enemy, you are confronted with a challenge. You can ignore him, or cause him harm. However, it will be far better to act towards him according to Christ's commands.

Your first obligation is to erase all hatred and bitterness from your heart. Open yourself up to the influence of the Holy Spirit, and you will achieve the impossible. If your bitterness is under control, pray for your enemy. Prayer offers healing and salving that will enrich your spirit.

An enemy, who is treated according to Christ's commands, enables you to develop spiritual maturity. Should your enemy become your friend, you have achieved a resounding victory for the cause of the King.

I plead guilty before You, Lord. Give me strength to actively display my love for You, for my enemies and my neighbors. *Amen.*

March

Christ First

I want to know Christ and the power of His resurrection and the fellowship of sharing in His sufferings, becoming like Him in His death.

~ PHILIPPIANS 3:10

Many of God's servants are so busy working for Him that they do not have time to spend a few quiet moments alone with Him. They are so busy working for God's Kingdom that their activities cancel the necessity for solitude and quiet time. They are working for God without experiencing the presence and power of the living Christ.

Trying to serve Christ without the inspiring strength of the Holy Spirit leads to frustration, and eventually to spiritual suicide. When the ideal of what you are trying to do for Him fades away, when your spiritual reserves are not supplemented by prayer and meditation, when you try to maintain a Christian testimony without making Christ the most important element in your life; then your service will become powerless, without any effect or impact on the world.

If you want to serve the Master, you must put Him first in everything you do. He must be placed first on the agenda of your life. The service you offer Him must be the result of experiencing Him firsthand and not the result of hearsay.

Only if you put Him first in everything, can you determine your goal in life according to His will. If you place Christ first in your life, it will make you a more effective and acceptable servant.

Lord, my Lord, I place You first in my life. You are my inspiration and my motivating strength in the service that I offer to You. *Amen.*

How Can I Serve God?

Your love has given me great joy and encouragement, because you,
brother, have refreshed the hearts of the saints.

~ PHILEMON 7

There are many people who fervently desire to serve the Lord, but they cannot think of a way to do so. As a result they experience a vacuum in their spiritual lives. They get frustrated and complain that they remain unfulfilled.

They seek in vain for ways to bear testimony to the Lord and to serve Him, but every search ends in a cul-de-sac. In their disappointment, they withdraw more and more, until they wave what they perceive to be a lost cause goodbye.

Every disciple of Jesus has a capacity for love. There is no emotion that is more important to serve the Master with than to share His love with others. Love can comfort, save those who are lost, and give hope to those who need it. It can break down barriers, build bridges, establish relationships and heal wounds. As Paul states: Love is the greatest.

If you are sincerely looking for a way to serve the Lord, why don't you start to love others in His name! A telephone call, a letter or a visit to somebody who is in distress, will provide unprecedented joy and comfort. Even more importantly, it will give a feeling of fulfillment to your life – while you serve the Master.

Lord, grant that I may be the manifestation of Your love to all those around me. *Amen.*

The Discipline of Service

We too will serve the Lord, because He is our God.

~ Joshua 24:18

The most important moment of your life is when you are born again, when you are filled with that wonderful, indescribable feeling of peace that can only come from Jesus, the One to whom you surrendered your life. The holiness of such a moment makes you inclined to place yourself at the service of the Master. At that moment, no sacrifice seems too big for you.

You must, however, be prepared for the afterglow of this experience. Shortly on the heels of the joy of being born again, moments of doubt and uncertainty follow. The more you get involved with the activities of the church, the more things there will be to disagree with. In all probability you will experience disillusionment and even discouragement.

All these things form part of the devil's armory. He continually bombards Christians with it in the hope that their faith will weaken and their testimonies to God will be silenced. To counter this, you must hold on steadfastly to the promises of Jesus, and believe that His grace will be sufficient for you at all times (see 2 Cor. 12:9).

Discipline yourself to look up to Jesus – the Author and Perfecter of your faith. Trust in Him at all times and not in man. He will lead you from temptation onto His eternal path of devotion. Give your life to Him once more and devote yourself once again to His glorious service.

Strengthen me through Your power, Lord. Grant that I may remain steadfast against sin. *Amen.*

Do You Have an HR Program?

How good and pleasant it is when brothers live together in unity!
~ PSALM 133:1

If you have to live with people, it is rewarding to understand them and to maintain a healthy relationship with them. In some cases this is relatively easy, but in others it could be exceptionally difficult. So much depends on the disposition of other people.

There are many people who are abrupt and difficult and it seems as if they derive pleasure from making things unpleasant for those around them. At one time or another, such people enter the sphere of your life. If you try and solve the problem by ignoring them, you avoid the problem. At the same time you might miss the opportunity to get to know a unique, although difficult personality.

Handling the problem of human relations constructively requires patience and sympathetic understanding on your part. You will keep quiet and give others the opportunity to talk and even if what they say hurts, you will maintain control over the situation by remaining calm. Under such circumstances you will learn and discover that behind the rough exterior and apparent rudeness, there is a life that yearns for love and friendship.

If you can help meet that need, then you have learnt the special art of freeing restrained personalities and making friends out of potential enemies.

God of grace and love, in Your strength I strive to obtain an understanding of all people so that I can live in peace with them. *Amen.*

Are You Seeking the Lord?

If only I knew where to find Him; if only I could go to His dwelling! I would state my case before Him and fill my mouth with arguments.

~ Job 23:3-4

Throughout the Christian world today we find people who are seeking the Lord so they can get to know Him better. You find them in care groups, revival campaigns, seminars, study groups, and those who meditate in solitude. Their desire for God is so great that they strive endlessly to find Him.

Many such people maintain that they have a relationship with God that originates from a dramatic form of worship where emotions reach a high and where emphasis is placed on excitement. Others maintain that they have found Him in the solitude of meditation.

If you truly want to find Christ, look at the world around you – where you live and work. When you help a beggar, or show compassion to somebody in distress, where you offer friendship to the lonely, when you dedicate your time to converse with the aged or to play with children, when you visit the sick and console the mournful, when you attempt to comfort the dispirited.

If you do any of these things and be of service to your fellow man: look deep into the eyes of the person that you minister to and there you will find Jesus who said, "Whatever you did for one of the least of these brothers of Mine, you did for Me'" (Matt. 25:40).

Lord God, let me find You in the world around me and amongst the people who need me. *Amen.*

Do You Have the Courage to Care?

Then the LORD said to Cain, "Where is your brother Abel?"
"I don't know," he replied. "Am I my brother's keeper?"

~ GENESIS 4:9

No one lives in isolation and only for himself. You are dependent on others for the food you eat and the clothes you wear. It is unrealistic to say, "I am self-sufficient." People are created to depend on one another, that's just how it is.

Due to this basic fact, human beings are essentially divided into two groups. Those who want to receive without giving: the takers; and those who find joy and fulfillment in making themselves available to others in service: the givers. It requires great courage to give of yourself through the act of love. It means that you must identify very closely with the person you want to help.

If you question the wisdom of becoming involved in the distress of someone who needs your help, what is the alternative? Will it make you happy to turn your back on someone who needs you? The knowledge that someone needs you should give you the courage to react without considering the cost.

It is an inspiring truth that when you react to the deepest distress of your fellow man, the Almighty God will give you the wisdom and strength to do what must be done. You can never care for someone in distress without experiencing the blessing of the Lord on your efforts.

This is the inheritance of those whose philosophy in life is: "I am not only my brother's keeper; I am my brother's brother!"

My God and my Provider, thank You that I am blessed in a unique way when I help others. *Amen.*

Delegated Responsibility

"I will take of the Spirit that is on you and put the Spirit on them. They will help you carry the burden of the people so that you will not have to carry it alone."

~ NUMBERS 11:17

There are many dedicated children of the Lord who serve their Master and their fellow man with dedication and enthusiasm, even putting their own health on the line by doing this.

They volunteer to do any task that arises and, eventually they have so many divergent responsibilities that they cannot do anything properly.

The intellectual and spiritual tension on their lives then becomes so big that it visibly affects the condition of their health.

Many pastors and church members are so conscientious and concerned about their God-given task that they are not willing to share it with anyone else fearing that it will not be done according to their standards. Therefore, they stubbornly refuse to delegate the Lord's work to other talented Christian disciples.

In the end there is so much to do and so little time in which to do it that nothing is done properly. If God has called you for a specific task, it is your privilege and duty to do it to the best of your ability. This does not mean you cannot ask for help from others. Accept your God-given responsibility, but never regard a request for help as neglecting your duty. With the help of others you can most likely serve God more effectively.

Master, when You give me a task, teach me to co-operate with others to complete it. *Amen.*

Relieve Someone's Needs

I devoted myself to study and to explore by wisdom all that is done under heaven.

~ ECCLESIASTES 1:13

The principle of identifying a need and then satisfying it, forms the basic philosophy behind many fortunes.

Everywhere in the world there are needs waiting to be relieved. God may ask you to do precisely that. The need you will have to satisfy will possibly not bring you a fortune or enable you to establish an empire, but it may be more important than both of these in the eyes of God.

Can you look around and honestly tell God that you do not see any need? That difficult person whom no one understands and whom everyone tries to avoid may have an urgent need for a sympathetic ear and an understanding heart. That widow, or divorcée who has been shut out from the community in a subtle way through no fault of their own, would certainly react to the offer of sincere friendship. There is probably a need in the life of the next person you will meet. You only need to be sensitive enough to the prompting of the Holy Spirit to notice it.

You may ask why you should tire yourself with the needs or distress of others while you have enough problems of your own. The answer is simple: you belong to Christ! As His follower, dare you neglect relieving someone's needs? He said that if we do it for the least important of His brothers, we do it for Him!

Teach me, Holy Spirit, to be sensitive towards my fellow man. *Amen.*

Lost Opportunities

"If you, even you, had only known on this day what would bring you peace – but now it is hidden from your eyes."
~ LUKE 19:42

There are certainly few people who can say in all sincerity that they have no self-reproach about letting opportunities for doing a friendly deed or speaking a word of encouragement slip past. A day seldom passes without the opportunity to cheer up someone who is depressed; to help someone who is going through a hard time; or to speak a friendly word to someone whom the struggles of life are threatening to overwhelm.

To be sensitive to the distress of others, and to do your utmost to relieve that distress is a definite way of preventing regret, when it is too late to do anything about it. To be offered the opportunity of doing a kind deed for someone, and then to turn away instead, will impoverish you more than the other person.

It is a basic rule of life that it is impossible to enrich other people's lives through love and good deeds without enriching your own life at the same time. Giving yourself in love and service to others is the privilege of everyone who loves and serves Christ with a sincere heart. It is a certain way to spiritual growth.

Find God's purpose for your life while you serve others in His glorious name. Throw yourself enthusiastically into the service of your fellow man. Use every opportunity in His strength, and the future will hold no self-reproach for you.

Holy Lord Jesus, make me sensitive to the distress of others and help me not to let any opportunity for service pass me by. *Amen.*

Are You Uninvolved?

Then the LORD said to Cain, "Where is your brother Abel?" "I don't know," he replied. "Am I my brother's keeper?"

~ GENESIS 4:9

Much of the evil in the world can be ascribed to uninvolvement in the face of distress in the lives of our fellow man. For a number of reasons, there are so many people who are inclined to follow the example of the priest and the Levite in the parable of the Good Samaritan. They prefer "passing on the other side", instead of feeling deeply sorry for the victim of the crime.

Their reasons may differ and their attitudes may be ascribed to embarrassment, inability or a fear of rejection. More often than not, they are so involved with their own affairs, or their own problems, that they do not have time to get involved with other people's problems. Even worse, they do not even notice the other person's distress.

Jesus gave us two commandments that He emphasized as the most important. The one is to love God with your entire being, and the other is to love your neighbor as yourself. A Christian cannot ignore his fellow man. Uninvolvement has no place in the Christian faith and your concern for the welfare of your fellow man is a barometer of your love for God.

It does not require much effort to notice the distress in today's world. Reach out a helping hand to others and experience the presence of God in your service done in His name.

Use me, Lord, to serve amongst my fellow man. *Amen.*

We Need Each Other

Let us not become weary in doing good, for at the proper time we
will reap a harvest if we do not give up.

~ GALATIANS 6:9

Scientific, academic and technological progress has created a sophisticated world to live in that has many advantages.

However, there are also disadvantages that follow progress. It
is difficult to live a simple and uncomplicated life in these modern times. Heavy demands are made on people of all genders and
ages.

Signs of stress and tension are noticeable as the qualifying requirements increase, greater productivity is required, and many
people are regarded as redundant in the prime of their lives. We
pay a high price for progress and people suffer psychologically,
mentally, physically and emotionally because of it.

Now is the time for Christianity to be active for the sake of
people in distress. We must draw from the wells of wisdom and
discernment that are granted to us by the Holy Spirit, and utilize
our talents to the full.

We must always be aware of the needs of others. Lend a helping hand where required; be ready to listen and, if you are so
guided, give advice; comfort those in despair and help to build
their self-confidence. Christ expects His disciples to listen to the
cries of distress around them and to do something about it!

Merciful Lord, stand by me while I try to serve You amongst those
who are in need. *Amen.*

Reach Out to Others

"Whatever you did for one of the least of these brothers of Mine, you did for Me."

~ Matthew 25:40

Let us thank God for those people who take pleasure in helping others. No task is too small for them, and they rejoice in doing good unobtrusively. They do not seek any reward, except for making life richer and easier for their fellow man. People like that are usually happy. It is seldom that you will come across somebody who makes life more pleasant for others, who is dejected.

To forget about yourself in the service of others, is not only the religious path of life, but also the path to a full and satisfying life. The only way in which you can be convinced of this, is by giving of yourself in the service of others.

Now is the best time to start. Find somebody who is in need. You will not have to look far, because the world is full of people who are destitute. A lonely person might welcome friendship; someone who is confused will appreciate a good and understanding listener; a lonely person might welcome visitors heartily; a single parent might welcome a responsible child-minder so as to go out for an evening.

There are so many different ways in which to help. While you are helping others, you will receive a rich blessing as your reward. Every good deed that is performed in the name of Christ bestows a blessing on both the giver and the receiver. Most of all, it brings glory to His name.

Lord and Master, make me sensitive to the needs of others. *Amen.*

The Ministry of Angels

Do not forget to entertain strangers, for by so doing some people have entertained angels without knowing it.

~ HEBREWS 13:2

The concept of angels does not meet with everybody's approval, but this does not mean that there aren't spiritual beings who serve God and assist people. There are many cases in the Bible where angels were sent as God's messengers to people.

However, the thought of a winged being, as portrayed in works of art, is unrealistic. If angels walked amongst us in our times, we would not be able to distinguish them from ordinary people. They would be known only by their conduct and not by what they wear or how they look.

The thought that there could be angels in this world, presents us with a fresh approach and a new appreciation for our fellow beings. Instead of looking for their faults, you will discover something of their God-given talents. Where the best in people is often concealed by layers of pride and self-glorification, you must look for something of the true glory that God has planted in the souls of all people.

God's serving angels often work unobtrusively as they attempt to make life easier and more pleasant for those they come into contact with: a visit to a lonely or depressed person, or caring for somebody who has nobody to care for him. These, and many other things, are all tasks that are being performed by serving angels. Has it ever occurred to you that you could be a serving angel of God?

Lord, help me to be an instrument of Your love. Help me to serve others in love. *Amen.*

Caring for Others Could Cure the World

Each of you should look not only to your own interests, but also to the interests of others.

~ Philippians 2:4

Selfishness or self-centeredness undoubtedly stands out as one of the major causes of disturbed human relationships. Regardless of the level of the community where it may manifest itself – either on the national or international stage, or in our relationships with one another – a lack of caring and consideration for others places a blot on society.

Jesus' whole life was devoted to caring for others. His love for people was all-embracing. This was obvious in His behavior and treatment of everyone He came into contact with. Despite the circumstances, regardless of the consequences, His first thought was always for others; even when He was nailed to the cross.

Jesus commanded His followers to love one another as He loves us. It is unavoidable that this will include self-sacrifice. In our ministry of love to one another, we must show others the same compassion and forgiving love that the Master has for us. Only in so doing, can the wounds of this world be healed.

Harmony between people can only be achieved through obedience to Christ's commands. In this way you can play an important role – through God's grace.

Holy Spirit of God, fill me with the desire and the ability to love my neighbor as You love me. *Amen.*

Live to Bless Your Fellow Man

"Love your neighbor as yourself."

~ MATTHEW 22:39

It is so easy to become self-centered. You talk about what you want and what you own, until you start to feel that this world has been created especially for you. If this happens, something of immeasurable value dies within you and people will no longer seek your company. Self-centeredness can destroy the beauty of your character.

If you want to live a full, satisfying and free life, you need other people around you whom you can love and serve. It is only through loving service to your neighbor that you can grow to spiritual and intellectual maturity. Jesus emphasized this fact when He said, "For whoever wants to save his life will lose it, but whoever loses his life for Me will find it" (Matt. 16:25). Live to bless other people, and you will be rendered speechless by how the quality of your own life improves.

If you want your life to have meaning and purpose, it is important to lose yourself in someone or a cause that is greater than yourself. It is at this level that Jesus Christ reveals Himself as the Great Inspirer of people like you and me, and who said, "Remain in Me, and I will remain in you" (John 15:4). He also said, "Love your enemies and pray for those who persecute you" (Matt. 5:44).

To bless in this way in the power of Christ, is to discover a full and satisfying life.

Lord, help me to live a life of service so that I can experience a full and rich life. *Amen.*

What Does Your "Caring" Mean?

"'Look after him,' he said, 'and when I return, I will reimburse you for any extra expense you may have.'"

~ LUKE 10:35

True sympathy is a heart-warming experience. When it is offered to others, it could console a sorrowful heart and comfort those who are discouraged. To be deeply touched by the misfortunes of others enriches your spirit, because true sympathy stirs the most profound emotions and enables you to understand the sadness and pain of others.

The Good Samaritan experienced such emotions when he "took pity on" the victim of the robbers at the roadside. However, he did not merely sympathize, but actively did something practical to ease the suffering of the unfortunate man. Sympathy is a splendid sentiment, but it is enriched when practically applied.

How practical sympathy could be applied, however, is not always clear. Sometimes it would seem as if all you can do is to say, "I feel for you." However, that is better than saying nothing. If possible, a short visit will have helping and healing results. Never hesitate to visit people who have experienced sorrow or disaster. Just showing that you care is already a consolation to them.

There is something which you can do that has healing qualities, and that is to pray for the person. To know that they are receiving support in prayer can be of great comfort to people. And the one who prays is enriched by the knowledge that he or she is a channel of God's healing grace and comfort.

Make me an instrument of Your healing grace, O Master, so that I may be a blessing to all who are in distress. *Amen.*

The Crucial Power of Love

"You have let go of the commands of God and are holding on to the traditions of men."

~ MARK 7:8

Rituals and traditions have always played an important role in the affairs of people. This is especially true in the church, where congregational life and practices are to a large extent controlled by the church ordinance and liturgy, the existence of which is attributable to human reasoning.

While it is essential, for the sake of order, that any group of people must adhere to rules so that everything can be run fairly, it is of the utmost importance that these things do not become a dominating factor in any Christian community.

The foundation of any denomination or congregation must be absolute surrender, devotion and obedience to God. It must be born from pure love for Him. Jesus Christ must be the central figure in all things and His will and wishes must always get preference, over the will of people, regardless of how well-meaning the latter may be.

In order to be a channel of the love of God, you must surrender yourself unconditionally to the influence and guidance of the Holy Spirit. If you surrender yourself to Christ, you will also be able to identify man-made rules with the wisdom of the Holy Spirit and implement them through the love of God. In this way, you will be able to serve yourself and your community according to God's will.

Holy Spirit, bring me to total surrender, devotion and obedience to the God of Love. *Amen.*

Love Can Rule the World

Live in harmony with one another; be sympathetic, love as brothers, be compassionate and humble.

~ 1 Peter 3:8

The world is filled with the noise of accusations and counter-accusations. Nation against nation; organization against organization; person against person. The threat of war hangs heavily over virtually all countries. Aggressive dispositions come to the fore and become the rule rather than the exception.

There is not much that ordinary people can do to suddenly calm the world down. However, it is the duty of every Christian to start somewhere. You must start in the neighborhood where you live and work.

It costs nothing to be courteous and friendly, obliging and kind. It is not difficult to offer sympathy to someone who is heavily burdened with problems. That is what Christian love is all about: caring about others.

If you are willing to allow Jesus to use you in the service of your fellow men, you can make an enormous impact on your environment. If everyone was willing to do this, love could rule the world.

All things are possible with God. Open your life to His Holy Spirit and start serving others with love. You could be the beginning of a flood of love that will submerge the world.

Lord God, let Your love submerge the world and rule it by conquering the hearts of people. *Amen.*

Share Another's Suffering

They sat on the ground with him for seven days and seven nights.
No one said a word to him, because they saw how great his suffer-
ing was.

~ JOB 2:13

Job's friends probably did not know why their friend had to suffer so terribly, but there's no doubt about the sincerity of their sympathy. They just sat with him for seven days and seven nights and their wordless presence was a balm for Job's distressed spirit.

The principle of compassionate assistance in suffering, shown by Job's three friends, is a true Christian virtue. In your life you might be confronted with the suffering and sorrow of a dear friend, but circumstances might prevent you from doing anything to alleviate the pain.

This is a heart-rending experience, and can cause frustration as well as inner confusion. Do not allow these distressing circumstances to undermine your faith. Just trust in the omnipresence and omnipotence of God.

Hold on to your faith in the face of every kind of adversity. Your sympathy will increase and you will become a source of power and faith to the person who is suffering – even if you are unable to express yourself eloquently. Just knowing that you are compassionately and prayerfully present will be a great comfort to the suffering soul.

Strengthen me, dear Lord and Master, so that I may become a source of power and comfort to those who suffer. *Amen.*

People's Needs

Let us then approach the throne of grace with confidence, so that we may receive mercy and find grace to help us in our time of need.

⁓ HEBREWS 4:16

The average Christian lives under very normal circumstances. He or she experiences joy, happiness, failure and success and also shares in the aspirations of the community he or she is part of. There are some followers of Christ, however, who stress the scriptural call for Christians to isolate themselves from this sinful world. They try to have as little contact as possible with non-Christians.

Such an attitude denies the very essence of Christ's incarnation, because He came to the world to save sinners. To do so He mixed with all types of people, even those who were considered unacceptable in His time. Scripture declares that Jesus died for sinners. How will they be able to know Jesus unless they see His beauty and power revealed in your life?

If you know Christ as your Savior, you develop an understanding for the needs of others. Because people don't talk about their needs, we should not take it for granted that they don't have any. Through the guidance of the Holy Spirit, Christians can become acutely aware of others' spiritual and everyday needs.

There are many ways in which you can discover and ease another person's burden if you ask God to reveal them to you. Disciples who live in continual harmony with the Holy Spirit will find this easy.

Please use me, Almighty Savior, to notice and alleviate the burdens of others by Your grace and under the guidance of the Holy Spirit. *Amen.*

Let Love Inspire Your Service

"Blessed is the King who comes in the name of the Lord! Peace in heaven and glory in the highest!"

~ LUKE 19:38

When we read the account of Jesus' triumphant journey into Jerusalem, we cannot help but feel the joy and excitement of those who offered Him such a sincere welcome. He was the long-awaited Messiah who would usher in an era of peace, joy, hope and liberation: "Blessed is the King who comes in the name of the Lord!"

Throughout the ages this same feeling of wonderment, awe and joy has been experienced by people who welcomed Christ into their lives. Jesus said that He came so that you may experience the fullness of life (see John 10:10). This means that you can live in peace and calm in the certain knowledge that He is with you at all times.

Just as the people of Jerusalem were a captive nation under the hated yoke of the Roman oppressors, so today many people are enslaved by habits that are extremely detrimental to their well-being. The living Christ offers to liberate you from these habits. Similarly, there are many people seeking love, grace and compassion in a world that can be very cruel at times. This is exactly what Jesus still offers today to those who accept Him as their Redeemer and Savior.

Welcome the Master into your life with the same joy as the people of Jerusalem did and experience the joy that Christ brings.

Redeemer and Friend, in love and compassion, by Your grace You raise me from sin and shame, so that I may be Your joyful child. *Amen.*

Encouragement

The Sovereign Lord has given me an instructed tongue, to know the word that sustains the weary.

~ Isaiah 50:4

Words have immeasurable power and influence. Because the effect of the spoken word can be so far-reaching, it is vitally important that we use our words carefully.

In every area of life you will find people who regard it their duty to discourage others. Unfortunately most of the time this is because they are jealous of, and begrudge, the successes of others.

As followers of the Master, who strive to follow His example, we must consciously try to say things that inspire and encourage. This does not imply that we must agree with everything, but that we speak a word of wisdom and encouragement to those who require help and guidance.

Sometimes it might be necessary to criticize, but this should never be done in an unfriendly or harsh manner. Let it always be in love, constructive and with Christ's attitude. To be a person who encourages makes you a blessing where you live and work.

When you start treating people in this way, you will inspire your own spirit and you will become gloriously conscious of the Lord's presence in your life. Therefore, start practicing the ministry of encouragement in His name. It is highly unlikely that you will experience despair yourself while encouraging others, especially if it is done in the attitude and love of the great Comforter.

Gracious Lord, You have encouraged me so often. Make me willing to be a source of encouragement to others. *Amen.*

Reflect the Presence of Christ

When Moses came down from Mount Sinai with the two tablets
of the Testimony in his hands, he was not aware that his face was
radiant because he had spoken with the LORD.

~EXODUS 34:29

People often say that every picture tells a story, and this also applies to a person's facial expression. Often it is possible to tell at a glance what kind of person you are dealing with, what emotions he is experiencing and whether this is the type of person you can trust – all by merely looking at a facial expression.

However, we often judge other people wrongly, with the result that we are sometimes disappointed. There are also those who formed a wrong first impression of someone only to regret it later. But you never have to doubt a person who has an intimate relationship with the living Christ. It will always be evident, because the love and compassion of Christ is visible in that person since he looks at you through the eyes of Jesus.

If you cultivate an intimate relationship with Jesus, you will become more and more like Him, because His Holy Spirit is working in you and reaches out to others through you. Allow Him into your life and allow His love to flow through you to others. Then you will live a life of plenty, which only Jesus can give you (see John 10:10).

Lord Jesus Christ, grant me the privilege of being an instrument of Your peace. *Amen.*

Practical Christianity

"Now that you know these things, you will be blessed if you do them."

~ JOHN 13:17

The communist Karl Marx professed that religion was the opium of the people; a candy-coated pill to make everyday life bearable; a pie in the sky when you die. What he actually meant was that people become so obsessed with religion that the things concerning their daily existence are of little value to them. Unfortunately it is often true that people become so heavenly-minded, that they are of no earthly use.

True religion acknowledges the authority of Christ in everyday life issues and applies His message practically. Praise to Christ must be visible in your relationships with other people. Without that your faith has no substance.

It is possible to become so enthusiastic about the content of the gospel, that you forget the call of the Master to apply His message in practical, constructive service. It is also possible to sidestep Christ's challenge to live a holy and committed life by surrendering only to the social application of His message.

Between enthusiastic discipleship and Christian service, lies the road that the Master has sanctified: living in total harmony with God and your fellow man. When you have accepted this challenge in His strength, the world will know whom you belong to and in whose service you stand.

Perfect Example, thank You for enabling me through the Holy Spirit to accept the challenges of practical Christianity. *Amen.*

Get Off the Grandstand

"If anyone would come after Me, he must deny himself and take up his cross and follow Me."

~ MARK 8:34

Paul had probably often watched the Isthmus Games in Corinth and looked on as unarmed Christians fought for their lives against wild animals in the Colosseum in Rome. While a few were fighting in the arena, thousands sat on the grandstand, cheering.

In the same way many of us have become spectators on the sidelines of life. Thousands upon thousands are sitting on the grandstand while a handful are fighting courageously. Many people call themselves Christians, but never think of getting involved, or of sacrificing anything for their convictions.

And how do the spectators react when their team's achievements fall short of their expectations? They jeer and criticize.

People who do things for God's Kingdom are certainly not perfect. Someone was once heard saying, "I've got nothing against Jesus Christ, but it's His ground staff that bothers me." We may not, however, remain neutral because we know that we are not perfect.

In this world a never-ending feud is raging between good and evil, right and wrong, truth and lie, light and darkness, life and death. That is why God's children dare not remain on the grandstand. Jesus Himself never remained neutral – even though it cost Him His life. He expects us to follow suit. Christianity involves dynamic action in life's arena!

Use my life O Lord, let it glorify You more and more. *Amen.*

The Titus-Ministry

God, who comforts the downcast, comforted us by the coming of Titus, and not only by his coming but also by the comfort you had given him.

~ 2 Corinthians 7:6-7

The world is teeming with people who are downcast. And with it prophets of doom; people who take a morbid delight in spreading disturbing prophecies and rumors. They are never happier than when they can upset others with their idle gossip.

When people are at their lowest, they need the company of someone who can encourage them. As an encourager, you should always find something positive to comment on.

A true follower of Jesus Christ will always try to have a stabilizing influence on a disturbing situation. Even though prophets of doom predict disasters, you can bring confidence and encouragement into the lives of those who are insecure and fearful of the future.

If you want to practice the Titus-ministry of encouragement and convey a spirit of stability to insecure, discouraged people, you need inner spiritual qualities that can only be obtained through continuous fellowship with the living Christ in your daily life.

If you live and work in the presence of Jesus Christ, your life will not only be enriched, but you will also bring comfort and blessings into the lives of those you meet. This is a glorious but important ministry, because by God's grace you have the ability to encourage, inspire and stabilize.

Through the strength I receive by Your grace, Lord Jesus, I will try to inspire and encourage others. *Amen.*

Life Partners

*"I no longer call you servants, because a servant does not know his
master's business. Instead, I have called you friends, for everything
that I learned from My Father I have made known to you."*

~ JOHN 15:15

It is only when you have earnestly requested the risen Christ to
become your life partner that you realize the full impact and implications of your Christian faith. A partnership implies the shared
responsibility to achieve a common goal. When Christ is in control, your life undergoes a change and transformation.

The purpose of the ministry of Christ is to unify you with the
Father. He asks for your cooperation to achieve this by acknowledging His sovereignty and His redemptive power in your life. If
you do, you will experience a growing awareness of His presence
in your daily life, because you are following the path that Christ
has mapped out for you.

Such a wonderful partnership, which is connected to such a
magnificent goal, may sound idealistic and impractical, but it is
the pinnacle of wisdom. To live your life in partnership with God
and with a focus on spiritual matters, brings an exceptional balance to your life.

With Christ managing and controlling your life, you possess
a code of conduct inspired by the Holy Spirit. You will not be a
sleeping partner, but eager to manifest the partnership in your life
at all times.

My Lord and Master, in partnership with You I will live and work in
victory. I thank You for Your love and grace. *Amen.*

Serve Christ Joyfully

"If you love Me, you will obey what I command."

~ John 14:15

Many people regard their surrender to Christ as a strict discipline that adds an unbearable burden on their lives. They feel that the cost of being a disciple is too high a price to pay. As the demands of their faith increase, their grip on Christ weakens until they completely lose it and relapse. They consequently lead an unsatisfying spiritual life that lacks fulfillment.

You must never regard your attachment to the cause of Christ as a burden. Your life in Christ should be joyful, and as you grow in Christ, your joy should increase. If you are truly devoted to Christ, your highest desire will be to get to know Him better and serve Him more effectively. As you grow in faith you will constantly strive towards ways of serving Him better because you want to – not because you have to.

To reach this point in your pilgrimage, you have to get to know Him increasingly better through Bible study and wholesome Christian literature. However, you also have to know the living Christ personally by talking with Him in prayer. Strive to be with Christ, and the more He becomes an inseparable part of your life, the more joy you will experience in His service.

I rejoice in Your service, O Lord. Thank You for this wonderful privilege. *Amen.*

Walk with Jesus

As they talked and discussed these things with each other, Jesus Himself came up and walked along with them.

~ Luke. 24:15

Tragic events paralyzed Jesus' first disciples. They were unable to see beyond the darkness of the crucifixion and therefore they could not remember Jesus' promises. Consequently, the road to Emmaus was shrouded in despondent darkness for the disciples.

Jesus joined them on this journey, but they did not even recognize Him. Initially He was only a stranger who astonished them with His ignorance of recent events. But when He started to explain the Scriptures, He became a Prophet to them, and they listened to Him with interest. After they had invited Him to spend the night with them, they recognized Him as the Master they loved.

The events on the road to Emmaus were not unique in Christian experience. Many have walked this path in His company without recognizing Him. He showered His blessings on them and they did not respond to His love. They may have listened to the gospel for years without grasping its full meaning. They may even claim to have been converted, and yet the joy and reality of true faith has passed them by.

The wonderful truth is that the Master is with you every step of the way. Even when He is regarded as a stranger, He remains your Friend; even when His blessings aren't recognized, He keeps giving; and if you listen to His Word He reveals Himself to you.

Powerful Redeemer, I no longer want to treat You as a stranger, but I accept You completely as my Savior and Redeemer. *Amen.*

We Belong to One Another

"God so loved the world that He gave His one and only Son."

~ John 3:16

It is a glorious and overwhelming truth that you belong to God. Undeserving and unworthy as you may be, the eternal Father has called you and made you His child. The love that He has poured out on you reassures your innermost being and frees your spirit, so that you unmistakably know that you belong to Him.

You might not be able to explain this experience, but you know to your own joyous satisfaction that you are God's child and that you belong to Him. Yet, there is a still greater and more glorious truth born out of God's love: not only do you belong to God, but He belongs to you.

God, in His immeasurable love, has made Himself available so that you can own Him to the extent in which you accept Him. Once you have accepted Him and made this truth your own, you enter a new dimension of life.

God gives you wisdom so that you can deal with your problems in a calm and constructive way. You become aware of a dynamic inner strength that is not your own or from yourself. This strength helps you to resist temptations and to live victoriously. God becomes a living reality as He starts to flow through you to others.

To be owned by Him and to own Him, are the two greatest experiences of the Christian faith. They bring the reality of God back to the everyday life.

Lord God, I rejoice in the fact that I belong to You and that I experience inner strength and power when I realize that You belong to me. *Amen.*

When Strangers Meet

You are to love those who are aliens, for you yourselves were aliens in Egypt.

~ Deuteronomy 10:19

There is a song with the title: "A stranger is just a friend you do not know." This reveals one of life's great truths. Every day you meet people you may never see again. Like ships in the night you move past each other. Yet circumstances sometimes force people to spend time in the presence of strangers, even if it is only for a short while.

You might stand in an elevator with strangers today. Each person is caught up in his own train of thought and nobody says anything. But when one person suddenly says something pleasant, the silence vanishes. A friendly word more often than not draws a friendly response.

Many people protect themselves in a cocoon of isolation. They believe that the less contact they have with other people, the less the chances there are of getting hurt. Such private people are very sensitive to the moods of others and react to them easily. When you move amongst strangers, it is important that you, as a Christian, radiate a positive and loving attitude. You don't have to say anything, but if you love people for the sake of Christ, they will instinctively feel the love and react to it.

With the attitude of Jesus Christ visible in your life, there would be more sunshine and joy in this harsh and unfriendly world.

Lord Jesus, You are my example. Help me to respect others and to accept them in love. *Amen.*

Gratitude

Rejoice in the Lord always. Again I will say, rejoice!
~ Philippians 4:4 (nkjv)

Many people experience their religion as a somber burden which they feel compelled to bear. They feel compelled to attend church services and to worship, and when they don't do it, they feel very guilty. Bible study and prayer have become a form of duty to them which they have to do in order to please a formidable God. The result is that their submission to the Christian teachings and objectives is simply a colorless habit which doesn't have any deeper meaning to them.

This approach is a total misrepresentation! There is nothing colorless or boring about Christ's life here on earth and there is nothing dull in the abundant life which He offers us. As with everything else in life, it depends on what you make of it. If you are experiencing a colorless spiritual life, you should take a serious look at yourself.

Jesus Christ invites you to become part of His life. He wants to become a part of your life, in order that, as He Himself said, "Your joy no one will take from you" (John 16:22 nkjv). Then the joy of Christ becomes full in our lives. The whole Christian experience is one of great joy because Jesus overcame sin and death.

With such a rich inheritance to look forward to, can you do otherwise than to rejoice in the Lord in such a way that the whole world will know who your Source of joy is? Let us stop cursing the darkness and rather light a candle of joy, thus helping to dispel the darkness.

O Lord, I rejoice in You. I take delight in Your presence. *Amen.*

Joy in the Lord

Serve the LORD with gladness; come before His presence with singing.

~ PSALM 100:2 (NKJV)

Strange as it may sound, most people feel worship is a burden and not a joy. They feel that they have to lay down so many things that are precious to them and enter into a life of seriousness and hardship. They forget the fact that when God asks us to lay down our old life, we can be confident that He will replace it with something much better.

Don't believe for one moment that when God requires total obedience from you, that your life will lose its joy and gladness. God probably finds it easier to use an obedient, happy person in His service than one who is overwhelmed by the idea of the heavy responsibility he believes is required to serve the Lord.

He promised to bear our burdens if we obey and trust Him. If He calls you to obedience, trust Him completely and have a positive and cheerful faith.

Many of God's servants have great responsibilities, but they don't bear them on their own, because they are thoroughly aware that His everlasting arms are supporting them.

If God has called you to a special responsibility in His vineyard, don't become despondent to the point where your life becomes a burden. Rejoice in the Lord and in His omnipotence and accept your duty with gladness and gratitude.

I want to accept my task with gladness, Lord, because I know that with Your help it will never be too burdensome for me. *Amen.*

The Power of Thanksgiving

"He who is joined to the Lord is one spirit with Him."

~ 1 CORINTHIANS 6:17

Joy and gladness are not the main goals of a Christian's faith, but important by-products of it. When you have experienced the inflowing of Christ's life-giving Spirit, the joy of a Christ-filled life becomes yours.

To be united with Him and to share in Christ's life, presupposes that you will have a relationship with Him and that you will experience the peace and power of His indwelling presence. Such an experience is much more than an emotion because it is founded on a living faith of someone who has accepted His forgiveness and only lives to portray Christ in the midst of life's harsh realities.

Forgiveness, which goes hand-in-hand with a Spirit-filled life, gives tremendous joy to all who strive to live "in Christ". But the summit of this joy is to be conscious of Christ's living presence.

You find yourself in fellowship with Him at all times and in every place. The more you become aware of His closeness, the stronger and more meaningful your faith gets. Then you realize that your faith is in actual fact your personal relationship with the living Christ.

There is no way in which we can express this pure joy in words – except to live in gratitude for His glory and to serve our fellow man as He did.

I want to express my gratitude to You, Father. Thank You that I can walk closely with You. *Amen.*

Grateful Obedience

"[I will] put breath in you; and you shall live."

~ EZEKIEL 37:6

If your faith has lost its energy, the time has come for you to take stock spiritually. It is not the will of your heavenly Father that your faith in Him should be a burden to you. Therefore, the cause of your spiritual deadness lies in yourself and not in Him.

Perhaps, in your zeal and enthusiasm to serve Him, you have set your mind more on getting things done, than on following the will of the Lord.

The courage of your faith carried you for a time, but has now decreased fast. You discover that though you were busy working for God, you have lost the consciousness of His divine presence in your life. Something indispensable has vanished from your life.

There is but one way to revival. In order for you to taste the joy of an experience with God through Jesus Christ again, you must make your heart the home of His Holy Spirit. Through God's indwelling Spirit, you will start living a victorious life in Jesus again.

The greatest joy, however, lies in the fact that your life is reflecting the glory of Christ again, even though it may be in a small measure. When this happens, your faith becomes an inspiration as well as the motivational force in your life. It becomes the most important matter of your life, because Christ is a glorious reality.

Holy Spirit, take control of my life so that I may reclaim my zeal and fervor for You. Inspire me through Your Holy Spirit. *Amen.*

Joy of Faith

Do everything without complaining or arguing.

~ PHILIPPIANS 2:14

The Christian's life is a life of service and submission. It may be that you are called to work among people in distress, or that your calling is administration, preaching or another form of service. Whatever it is, it will demand that you sacrifice your time and yourself in the service of Christ.

Unfortunately many people have the habit of performing their task for Christ with a negative attitude. They will do their work and often do it well, but they are unpleasant people with poor interpersonal relationships. This spoils the quality of their deeds, which should be manifestations of compassion or mercy in the name of Christ. The result is that people hesitate to approach them because of the attitude that they encounter.

You must always remember that whatever task you are assigned to do for Jesus is to be done in His name, and therefore your attitude will have a positive or negative influence on the Christian faith. To ensure that you reflect the glory and love of God in everything that you do, you must do it in the strength of the Holy Spirit.

Follow the example of love, compassion, understanding and humility that Christ set in His ministry. In this way your discipleship and service will be fruitful and effective, and fulfill its ultimate purpose to exalt God.

Master and Guide, I newly dedicate myself and my strength to Your service. Make me a joyful servant because I find my joy in You. *Amen.*

Practice Praise and Thanksgiving

Then the people of Israel – the priests, the Levites and the rest of the exiles – celebrated the dedication of the house of God with joy.

~ Ezra 6:16

Unfortunately, there are many people in the world who associate worship with despondency, cheerlessness and even fear. Their attendance of church services is little more than a duty done for habit's sake. The tragedy of an attitude like this is that it deprives people of the greatest of all joys – joy in the Lord.

Through Christ, God invites you to find peace in Him and to receive the fullness of life that He offers you. If you turn to Him you become increasingly aware of His life-giving Spirit that works in you. Seemingly unattainable goals are suddenly within your reach. Adversity does not overwhelm you because in Him you find the strength to overcome it; a newly found confidence replaces your nervous pessimism and feelings of failure. Day by day your faith grows stronger.

As you open yourself to the Holy Spirit, you will find that your worship, Bible study and prayer life gain new meaning. If you place your trust in the living Christ, you will discover that God is no longer a far-away figure, but an integral part of your life. He will lead you on the path that He has mapped out for you.

Worship ought to be a joyful experience. Open yourself to the Holy Spirit, and He will raise you from despondency to ecstasy in Christ.

O Holy Spirit, help me to find peace in You so that I may enjoy fullness of life. *Amen.*

Live Life to the Full

My soul glorifies the Lord and my spirit rejoices in God my Savior.

~ LUKE 1:46-47

Many people view their religion as a heavy and sometimes even unbearable burden. They easily frown upon any semblance of light-heartedness in spiritual matters. They stoop somberly under the heavy burden of their spiritual conscience. This is definitely not what God intended.

The faith of the Christian should be a joyous experience. Your Father takes joy in and is interested in your life. He is happy when you are happy; He consoles you in sadness and grief; He supports you when the burden becomes too heavy for you; He helps you up when you stumble over obstacles; He enjoys your successes as you enjoy them yourself.

Christianity does not eliminate joy and happiness from your life. On the contrary, it returns happiness to your life. Through your communion with the living Christ, you realize the blessing of His presence every day. The more you praise and thank Him, the more happiness you glean from your spiritual life.

Happiness is the fruit of the Holy Spirit (Gal. 5:22). Your surrender and devotion to the Lord should be revealed across the entire spectrum of your life. Then every day becomes a celebration of Him.

Dear Lord Jesus, I continually delight in the knowledge that You are always with me. *Amen.*

Count Your Blessings

Though the fig tree does not bud ... yet I will rejoice in the LORD, I will be joyful in God my Savior.

~ HABAKKUK 3:17-18

Many people have a problem linking Christianity and joy together because they think of religion as solemn, serious and rigid. The result is that they miss out on many dimensions of a balanced Christian life.

Some people think that Paul's call to the Philippians to rejoice in the Lord does not suit this worthy man of faith, and that it was also out of place in those times of bitter persecution.

However, Scripture teaches us that there is always joy to be found in God's presence. To experience this joy, it is imperative to live in total harmony with Him. Then you can rejoice in times of prosperity and adversity.

How we express our Christian joy depends on each individual's temperament. There are those who will express their joy in a spontaneous, jubilant manner, while others will experience it in a more subdued or reserved manner.

Yet it is not the expression itself that is important, but the actual experience. Never judge people's inner feelings by their outward expressions. Whether you are outwardly vocal about the wonder of being God's child or whether you experience unspoken joy – the main thing is to praise Him from a heart filled with gratitude.

Jesus, Source of all my joy, thank You that my joy is not dependent on my circumstances, but on my relationship with You. *Amen.*

Be Joyful

Rejoice in the Lord always. I will say it again: Rejoice! Let your gentleness be evident to all. The Lord is near.

~ PHILIPPIANS 4:4-5

Perhaps the time has come for Christians to take stock of their attitude towards life. Galatians 5:22 lists the fruit of the Spirit. First we find love: the greatest of all. Secondly Paul mentions joy: an equally important sign of redemption.

However, we find very little of this Christian joy in everyday life and tend to be somber, reserved, and morbid. This is a sad denial of the life of joy for a Christian.

Many people think we simply have to endure this life so that we can go to heaven one day. If, however, we do not practice the art of cheerfulness now, we will not appreciate the joy in heaven.

What the prodigal son in Jesus' parable missed most in the joyless country of sin was the joyful feasting in his father's house. That is why we, the redeemed, should become part of God's feast here and now. We do accept that our sins are forgiven, but refuse to express our joy daily. We cautiously and longingly remain on the edge of receiving invincible Christian joy, thus robbing ourselves and others of one of God's greatest gifts of grace.

The Christian's joy is in Christ Jesus – founded on an encounter with the Savior. In Christ, God not only came very near to us – no, God came *into* us. Christ met God's demands and filled our past, present and future with joy. Therefore, our joy should be unceasing and everlasting, because Christ is its Source.

Jesus, Joy of our lives, Source of all true goodness. We want to rejoice in You here on earth in preparation for heaven. *Amen.*

Rejoice in the Lord

You have made known to me the path of life, You will fill me with joy in Your presence, with eternal pleasures at Your right hand.

~ Psalm 16:11

For some people prayer is boring. This is especially true if the beauty of prescribed prayer has waned and it has become nothing but a habit. It smothers your longing for God. Prayer can also become an unbearable burden if it is only a meaningless repetition of words and phrases.

Prayer must be kept fresh and vibrant if you want it to achieve God's purpose. He never intended conversing with Him to be boring and dull. That is why the living presence of God and never our own needs and desires must always be at the center of our prayers.

You cannot be involved in praising and worshiping God without becoming intensely aware of the fact that you are in His holy presence. Praise is the doorway that leads you into the throne room of God. When you become conscious of being in His holy presence, you experience exceeding joy and glory like nowhere else on earth!

It is also praise that prevents our prayers from becoming meaningless. Praise uplifts you, despite your shortcomings, and creates a totally new relationship between you and God. It strengthens your faith, joy, zeal and interest in life. Learn to praise God – and start living on victorious ground. "Praise the Lord. Give thanks to the Lord, for He is good; His love endures forever" (Ps. 106:1-2).

O God who answers prayers, teach me to appreciate the power and real value of praising and worshiping You. *Amen.*

Joyous Christianity

All the days of the oppressed are wretched, but the cheerful heart has a continual feast.

~ PROVERBS 15:15

Paul was sitting in a cold cell of a Roman jail when he encouraged the Philippian Christians to be cheerful, "Rejoice in the Lord always. I will say it again: Rejoice!" (Phil. 4:4).

One of the most valuable gifts that the Holy Spirit has bestowed upon God's children is the gift of contagious gladness and joy.

Yet even the Christian's life is subject to tides of ever-changing emotions. The life of our Lord is an excellent example of this as He also experienced the heights and depths of the spirit.

The joy that Christ brings into our lives is much more than just a smile. There are times when you would much rather cry. However, when we set our minds on Christ, a peaceful spirit is established and this generates real joy and gladness. You live in the assurance that God is in control even in the most confusing times of your life. This blessed assurance is worth more than a mere smile or passing emotions.

Christian joy does not depend on emotions, but on the unchanging Lord. That is why you can say:

When wild, wild storms were raging
I found a steadfast Rock deep down:
The Word that saved me from disaster –
God is my Father; I His child!

I praise and thank You, Lord my God, that I can live joyfully and trustingly because Your Spirit dwells in me. *Amen.*

Christlike Happiness

He who has clean hands and a pure heart, who does not lift up his soul to an idol or swear by what is false. He will receive blessing from the Lord and vindication from God his Savior.

~ Psalm 24:4-5

Christ's happiness, blessing and joy are indestructible (see John 16:22). Christ's happiness is a blessing, even when we are in pain. It is a happiness that cannot be erased by sorrow, loss, disappointment or failure. It is a happiness that still sees a rainbow through your tears. It is something that nothing in life or death can deprive us of.

Christ's happiness is born from an intimate walk with God: today, through the dark night, tomorrow and every day. It is like the depth of the ocean that surges and seethes above, where waves toss and break, causing rough waters. However, underneath, it is quiet and calm. It is like the little bird that builds its nest on the rocky ledge under the thundering roar of the waterfall and, in the midst of the storm, serenely sits on its nest, hatching its little eggs.

Christ's happiness does not necessarily coincide with our circumstances. It is a deep joy – everlasting and steadfast. It is furthermore not something that we could cultivate through effort. It is a gift of God in our lives. The Holy Spirit will guide us to be obedient to the demands of Christ, so that His happiness and blessing will become our portion.

Loving Master, thank You that the happiness that You bestow is steadfast and indestructible, unlike the temporary and transient happiness of the world. *Amen.*

Indestructible Joy

Rejoice in the Lord always! I will say it again: Rejoice!
~ PHILIPPIANS 4:4

Life would have been very dull and monotonous without humor and smiles. But we were not all born with a well-developed sense of humor. As with any other gift, it too has to be nurtured and developed.

The ability to be amused by life is an art that can keep a person's mind balanced and even save one's life. Anyone who has experienced suffering will confirm this truth.

The old saying that laughter is the best medicine, holds much truth. To have a good sense of humor implies much more than the ability to laugh at a joke. It means to have sympathy towards other people's misfortune and to never take your own success or failure too seriously; to find pure joy in the thrill of life itself and in the humor of everyday events. True humor never laughs at a fellow human being, but with him. That is why humor has been defined as laughing with a tear.

A person who is only concerned about himself most probably has no sense of humor. We have to be sincerely interested in people and be sensitive to their mindsets and distress before we can see the humor in their situation. Then we are bringing a little sunshine into the world around us.

Do not allow your sense of humor to become rusty because you don't use it. Ask God to put some sparkle into your life through the Holy Spirit.

Heavenly Father, thank You for the joy You bring even in the darkest circumstances and situations. *Amen.*

Joy in Prayer

Teach us to number our days aright, that we may gain a heart of wisdom.

~ PSALM 90:12

Dr. Kathleen Heasman says in her book *An introduction to Pastoral Counseling* that there are three stages in man's life.

The first reaches its climax during youth, when achievements are reached in the fields of physical strength and speed. The second is middle-age, when a condition of maturity and self-confidence is achieved and the pinnacle of a chosen career is reached. The third is old age, when qualities of reasoning and experience are of the utmost importance and wisdom comes into its own.

One of the biggest mistakes one can make in life is trying to stay in a phase when you should have moved on a long time ago. Youth is a wonderful and beautiful time, but it passes. We must accept this fact. "A man amongst children, is a child amongst men!"

Middle age is the age when we have reached the top of the ladder in our careers. Here we are also tempted to linger for too long. No one is indispensable. Leaving while still at the pinnacle of success, is a clear form of success in itself.

Old age also has its own problems. One can so easily become self-centered and difficult. To be yourself and to constantly clash with others are recipes for loneliness and unhappiness. Remember that your children are maturing and that you should treat them as equals and not as little children. Only the grace of God and the Spirit of the living God can give you this wisdom.

Thank You, Creator Lord, for the phases of life. Give me the wisdom to move from one to the other with dignity. *Amen.*

Cheerful in Adversity

I will rejoice in the LORD, I will be joyful in God my Savior.

~ HABAKKUK 3:18

Many people have serious problems when they have to re-concile their Christianity with their joy. Ceremony, dignity and solemnity are all associated with our service to the heavenly Father. Many people think that Paul's call to rejoice in the Lord is somewhat vain.

The Scriptures teach us time and again that there is joy in the presence of our God. In order to experience this, however, we have to live in complete harmony with Him. This harmony is born from a pure love for the Father; a love which motivates and brings energy and joy to our lives. How we express this Christian joy will depend on every individual's temperament. In the family of God there is room for all types of people.

There are those who celebrate their joy with gestures and the clapping of hands. Others experience the joy and strength of God in silence. However it may be expressed, it is the experience itself that matters – not the way in which it is revealed.

Do not judge people's inner feelings by appearances. You may shout for joy and bow before God in astonishment because you are His child, or you may experience joy in silent, unspoken gladness. The most important part is that you praise Him in heartfelt gratitude. May you experience God's joy today and every day.

Jesus, Joy of my heart, I thank You that the love You pour into my heart leads to a joy that is not dependent on my circumstances. I thank You that I can express my joy in songs of praise. *Amen.*

Sense of Humor

Blessed is he who trusts in the LORD.

~ PROVERBS 16:20

Happiness is the one thing that all people anxiously seek. Yet it seems as if it constantly escapes most people. Someone once said, "Happiness is like a butterfly: if you hunt it, it will evade you; if you sit down quietly, it will come and sit on your shoulder."

We find it difficult because we forget that happiness is something that comes from deep inside when our spirit is in harmony with God. With God in the center of our lives, it is possible to find lasting happiness, even in the most trying circumstances.

Many people seek happiness in material things. To put your trust in earthly possessions is to elevate things that can be destroyed. Such people often find out too late that they do not own their possessions, but that their possessions own them. "What good will it be for man if he gains the whole world, yet forfeits his soul?" (Matt. 16:26).

Others think that freedom from all restricting laws brings happiness, but one should guard against confusing freedom with immorality. You can also seek happiness by isolating yourself from the world and living for yourself only, but this will just leave you feeling lonely and unfulfilled. Love finds its highest fulfillment in service to others and this service is a requirement for happiness.

A life where God has complete control, is a life of happiness and inner peace.

I seek You with all my heart, O Lord, because I know that with You alone can I find true happiness. *Amen.*

The Majesty of God

Rejoice in the Lord always. I will say it again: Rejoice! Let your gentleness be evident to all.

~ Philippians 4:4-5

Let us enter this new day with joy in our hearts. Come, let us share the glory of this joy with everyone we meet today, because joy is an important virtue for Christians and one of the fruits of the Spirit (see Gal. 5:22).

If your faith is making you a happy person, you will not be able to keep this experience to yourself. If what you believe in does not increase your joy, you should earnestly ask yourself where the fault lies and pray for the Holy Spirit to guide you in truth. Thomas à Kempis said, "If there is joy in the world, then the person with a pure heart undoubtedly has it."

To share your joy with others is an outstanding privilege. He who brings sunshine to the lives of others, cannot keep the reflection of that joy from his own life.

To generously hand out friendliness is a way of life that makes our existence worthwhile. It builds friendships and makes us sensitive to the needs of others. You act positively because you see the positive things in life. It is a gift of God to His faithful children. God is, after all, the Source of all true and lasting happiness.

Robert Louis Stevenson claimed, "When a cheerful person comes into a room, it is as though a light has been switched on." Christ said, "You are the light of the world!"

Redeemer and Friend, help me through Your love and mercy to always be a cheerful person. Give me the desire to share my joy generously with others. *Amen.*

Find Joy in the Lord

"The joy of the LORD is your strength."

~ NEHEMIAH 8:10

Our Christianity, and especially the reading of the Word, is important. Through it, we experience something of God's grandeur and so call upon Him with awe. We become aware of our sins and rejoice in the God who forgives us our transgressions, who listens to us, who hears our prayers, who cries with us and rejoices with us, who wishes to grant us joy.

With the reformation in Israel through the reading of the Word, the people were initially sad and disturbed, and Ezra and Nehemiah had calmed them with the words of our text today.

There are times when we feel powerless and weak, and grief and dejection seem to take hold of our hearts. Maybe you have had a difficult day or faced a disappointment, making it hard – if not impossible – to keep a smile on your face.

Note that the Scripture verse does not state that our joy lies in our own strength. It says that, if we serve the Lord joyously, He will protect us. That is something entirely different. Our feelings are uncertain and unstable, but the Lord never changes. He is always there. We must never allow clouds of uncertainty to hide God's face.

If we live in loving fellowship with our Father, allowing nothing to come between us, we will be able to say, "I serve the Lord joyously and I am sheltered by Him. Praise the Lord!"

Lord Jesus, let me serve You with happiness and joy and, in so doing, become a powerful testimony to You in the world. *Amen.*

A Legacy of Prayer

*By faith Jacob, when he was dying, blessed each of Joseph's sons,
and worshiped as he leaned on the top of his staff.*

~ HEBREWS 11:21

Eternity will one day reveal how many blessings flowed over generations from the loving prayers of grandparents for their children. Three generations are brought together here.

Jacob, the gray old man, over a hundred years old, is the binding factor. He lives at peace in the land Goshen. His son and grandsons live in the city. But he does not write them off. He trusts them and believes in them. The power of his prayers reaches out to include them in his blessing.

Joseph is Jacob's son, but he is also the governor of Egypt. He is a busy man with great responsibilities. He is summoned to his old father's tent. He offers no excuses. He does not forget his father. He comes and brings his children with him to preserve the bond between the generations. Joseph is great before man, but small before his parents and before his God.

Ephraim and Manasseh, Jacob's two grandsons are in their prime years. They are the promise of a future for the generation. Despite their youth they feel the wonder of what is happening in Jacob's tent. They chose God as their share and their future. In Jacob's tent, they were ensured of descendants and of an eternal blessing, because the God of their fathers also became their God.

Our heavenly Father, we praise You for the wonder of family ties and the power of elderly people's prayers. I thank You for the blessings that flow from their prayers to generations of descendants. *Amen.*

Joyful Christians

Blessed is the man whom God corrects; so do not despise the discipline of the Almighty.

~ Job 5:17

All of us want happiness. Many people believe that if they were wealthy and could do what they wanted, they would be very happy. This is not true The fun-seekers of this world are usually the most bored people and they are always on the lookout for new enjoyment. Wealth and exciting, daring experiences can never guarantee permanent happiness.

The inner happiness for which most people long, arises from man's spirit. If the spirit is immoral and wants to pursue every passing fancy, you become frustrated and disillusioned. Instead of true happiness, a gray curtain of monotony descends on your life.

Happiness is a by-product of a life that is obedient to the laws of God and is led in fellowship of the living Christ. It does not necessarily mean that your path will become easier and that you will experience sunshine all the way. But while you walk daily in the awareness of Christ's presence in your life, you will face the future with confidence. You know you are walking the path that He has set out for you and on which He will guide you.

On this path, you will obtain an inner balance which no evil force can destroy. Peace of mind is your rich portion, and from peace of mind happiness is born. This happiness is known only to those who love and serve God.

Merciful God, I accept with joy and thanksgiving the happiness which is the result of a committed and disciplined life. *Amen.*

Healing Power of Joy

He came to that which was His own, but His own did not receive Him.

~ JOHN 1:11

There are few experiences that hurt more than being rejected by someone whom you love dearly. To give love and then be rejected, is painful and difficult to handle. However, we must take care not to suffocate people with our love. If you truly love someone, you will allow him the freedom that he needs. It is only by setting someone free that the bonds of mutual love may be strengthened. It is love with a tender touch.

The principle of generous love forms the basis of the Christian gospel. God allows you the freedom of choice to either believe in Him or reject Him. Christ does not want to compel you to love Him. He invites you from His grace to accept Him and to associate with Him through a new relationship of love.

If you accept His love and make His new way of life your own, you will discover with delight that your imperfect love reacts to His divine love. Your relationship with Him strengthens and deepens steadily. Such a love brings about freedom, joy and peace in your life. If you reject His love and turn your back on the gratifying life that He offers you, you not only accept a lower standard of living, but you also turn your back on God's love.

He will continue to love you, even though you have rejected His love. In this way you sacrifice your precious freedom. Can you still afford to do so this year?

Take away my weariness, Lord, and allow Your strength to flow through me. *Amen.*

Source of True Happiness

Hosanna! Blessed is he who comes in the name of the Lord! Blessed is the coming kingdom of our father David!

~ Mark 11:9-10

Jesus is the source of all true happiness and blessings. To be blessed, we must know Jesus as our personal Savior and Redeemer; we must devote our lives to Him; we must be obedient to His will under all circumstances. Without Jesus there will be no happiness or blessings awaiting us.

Our expectations regarding blessings, and God's way of providing them, often differ widely. Through the ages, this has presented man with a problem: Adam and Eve, the people of Israel, and even the disciples searched for a worldly kingdom while Christ came to build a heavenly one. The same mistake could manifest in our lives.

While we are all searching for happiness, we run the risk of missing Christ's blessing. Christ's happiness is a "singular happiness", a happiness in Christ. Our happiness as humans often depends upon "chances" or "luck": a sudden and unexpected change in our condition. One moment we have nothing, and then, suddenly, we have wealth and abundance. This easily results in materialism.

Human happiness is something that life can offer, and then, just as suddenly, take away again. Man, in his short-sightedness, calls it "happiness" when things are in his favor for a while. But that is not what God's happiness or blessings mean.

Lord Jesus, I praise You for You are the source of all my happiness. You delivered me and made me a child of God. *Amen.*

Calling to Chiefness

To know this love that surpasses knowledge – that you may be filled to the measure of all the fullness of God.

~ EPHESIANS 3:19

Life is filled with many enriching experiences. Some happen so often that they are taken for granted – the love of family and friends; the miracle of a beautiful, sunny day; fellowship with friends; feeling satisfied when everything is running smoothly; having nothing to worry about – these are a few experiences that enrich us and add to our joy.

You can't define what the greatest experience is; What is exceptional to one might be ordinary to the next. However, regardless of who you are, the one experience that exceeds all others by far is to be united with God through Jesus Christ. Nothing whatsoever can be a greater experience than getting to know God in Christ.

The level of this knowledge will depend on the quality of your commitment and surrender to Him. God gives Himself abundantly to all who accept Him in truth. His gift can only be restricted by your refusal to fully accept Him.

To be aware of God's indwelling presence is an experience that changes lives. You develop a fresh appreciation for the meaning and purpose of life. You start every day with a spirit of anticipation instead of getting caught up in the quicksand of self-pity and depression. This experience uplifts your spirit and gives you a fresh attitude and your daily existence is renewed because you are filled with the fullness of God.

Lord, because You live in me, I strive to honor and glorify You through my life. Let me grow in my knowledge and love for You. *Amen.*

Great Experience

Give thanks to the LORD, for He is good; His love endures forever.
~ PSALM 106:1

I know in whom I trust,
even when day turns to darkness;
I know the Rock on whom I have built,
He is my salvation.
When I reach the end of my life,
totally free from all my cares and sorrow,
I will praise You with a purer song of praise
for every day of grace You granted me.

With these words we can leave the old behind us and enter into new beginnings. But more than that: we can approach the end of our lives with these words on our lips and eternity with them in our hearts.

Recall the path on which God has led you so far. Thank Him for leading you on the right path and loving you every step of the way.

May we be inspired by Marie Louise Haskins's words, "I said to the man who stood at the gate of the year: 'Give me a light, that I may tread safely into the unknown!' And he replied: 'Go out into the darkness and put your hand into the hand of God. That shall be to you better than light and safer than a known way.' So I went forth, and finding the hand of God, trod gladly into the night and He led me toward the hills and the breaking of the lone East."

O Lord, we thank You abundantly for all You've done and we enter the future holding Your almighty, loving hand. *Amen.*

Be Thankful in Everything

Better is a little with the fear of the LORD, than great treasure with trouble.

~ PROVERBS 15:16 (NKJV)

Inspirational phrases such as, "Expect God to do great things," or "We serve a miracle-working God," or "Nothing is impossible for those who believe," and many similar expressions emphasize the greatness of God.

However, it seems as if the average Christian derives more inspiration than practical experience from these sayings. He steadfastly believes that they are true, yet in his personal life he still has to get to know the great deeds of God.

One of the main reasons for this is that he is so anxious to look for a revelation of the miracle-working God that he is not able to see God at work in the common, everyday matters.

It is when you have learned to appreciate the small blessings from God that you are able to see how God is at work in your life. The wonder of true friendship, the basic goodness of people, an understanding heart, the marvel of joy and laughter, are all expressions of the greatness of God who bestows His blessings upon us.

Therefore, decide now that from today on you will not take anything for granted. Thank God for blessings as you become aware of them. By doing this, you will unlock a treasure chamber of God which will add new beauty and riches to your life.

Lord, help me not to take the small things in life for granted. Reveal their beauty to me every day. *Amen.*

Reach for the Sky

Simon Peter answered, "You are the Christ, the Son of the living God."

~ MATTHEW 16:16

There are many people who wish for stronger faith. Many of them attend services and are active in church affairs; some have been involved with the Christian faith for many years. But their spiritual lives have become lukewarm and their relationship with Christ monotonous.

There comes a time when all of us are confronted with the question that Jesus asked Simon Peter: "What about you? Who do you say I am?" This question may be presented to us at a time in our lives when we do not know who to turn to for help or what we must do; it might loom before us when we are frustrated and dissatisfied with our own seemingly empty, spiritual lives. This is a question that you cannot avoid; you have to answer it.

In order to get the maximum benefit from Christian experience, and to know the fullness and abundance of true life that Jesus offers us, it is essential for you to have a personal relationship with the living Christ. This does not only mean to learn everything about Him that there is to learn; it means to know Him personally and to surrender to Him; to open your life and allow His Holy Spirit to take control.

Acknowledge Christ's sovereignty and then abundant life will be yours. That is why Jesus came to this world.

Make me Your prisoner, O Lord, because only then will I be truly free. *Amen.*

Find Joy in Small Things

Teach me Your way, O LORD; lead me in a straight path.

~ PSALM 27:11

There is an essential difference between laying your requests before God and making aggressive demands on Him. To ensure that God will be present in your heart, you need to be obedient to His demands, to believe that He knows what is best for you, and willingly submit yourself to His judgment. This acceptance creates a firm bond between you and your heavenly Father. As your faith grows, you will be increasingly willing to meet the demands that He puts to you.

When you are tempted to approach His throne of mercy with demands, you should remember that sincere humility is a virtue. However strongly you may feel about the matter, you really have no right to demand anything from Him. Irreparable damage has been caused by people making aggressive demands on God that He has chosen to leave unanswered. In such cases it is easily said that people's prayers are not answered because they lack faith.

It is not the person who storms the gates of heaven, but the disciple who in humility lays his requests before God, who experiences the joy of God's guidance in his everyday life – those who say: "Lord, this is my humble prayer, but let Your will be done."

This is not an approach of blind fatalism, but one of deep trust, born from the profound conviction that God knows best and that He wants to do what is best for you.

O Hearer of prayers, help me not to walk my own path, but Yours, so that I can come to a deeper understanding of Your love and Your purpose for my life. *Amen.*

Joy in Service of the Most High

So we fix our eyes not on what is seen, but on what is unseen. For what is seen is temporary, but what is unseen is eternal.

~ 2 CORINTHIANS 4:18

Many people find that their experience of the beauty of life is spoiled by the narrowness of their spiritual perspectives. They cannot appreciate beauty or any form of goodness unless it conforms to their religious convictions. However, a life and character that has been created by inner piety cannot be narrow in either perspective or practice. The beauty of piety transcends narrow-mindedness and reflects the glory of God in the life of His disciple.

When your thoughts are focused on Christ and you try to live for His glory, your spirit is elevated beyond place and time and you develop a greater understanding of eternal truths. You appreciate love, honor, purity, unselfishness and other noble qualities, despite the fact that they reside in the realities of a rough and often crude life.

As your appreciation for the intrinsic values of life increases, you develop the ability to distinguish between that which is genuine and that which is feigned.

Then you realize that the things that you cannot see or touch are actually the most important things. He who claims only to believe in what he can see, touch and understand, has a very limited perspective on life, because the great wealth of God does not fall into any of these categories.

Beloved Lord, may I always have a deep appreciation for the value of things that remain unseen and untouched. *Amen.*

Joyous Assurance

The LORD is my light and my salvation – whom shall I fear? The LORD is the stronghold of my life – of whom shall I be afraid?.

~ PSALM 27:1

When thinking of God, we involuntarily think of a bright light that dispels all darkness. Christ declared that He is the Light of the world and His Word assures us that heaven is a place where God Himself is the light.

It is wrong to think that God is not present in the dark places of our lives. Psalm 23:4 assures us that, "Even though I walk through the valley of the shadow of death, I will fear no evil, for You are with me." In Exodus 20:21 we read that, "Moses approached the thick darkness where God was."

At all times and under all circumstances we can hold on to the comforting truth that God will meet us even in the darkest moments of our lives. No matter how dark your life seem, God is there. In His own time He will miraculously transform the darkness into light.

Are you experiencing a dark moment? God is there for you! He is there to take your hand and to lead you out of the darkness into His marvelous light.

May you experience God's presence abundantly in your life. Those who serve and love Him will not dwell in darkness forever. The light of His grace will always penetrate the gloom.

God of light and love, thank You that I may know that in my darkest hour Your light can and will brighten even the most intense moment of sorrow. *Amen.*

Are You Happy?

You are a chosen people, a royal priesthood, a holy nation, a people belonging to God, that you may declare the praises of Him who called you out of darkness into His wonderful light.

~ 1 Peter 2:9

Do you sometimes feel unsure of your faith and experience times of doubt and depression? When this happens you may be tempted to give up.

Remember, there are two distinctly discernible sides to your Christian life: God's side and your side. At your conversion and rebirth it was God who called you to live in harmony with Him; you reacted and became His disciple. This alone is reason enough for you to stand strong in your faith and to live the spiritual life with confidence and courage.

You belong to the living Savior. He bought you with His blood and accepted you as His own. Always remember your rich inheritance and the kind of life God has called you to live.

Nothing will ever be able to bring as much satisfaction into your life as the right relationship with your heavenly Father. This world might offer you seemingly attractive temptations, but remember who and what you are in Christ.

You have been "chosen"; you belong to a "royal priesthood" and you have been "set apart". Muster all your strength to be true to this high and lofty calling. Even if you sometimes find it difficult to faithfully hold on to God – rest assured that He will never let you go!

Gracious Lord, thank You for my high calling. Grant me, through the Holy Spirit, inner strength to live accordingly. *Amen.*

May

Praise the Lord!

One generation shall praise Your works to another, and shall de-
clare Your mighty acts. I will meditate on the glorious splendor of
Your majesty, and on Your wondrous works.

~ PSALM 145:4, 5 (NKJV)

In these eventful times where the voices of the prophets of doom seem to rise above all other voices, and like Job's comforters are casting a heavy gloom over life, very little gratitude is expressed towards God for the assurance that this is still His world. That He still controls it and still determines the fate of mankind.

When problems strike and the future suddenly seems unsure and ominous, man so easily forgets the mighty acts of God. Time and time again in the past He has saved man in his time of need.

The Bible speaks of the mighty acts of the Most High and history mentions numerous occasions where God's hand helped when man's foolishness drove him to the brink of extinction and chaos. In every catastrophe He saved the world.

When those who are in favor of doom and despair start doing their death-dance, it is time for the Christians to praise and thank God for everything that is good and noble. Then it is time to call on the living Christ and to plead that He fill you with His Holy Spirit.

The Spirit will strengthen your faith and cause your hope to burn high. Negative thoughts can be wiped out by reminding yourself with gratitude of the mighty acts of God and by remembering that He cares for His Creation. Be grateful to God for His nurturing love!

I thank You for Your greatness and omnipotence. You are a mighty God who loves us. *Amen.*

Gratitude Glorifies God

I will praise You, O Lord, with my whole heart; I will tell of all Your marvelous works.

~ Psalm 9:1 (nkjv)

Whatever you do, never allow a situation to develop where your faith makes you arrogant. Religion is a serious matter, yet some of God's most dedicated servants have been high-spirited, happy people. A religion which is void of humor can hardly express the spirit and attitude of Jesus Christ.

One of the most beautiful things we read about Jesus is that ordinary people enjoyed listening to Him and that children were at ease in His presence. Could this have happened if He had constantly expressed an attitude of heavy-heartedness? His personality must have emanated a deep peace. Happiness, joy and quiet humor enabled Him to love and appreciate people.

Your sense of humor, enriched by your gratitude and love, is undoubtedly a gift of God. It is difficult to think that a God, who reveals His beauty in the setting sun, who confirms His eternity in the freshness of day-break, who causes birds to sing and children to smile, does not have a sense of humor.

While, in the attitude of Jesus Christ, you learn to thank God with joy, you will make the exciting discovery that there is true joy in His service and that gratitude and gladness can glorify God much more than verbosity and arrogance could ever do.

I am so grateful for Your example of an attitude of peace, and Your sense of humor. *Amen.*

Praise the Lord in Gratitude

Yours, O LORD, is the greatness, the power and the glory, the victory and the majesty. And You are exalted as head over all.

~ 1 CHRONICLES 29:11 (NKJV)

The Scripture verse for today appears in a very touching prayer of gratitude by David. When the Christian comes before his Lord, much time is spent in intercession. Requests for the one who is praying, and on behalf of others, are brought to God's throne of grace. Worries, fears and anxieties are brought to God while seeking His assistance and guidance. Indeed, many people's prayers to God consist of personal requests only.

Don't make the mistake of neglecting to praise and thank the Lord in your prayer life. Remember all the love He has shown you; take note of the blessings which He lavishes upon you; remind yourself of all the instances when Jesus helped you to overcome obstacles and how He provided for your everyday needs. And for how many years has He been doing all this? Do not belittle these blessings simply because they are ordinary.

Never for a moment think that God doesn't need your praise and thanksgiving. By faithfully worshiping, you will find that your spirit is constantly drawn closer to the risen Savior. Your worship, praise and gratitude should not be lip-service only, but should flow sincerely from your heart.

While you are praising God's holy name and thanking Him, you will find yourself being surrounded more and more by His love, until you eventually experience the unity with the living Christ that is the deep desire of every true disciple of the Master.

Today I worship and praise You for You bless me abundantly! *Amen.*

Power of Thanksgiving

Heal me, O LORD, and I shall be healed; save me, and I shall be saved, for You are my praise.

~ JEREMIAH 17:14 (NKJV)

The person who has not yet lifted his heart and mind to God in an act of grateful praise has missed out on one of the greatest experiences of life. Unfortunately most people experience the time of praise and worship as a time of gloominess, something to be endured rather than enjoyed.

"Oh, clap your hands, all you peoples! Shout to God with the voice of triumph!" (Ps. 47:1). It is impossible to clap your hands and sing exultantly to the honor of God and still be gloomy. The speaking of praise is a powerful inspiration. If you are feeling downhearted at this moment and it seems as if nothing is working out well for you, then start praising and thanking God now.

True praise and thanksgiving to the Almighty God should not depend on your feelings. When you are downhearted and depressed, these are the very moments that you need to praise Him. Then you will experience the wonderful, elevating power of praise and thanksgiving. It is the key which God provides you with to open the treasure chambers of life in Him.

You don't need an organ or the church choir to truly praise and thank God. The simple lifting up of your heart to Him brings you into His presence immediately.

I want to lift my heart and mind to You and exalt You. Even in my lowest moments I will give You praise. *Amen.*

Start Your Day

Continue to live in Him, rooted and built up in Him and established in the faith, abounding in it with thanksgiving.
~ COLOSSIANS 2:6-7 (NKJV)

It is of the utmost importance that we, as children of God, maintain a positive and constructive attitude towards life. There are many things, however, that cause you to develop a distorted picture of what your life can and should be: poor health can influence you negatively so that you become difficult to live with, yet, numerous invalids are channels of blessings for those who take care of them. Your attitude towards life is of the greatest importance to yourself and those you live with.

A healthy approach and positive attitude towards life is not something that comes naturally to the average person. When we wake up in the morning, we are subjected to the whims of our emotions. If we didn't have sufficient sleep, we tend to look at life from a jaundiced point of view.

When you wake up in the morning your first responsibility is to take positive control of your thoughts and to thank God for the privilege of giving you a new day. Recall some of the blessings which you take for granted: your home, your friends and loved ones, your job and many more things.

Gratitude brings your heart into harmony with your heavenly Father. If that happens, then every day is filled with true gladness in the Lord. However, it requires an act of your will to start every day with true thanksgiving – but it is worthwhile.

Lord, thank You for this beautiful new day and for all the abundant blessings that You bestow on us. *Amen.*

Miraculous Power of Praise

My heart is steadfast, O God; I will sing and make music with all
my soul. Awake, harp and lyre! I will awaken the dawn.

~ PSALM 108:1-2

We often use prayer to thank God for what He has done for us, to lay our needs before Him, and to confess our sins and shortcomings to Him. It is sad, but true, that we often neglect to express our praise of Him in prayer.

Never underestimate the power of praise in your prayer life. If someone impresses you, you speak words of praise towards Him or other people. Good artists, sportsmen, musicians and singers are showered with praise. There is always a connection between the giver and the receiver of praise.

Why shouldn't we then shower the benevolent God with praise? Think of all the remarkable things that He has done; the miracles that flow from Him; the extraordinary extent of His love. Ponder for a moment the wonders of the universe and Creation; of human life and achievement – and praise and glorify Him. More than anyone He is worthy of our love and thanksgiving.

If you concentrate on praising and glorifying God, you will create a very special relationship with the living Christ, which will transform your prayer life and intensify your love for Him. Through your praise you will become a stronger witness for Him.

Great and wonderful God, we want to exalt Your name without end, and praise and glorify You for all the wonders of Your love and grace that You give to us even though we don't deserve it. *Amen.*

How Great Thou Art!

Since ancient times no one has heard, no ear has perceived, no eye has seen any God besides You, who acts on behalf of those who wait for Him.

~ Isaiah 64:4

Throughout history Christianity has come under fire from all quarters. The validity of our faith and even the existence of God have been challenged and questioned.

Many have suffered torment and persecution for the sake of their faith, and thousands have chosen death rather than to deny their God. This surely indicates the greatness and strength of God's love for the Christian and the Christian's love for God.

As you live your life faithfully in Jesus Christ, you will become more and more aware of His presence with you. When you place your trust in God and dedicate your life to Him, you become increasingly aware of the fact that His hand rests upon you and guides you through the maze of life. The healthier your relationship with the Master, the more aware you will be of the Holy Spirit who speaks to you and leads you through each day.

A life that is lived in, with and for the living Christ will strengthen your faith and allow you to seize each day joyfully. Nothing else can provide you with this joy and peace. And then you can do nothing but whisper in grateful prayer, "How great Thou art!"

Savior and Redeemer, I kneel in wonder before Your greatness and majesty. I truly love You, O Lord! My Rock and my Redeemer. *Amen.*

New Life

I heard You in the garden, and I was afraid because I was naked; so I hid.

~ GENESIS 3:10

There are times in our lives when we are burdened by feelings of guilt. In these times we find it very difficult to live with our conscience. The most common causes of these kinds of experiences include acts based on lies, deception, jealousy and envy, and there are many other causes, too numerous to list. Some of these acts may seem trivial, but whatever form they take, the human conscience will reprimand the wrongdoer in no uncertain terms.

Because of these feelings of shame and self-reproach, most of us instinctively try and hide from our wrongdoing by turning our backs on it or excluding it from our thoughts. Some people try to justify their behavior, while others think that an external façade of bravado will calm their inner storm.

One thing is absolutely sure: whatever you do and however hard you try, you cannot hide from God. Whatever you do to erase your footsteps, you can be sure that the blinding light of Jesus Christ will reveal it before your heavenly Father.

Never try to hide from God. Be assured of His undying love; confess to Him in repentant prayer those things that cause you shame and fear; then receive from Him the peace of mind that springs from the true confession of your sins. Listen to your conscience!

Lord Jesus, because I am assured of Your loving forgiveness, I reveal my soul to You in confession. Thank You for Your boundless forgiveness. *Amen.*

Why Praise?

Praise, O servants of the LORD, praise the name of the LORD. Let the name of the LORD be praised, both now and forevermore.

~ PSALM 113:1-2

Why should God be praised and glorified? Why should we tell Him how almighty, all-knowing and omnipresent He is? Why should we waste time telling Him things that He already knows? And yet He commands us to praise Him. God never channels our energy into dead-end streets. There is more to praising and glorifying God than simply repeating His divine attributes.

The complexity of the human temperament compels it to reach out to something higher and greater than itself. This yearning can be fulfilled by praising and glorifying God, through which we connect ourselves to Him who knows and understands the desires of our hearts. God can manage fine without our praise, but we cannot manage without the uplifting strength and inspiration that emanates from our praise to Him.

True praise is one of the greatest inspirational forces in life. It raises you up from your spiritual despondency and enables you to live in communion with your heavenly Father. Praise can occur in many different ways: during the excitement of a revival service; during the sanctification of the communion; or in those quiet moments when you are alone with your heavenly Father. The method is of little importance, as long as it allows you to enter into the holy presence of God.

Holy Father, with praise I go into Your temple court. I enter into Your presence with joy and thanksgiving. *Amen.*

Our Wonderful God

To our God and Father be glory for ever and ever.

~ PHILIPPIANS 4:20

The words "Praise the Lord" are repeated often in the Psalms – also in other parts of God's Holy Scriptures. Therefore, we should pay close attention to it. There are many Christians who praise and thank Him daily. Unfortunately there are also many who take His goodness for granted.

Some people urgently and impatiently seek God's help when they experience a crisis and take it for granted when God answers them. They carry on with their lives exactly as before and never give a second thought to the fact that God created the universe for His glory – and that their gratitude adds to that glory.

It will be worthwhile to become quiet for a while in this rat race and consider what your life would have been like without God's love and faithful care. How would you have handled insecurities and disappointments? What would have happened if you had lost your job and had no income? What would the quality of your life have been if you constantly feared suffering from a terminal disease or death or uncertainty about the hereafter?

As a Christian, you know that you don't have to worry about any of these things because your heavenly Father knows exactly what you need. You have been redeemed through the blood of Jesus and can echo the words of Psalm 106:1, "Praise the LORD. Give thanks to the LORD, for He is good; His love endures forever."

Praise the LORD, O my soul; all my inmost being, praise His holy name. Praise the LORD, O my soul, and forget not all His benefits (Ps. 103:1-2). *Amen.*

The Blessings of a Grateful Heart

"He who sacrifices thank offerings honors Me."

~ PSALM 50:23

There are many people who complain incessantly. Constant complaining can become a lifestyle. Eventually you forget that there are more things to be grateful for than to complain about. If you are currently complaining more often than expressing gratitude, you are living an inferior life.

It is impossible to have a grateful heart without also possessing a grateful spirit. Such a spirit makes getting along with others easier and more rewarding. It also deepens your understanding of life and makes those who live and work with you happier as well. Never let a day go by without consciously expressing your gratitude.

Open your eyes to what is beautiful around you and praise God for what you see or experience. Such an attitude not only enriches your life but also adds joy and satisfaction to it. God's treasures are then at your disposal because praise and thanksgiving are the keys to God's storehouse of treasures.

It is almost impossible to find someone who praises and thanks God constantly, yet remains depressed. Human experience has proved over and over again that when you start thanking God for His gifts of grace, He is already planning the next blessing for you.

If you concentrate on practicing the art of praise and thanksgiving, you have discovered the secret of a creative, inspired life.

I will praise You, O LORD, with all my heart. I will be glad and rejoice in You (Ps. 9:1-2). *Amen.*

Make Today Wonderful

This is the day the LORD has made; let us rejoice and be glad in it.

~ PSALM 118:24

Regardless of how things may seem, you are greater than any circumstances and any situation that you may find yourself in. You might doubt this truth, and as a result your life will be filled with fear and insecurity and every new day will become an unbearable burden. You start the day more conscious of your heavy burdens than of the One who offered to bear them for you (see 1 Pet. 5:7).

Every new day is a unique gift to you from God. What you make of it is your responsibility. You may be influenced by your past and be filled with hope for the future. How you welcome each new day will depend on your mood and attitude towards life.

Fortunately as a Christian you don't have to leave your mood in the hands of fate or coincidence. You don't allow it to descend upon you without channeling it into a creative, constructive power. You were never meant to be the victim of changing emotions or fluctuating circumstances. God has given you the ability to determine your mood as well as the pace of your life. Therefore, you can live a happy, victorious life!

When you wake up in the morning it is important to start the day on a positive note by praising God for His presence and His goodness. Then you will approach the day with joy and expectation.

Father, I experience Your presence every moment of the day. Teach me to welcome each day with enthusiasm and praise. *Amen.*

Nevertheless I Shall Rejoice

Though You have made me see troubles, many and bitter, You will restore my life again. I will praise You with the harp for Your faithfulness, O my God.

~ Psalm 71:20, 22

We need not be overcome by depression or collapse under the load of our adversity. For all who are depressed by life, there is liberating advice. Praise is one of the most remarkable forces in your spiritual life.

The Holy Spirit leads us to the discovery of this dynamic power. In the book of Psalms we find proof of the strength that arises from praise time and again.

You can try this remedy with confidence. When you go through dark and difficult days; when your spirit has reached a new low and you start doubting the wisdom and goodness of God, it is time for you to start exchanging your doubt, self-pity and complaints for praise and thanksgiving.

Do not in your depressed state convince yourself that there is nothing you can thank God for. God is still there, He has not rejected you, His love still shines upon your life. When you realize this, you will discover God in nature, in the Scriptures and in your fellow man. Life will smile on you once again and you will discover that faith in God is a prerequisite. With Habakkuk you will confess, "Yet I will rejoice in the Lord, I will be joyful in God my Savior" (Hab. 3:18).

Give me a grateful heart, O Lord, so that I can triumph over depression in the name of Jesus Christ. I praise You, heavenly Father, and I will not forget Your mercies. *Amen.*

My Heritage Is Beautiful!

LORD, You have assigned me my portion and my cup; You have made my lot secure. The boundary lines have fallen for me in pleasant places; surely I have a delightful inheritance.

~ PSALM 16:5-6

In Psalm 16 David states unequivocally that he believes there is no good in life outside the will of God. He praises God for the beautiful inheritance given to him by God's loving hand.

The same is true for us today for our history and for our country. Our heritage is outstandingly beautiful, "Soli Deo Gloria!" – To God be the glory! We have abundant reasons to be grateful.

That is why we kneel in thanksgiving before God. Like David, we confess to the Lord, "You have made known to me the path of life" (Ps. 16:11). We commit our family life to God because if He does not build the house, those who build it work in vain. We re-commit our work, relaxation, culture, politics, economy, the entire lives of our people, and place it under His blessing.

We give our love anew to our country, to our fellow man and to our God. We serve this love with a pure heart; a love that seeks unity amidst diversity; morality without hypocrisy; dignity that is not self-righteous; truth and not propaganda; justice which has not been bought with injustice; faith which is not vague sentimentality. With such a love, we can live with dignity in the place that God assigned to us.

Creator God, I thank You for the beautiful part of Your Kingdom that You have assigned to me. Make me worthy to occupy it to Your honor and glory. *Amen.*

Majesty of God

I will be glad and rejoice in You; I will sing praise to Your name, O Most High.

~ Psalm 9:2

We are so used to hearing about everything that is wrong with the world that it is difficult to believe that there is any good left. Emphasis is placed on the fact that man has many weaknesses and shortcomings but little time and effort go into finding the good in life. Subsequently we are in danger of becoming cynical and skeptical, with a pessimistic and negative outlook on life.

But good is still there if you would just take the time to look for it. You will find warm-hearted, generous people who really care. People who offer their service to their fellow man out of love and not out of personal motives of gain. The Creation of God is still the wonder it was at the beginning of time. Science and progress have made an unprecedented lifestyle possible.

When life seems depressing and it appears that everything is going wrong, if a spirit of despair descends on you, if you feel powerless against the evil of the world, when you feel that all is lost, then take note of the breathtaking achievements of science and art.

Think how the seasons come and go, and how each season offers its own enchantment and beauty, listen to the carefree laughter of a child or the pure song of a bird. Behind all these things you will see the majesty of God. Then praise Him and glorify His holy name.

How great You are, O Lord, and how glorious is Your name in all the earth. *Amen.*

With a Song in the Heart

Be filled with the Spirit. Speak to one another with psalms, hymns and spiritual songs. Sing and make music in your heart to the Lord.

~ EPHESIANS 5:18-19

We are told to sing a new song to the glory of the Lord. A song involves joy and love. A person who does not sing, is like springtime without blossoms; like a day without sunshine. Song and gratefulness go hand in hand. A grateful person sings and a person who sings is happy, regardless of his circumstances.

Music is present everywhere in God's Creation: the wind singing through the trees; the rhythmic movement of the waves; the sound of raindrops against the window; the waving wheat fields. To them who want to listen, there is singing all around us.

The world can tell by our singing that God is present in our hearts and lives.

Angels rejoiced at the birth of Christ. Jesus sang a song of praise with His disciples on the Thursday evening before He was crucified. One day in heaven there will be continuous singing by the redeemed. Meanwhile we must practice our songs.

Singing gives us courage in times of suffering. Like Paul and Silas we should sing in times of trial. Encourage and strengthen other believers with your song.

"May the road rise up to meet you. May the wind always be at your back. May the rain fall soft upon your fields. And may God hold you in the palm of His hand" (Old Irish Blessing).

Holy God, and heavenly Father, enable me to encourage others. Never let my song be silenced. *Amen.*

Glorify the Lord!

"I have brought You glory on earth by completing the work You gave Me to do."

~ JOHN 17:4

Some people just accept their faith as a matter of course. Over the years their worship has become a matter of routine and it is monotonous and meaningless.

When you worship God, whether in the fellowship of believers, in prayer, in Bible study groups, or in your private quiet time, you should never lose sight of the glorious reality of His holy presence. Your hymn book may inspire you, but the joy of worship can only come from the Source of that inspiration – the living Christ.

Think of the enormous impact the angels had on the shepherds of Bethlehem; or of the imposing figure of Christ preaching with so much authority, healing with so much power and caring with so much love. Meditate on the wonder of the resurrection and ascension. In view of these thoughts, your worship should become a joyous and triumphant experience.

When you worship remember that you are in the presence of the King of all kings. He is not tied to the pages of the liturgy, but He lives in your heart. Therefore, give Him the glory and honor His name deserves. Glorify the Lord!

All praise and thanks to God the Father now be given the Son and He who reigns with Them in highest heaven: The one, eternal God whom heaven and earth adore: For thus it was, is now, and shall be evermore. *Amen.*

Notice the Beauty

Finally, brothers ... whatever is lovely ... think about such things.
~ PHILIPPIANS 4:8

The state of the world today is shown through shocking headlines in newspapers, sickening revelations in the media and the lack of elegance and grace in our society.

Shocking fashions and lifestyles which are reprehensible and tasteless are taking the limelight. It seems as if decency has been replaced by rudeness and arrogance to such a degree that everything civilized and lovely is under the threat of being destroyed. The kind heart finds this sorrowful and disconcerting.

If you feel like this, you should guard against being overcome by negative tendencies and yielding to the temptation of believing, although hesitantly, that this degradation of values has become the norm and standard of modern society.

You should rather try to look past the filth and sordidness of the world. Look around you and search for the beautiful things in life.

Seek the glory of our Creator God in the song of birds; in the breathtaking miracle of sunrise and sunset; the mountains and fields; the ebb and flow of the tides; the abounding wildlife and the inspiring beauty of flowers.

Listen to soothing music and concentrate on the good things that are still present in the world. Then you will experience the peace of God that surpasses all understanding.

By paying attention to beauty, holy Master, I want to take away the sordidness of this world through the help of the Holy Spirit, and replace it with beauty and goodness. *Amen.*

Songs in Praise of Faith

I will praise the Lord all my life; I will sing praise to my God as long as I live.

~ Psalm 146:2

The purpose of all of Creation is to proclaim the glory of God. The most uplifting thing you can do is to contribute to that praise. It is a sad fact that we give an inferior place to praising God in all areas of life – even in the practice of our religion.

When someone mentions praising and worshiping God, the average person involuntarily thinks of a formal church service: hymns; the reading of Scripture verses; communal prayers and sermons. A faith that brings praise to God is, however, much more than formal religious ceremonies. It is an attitude towards life, inspired by our faith in Christ Jesus. To praise God is to gain the power of faith which sanctifies our everyday lives, because then God is in the center of our lives and all other things are arranged around Him.

There are many things that small children or very old people cannot do. But one thing we can all do with all our hearts, right from the beginning of our lives to the very end, is to praise the Lord.

Honoring and praising God happens with every simple, noble deed we do in His name, and with every uplifting thought in our minds. Let us then leave this month behind with rejoicing in our hearts and enter the new month with the motto, "Praise the Lord!"

Lord, I want to praise Your holy name. Thank You for all the blessings that You bestow upon me. *Amen.*

Yet I Will Rejoice

Though the fig tree does not bud and there are no grapes on the vines, though the olive crop fails and the fields produce no food, though there are no sheep in the pen and no cattle in the stalls, yet I will rejoice in the LORD, I will be joyful in God my Savior.

~ HABAKKUK 3:17-18

It's easy enough to be pleasant when life flows along like a song; but the man worthwhile is the man who can smile when everything goes dead wrong" (Anonymous).

It is easy to praise God when the sun shines. However, when threatening storm clouds gather and your prayers remain unanswered; when you are convinced that no one understands your problems, then praise appears to be impossible and life becomes a burden.

True praise is more than an emotional lifting of your heart to God. Figuratively it means looking up into the face of God and sincerely asking, "Lord, what do You want me to do?" When you ask this of God, the answer may be surprising.

He may reveal to you truths about yourself that have been hidden from you for a long time: an unforgiving spirit; arrogance; or some other pet sins that you refuse to let go.

When your life has been cleansed by the grace of God and the blood of Christ, you will experience a cheerfulness that will make it easy for you to praise God. Then you will experience new spiritual growth as well as an unknown joy which will call forth songs of praise from your heart.

Redeemer, Jesus Christ, I thank and praise You for Your cleansing power that enables me to praise You even in times of misfortune and disaster. *Amen.*

Wake Up My Soul!

"Our friend Lazarus sleeps, but I go that I may wake him up."
~ John 11:11 (NKJV)

How appropriate are these words that Jesus uttered in the past! He was on His way to Lazarus' grave to perform the great miracle of raising someone from the dead. They are appropriate today because there are so many people who need to be raised from their indifference, their general attitude of throwing in the towel, their hopelessness and helplessness. They willingly submit themselves to the worries and anxieties that torture them daily.

Yet, in the midst of all the problems encountered in the world today, it is not only important, but imperative, that your whole life and total existence be founded on your faith in the living Christ. This is your guarantee of a new life of powerful faith.

In an era where standards continually decline, it is easy to give in to the temptation of taking the easy road of compromise and disinterest; or just to give up the fight and drift along with the current rather than living the life God expects you to. If you are trusting in your own resources and ingenuity, there is little doubt that you will go under.

Nevertheless, just as Christ raised Lazarus from the dead, He will raise you from your spiritual sleep and inspire you to live a life of victory and achievement in His service. The only thing that the life-giving Savior asks of you is that you accept Him as the Lord of your life. Can you afford to refuse an offer so rich in mercy?

Lord Jesus, I worship You as the living Savior. Please raise me from my spiritual slumber so that I may serve You. *Amen.*

Songs of Praise

When they had sung a hymn, they went out to the Mount of Olives.

~ Mark 14:26

Jesus sang a song of praise before He was crucified for us. How could Jesus sing? Because His heart was in harmony with the will of God. He knew that God only wished the best for Him, as well as for all mankind. He could sing because He had a clear conscience.

Many lose their song because sin silences their voices. Jesus could sing because He believed with conviction in His final victory. Just before He was taken captive, Jesus sang a song of praise, not a song of sorrow or suffering. He could sing under the bleakest circumstances because His hand was steadfastly in the hand of His Father.

What is Jesus' song testimony about? His unimpeachable obedience to the will of God, and of His complete surrender to His Father's wishes. It is a striking testimony to His voluntary sacrifice on behalf of all sinners.

Jesus teaches us that, even in the darkest of days, we should not lose our song – to sing even in the face of death. He is aware of the cross, but He is also aware of the glory to follow. God is faithful! In similar fashion, the early Christians sang as martyrs on the stake and in the arenas; likewise, Paul and Silas sang songs of praise to the Lord, with scourged backs, at midnight, in jail. And so God's faithful and obedient children will sing through the ages, because the Master has showed us the way.

Father, help me to celebrate in suffering, because I know that I am en route to a life of joy beyond words. *Amen.*

Above Every Name!

"By those who come near Me I must be regarded as holy; and before all the people I must be glorified."

~ LEVITICUS 10:3 (NKJV)

It is an incalculable gift of grace from God that we may worship Him. Lately many people imply that they have come to such a new unity with the living Christ, handling their relationship with the Master with so much familiarity that the traditional believers stand in awe of their jovial relationship with God.

Expressions such as "the Boss" or "the Man upstairs" when referring to God, cause many Christians to feel upset or uneasy because of the seeming lack of respect or formality which we are used to when we worship God.

As a disciple of the Lord Jesus Christ, your relationship with the Master is something personal and intimate and it is a relationship which exists exclusively between you and your Lord. The same applies to other Christian pilgrims, even though their relationship with, and attitude towards, God may differ drastically from yours.

However, what is most important in your relationship with God, is to ensure that, even in these modern and enlightened times, your attitude towards Him is always one of respect, love and worship. That you continually praise and thank Him for His grace, and that you will never allow your familiarity with Him to trivialize your worship. That would be a serious abuse of His great grace.

Holy Spirit of God, please keep me from abusing Your grace. I honor and respect You above all things. *Amen.*

Sublime God

My speech and my preaching were not with persuasive words of human wisdom, but in demonstration of the Spirit and of power.

~ 1 Corinthians 2:4 (nkjv)

One of the greatest dangers threatening the church today, is people who attend worship services to listen to a popular speaker instead of the Word. People should not go to church to be entertained. Above all else, it must be an opportunity to meet with God and fellowship with other believers.

When founding the early church, Christ mainly used simple people with little or no education. Through the ages many of the spiritual giants had very little schooling, but still brought thousands to salvation. God often uses simple instruments.

This again serves to stress the fact that it is the Holy Spirit, and not a human being, who moves people to commit their lives to Jesus Christ. In all preaching it is the honor and glory of God through Jesus Christ, which must be accentuated. Christ not only needs to be the center of all preaching and worship, but the whole message must glorify Him. In your grateful worship you must always seek the guidance of the Holy Spirit.

If you have prayerfully wrestled a message from Him, you will feel compelled to submit yourself to His service as a form of gratitude for His great sacrifice. Then you will know for sure that you are worshiping in spirit and truth and with a heart filled with gratitude.

I want to worship You because I am filled with gratitude for all the great things You have done for me. *Amen.*

Celebration of God's Grace

The angel said to her, "Do not be afraid, Mary, you have found favor with God."

~ LUKE. 1:30

The Scriptures teach us that God is no respecter of persons and that all people are equal before Him. He shares His love equally with all who acknowledge Christ's sovereignty. They all receive the joy and privilege of His Holy Spirit in their hearts.

Some biblical characters found special favor with God and we might think that God favored them over others. But God has no favorites.

We must remember that when He lays His hand on someone for a special task, He also expects loyalty and obedience in humility, love and devotion.

Mary's life revealed her devotion to the heavenly Father. As far as it is known, she led a quiet life somewhere in the hills of Judea, unknown, except to her family. And yet she was chosen above all women as God's instrument through which He revealed Himself to the world.

Your love for and devotion to God may seem insignificant, but if you offer Him your very best, He will use you in His own unique way. Then you will rejoice in God's grace.

I praise and thank You, Father, that You reveal Yourself time and again to me. Use me to spread Your love throughout the world. *Amen.*

Source of Inexhaustible Power

Do not forget to do good and to share with others, for with such sacrifices God is pleased.

~ HEBREWS 13:16

So many relationships lapse into a monotonous rut because communication dies. The disintegration of communication with the Lord is a sure way of pulling away from Him.

When prayer becomes the repetition of meaningless phrases piously spoken, true communication dies. Then prayer becomes words without meaning, and fellowship with Christ is no longer enriching.

Meaningful communication does not happen easily or as a matter of course. It has to be cherished and developed. Husbands should share their experiences with their wives, because by talking to each other love and understanding are strengthened.

In prayer and communication with the Lord, in the good deeds we do in His name, we are making sacrifices that please God. Talk to your Redeemer as you would to a friend; tell Him of your hopes and fears; tell Him that you love Him. This will keep your communication with God and others alive and strong.

O Holy Spirit, prevent my communication with God and with others from becoming meaningless. Make my prayers meaningful, so that my human relationships can also be healthy. *Amen.*

Your Personal Worship

Come, let us bow down in worship, let us kneel before the LORD our Maker.

~ PSALM 95:6

Worship can entail the interaction of conflicting emotions. Sometimes you will be filled with a sense of awe that causes an irrepressible feeling of spontaneous praise. You then meditate on the greatness of God and feel like exclaiming with the psalmist, "When I consider Your heavens, the work of Your fingers, the moon and the stars, which You have set in place, what is man that You are mindful of him?" (Ps. 8:3-4). The greatness and omnipotence of God makes you aware of how fragile a person really is.

At other times you lack the inspiration that sparks off worship and you wonder what you should do to create an atmosphere of prayer and adoration. While attempting to understand the eternal God through the life, words and works of Jesus Christ, your worship necessarily becomes more intimate. Jesus enables you to call the holy God your Father.

Through the teachings of Christ a bond of friendship develops between creature and Creator. Then worship becomes a personal and holy matter.

To see God through the eyes of Jesus Christ in your personal times of worship will enable you to worship Him more intimately and affectionately. Wonder, awe, adoration, love and affection are experienced simultaneously when worship is offered in spirit and in truth.

Holy, Holy, Holy are You, Lord God of hosts. Draw me forever closer to You in worship. *Amen.*

Fresh and New

Sing to the Lord a new song, His praise from the ends of the earth.

~ Isaiah 42:10

It is very easy to fall into a rut when worshiping. Worship in your church might be conducted rigidly without any variation whatsoever; your personal devotions may follow the same pattern day after day and even your prayers may seem the same. The result of all this will be a dull, monotonous relationship with God.

Your times of worship should be vibrant and exciting. If this is not the case, you should seriously examine your pattern of worship and prayer.

Do not hesitate to experiment with new approaches. Even if seasoned, tested methods of worship have stood the test of time, variation in worship will prevent it from becoming lifeless.

When doing Bible study, use different translations – even another language can be exciting. Try using a concordance to shed more light on the meaning of Scripture, thus revealing deeper truths to you. Make use of spiritual literature that will explain parts of Scripture to you or highlight new concepts. Read songs in different languages and from different denominations. Read your Bible aloud. If you are used to meeting with God in the privacy of your room, move out into nature and allow God to speak to you.

Never be hesitant to vary the form or type of your worship. Change will bring a deeper dimension to your praise and worship. Just make sure that Jesus Christ remains the center of your worship.

Glorified Lord, I want to sing You a new song! Lead me through the Holy Spirit to worship You in Spirit and in truth. *Amen.*

God's Triumphant March!

Now thanks be to God who always leads us in triumph in Christ.
~ 2 Corinthians 2:14

In contrast to what some of Christ's disciples suggest, the Christian life can have its moments of depression and defeat. Such times can have devastating results if a follower of Christ allows them to cloud his spiritual view.

Regardless of how dark and difficult the present moment may be, keep your eyes focused on Jesus Christ and always remember that in His power you will overcome your weakness and victory will eventually be yours too. Remember that Christ is sufficient for you. Therefore you should not depend on your feelings or emotions, but on the faith that you have in His ability to hold on to you. Then you become victorious in spite of your emotions.

Be grateful that your faith doesn't depend on how you feel. It depends on what you believe about Jesus Christ. If you believe that He is what He says He is – the Son of God, that He lives today and that your future is in His omnipotent hands – then you can share in the grace of His victory. You have already overcome the powers that want to oppress and defeat you. Lift up your heart and remember to whom you belong and live triumphantly in His strength.

Thus, by the grace of God you become a companion of Christ in God's triumph through the ages.

Thank You that my discipleship doesn't depend on my emotions, but on my faith in Your ability to overcome all things. *Amen.*

God Performs His
Wonders through You

Cast all your anxiety on Him because He cares for you.

~ 1 Peter 5:7

You may be concerned about your job or your co-workers, about an increase in taxes or rent, or about the conduct of a loved one. You see only gloom and an unsure future. When your life is paralyzed by fear, you cannot experience the freedom and joy that God offers to those who love and trust Him.

If you are anxious and worried, remember that God is greater than anything that happens to you. Clouds of anxiety, fear and uncertainty might currently obscure your image of God, but He is always the same.

With thanksgiving, take your anxieties, fears and worries and share them with your merciful God. Give these things over to Him unreservedly. Accept the challenge to follow God's plan of action.

God's omnipotence will sweep away all irrelevant thoughts, and all uncertainty will disappear. The true greatness of God is not only revealed in His majestic universe, but also in His immeasurable love and concern for people like you and me.

Your works are perfect, Lord, and even when I drink from the cup of bitterness, You will never forsake me, but You will help me to understand eventually that with You, I will live forever. *Amen.*

Spontaneous Thanksgiving

Your ways, O God, are holy. What god is so great as our God? You are the God who performs miracles; You display Your power among the peoples.

~ PSALM 77:13-14

We serve a wonderful God and King! But, unfortunately, we sometimes lose sight of His greatness. Then we end up leading petty, unfulfilled lives. Instead of growing into the fullness of His stature through focusing on Him, we try to reduce Him to our level.

God is great and Scripture resounds with His invitation for us to share in His greatness. Jesus promised to dwell in those who love Him and to be revealed through them to the world. Surrendering to His presence transforms petty dwarves into spiritual giants. It requires steadfast faith in the promises of God and the courage to live out those promises to grow in Christ.

When you are aware of God living in you your attitude towards life changes. Trust and confidence replace a sense of inferiority, love overcomes hate, compassion conquers bitterness.

And as you honestly and sincerely acknowledge the greatness of God in you, your heart will overflow with gratitude for the glory and the beauty He imparts to your daily life.

Wondrous God, because You dwell in me through Jesus Christ I can overcome all the negative things in life and be filled with all the goodness of Your Holy Spirit. *Amen.*

June

Peace through Prayer

Continue earnestly in prayer, being vigilant in it with thanksgiving.

~ COLOSSIANS 4:2 (NKJV)

There are many people in this world who are living under a cloud of anxiety, concern and fear. Their anxiety may be caused by fear with regard to the future of their country or the world. Their concern, anxiety and fear is increased by violence, unrest, terrorism, political and economic insecurity. How can one find peace in the midst of such situations?

The apostle Paul answers our question when he says, "Be anxious for nothing, but in everything by prayer and supplication, with thanksgiving, let your requests be made known to God, and the peace of God, which surpasses all understanding, will guard your hearts and minds through Christ Jesus" (Phil 4:6-7 NKJV).

In difficult circumstances it is especially true that you can do nothing in your own strength to solve your problems. Jesus, our Master, has said that we can do nothing of ourselves, but He also said that with God all things are possible (see John 15:1-8).

In spite of your difficult circumstances and regardless of how unsure the future might seem, your peace of mind will only be secured when you become still before the Lord in prayer. Prayer and meditation, in conjunction with praise and thanksgiving, is the only infallible method to ensure that you will be able to accept and overcome life's challenges.

Even though the future is unknown, O Lord, I will be anxious for nothing for You are with me, guiding and watching over me. *Amen.*

Prayer Obedience

Lord, teach us to pray.

~ Luke 11:1

In its deepest essence, prayer is the soul of man reaching out to the living God. When circumstances and situations are beyond our control, then we pray – even though we have not spoken to Him, or listened to Him, for a long time. Of course God is able to do it. Yet effective prayer places certain requirements on us – one of which is that we should listen to God and do His will.

True prayer consists of two components: you have fellowship with the living God, and He has fellowship with you, an insignificant human being. Unfortunately in our prayer lives many of us are so busy talking, that we don't hear what God wants to say to us. Listening reverently to the voice of God is an important part of the discipline of prayer. He reveals His will to you through the working of the Holy Spirit – if you would only become quiet in His presence and receive His voice in your heart.

To be sure of His guidance, you must be willing to practice being obedient to His will, as revealed to you through the Holy Spirit. Too many people seek God's will and then sit back, waiting for God to act. Through our prayers we need to be inspired and motivated, and a spirit of anticipation needs to take hold of us.

As your prayer life develops and grows gradually in a disciplined way, you will become more sensitive to what God expects from you. Then you will find joy and happiness in just living for Him.

Lord, teach me to be obedient to You and to follow where You lead and guide me. *Amen.*

Make Your Prayer Life Effective

Continue earnestly in prayer, being vigilant in it with thanks-giving; meanwhile praying also for us.

~ COLOSSIANS 4:2, 3 (NKJV)

The majority of people experience prayer as something of a drudgery. As a result, their prayer lives are without power and color – a repetition of hackneyed phrases. They pray to God only because they want something special, or because their prayers originate from a habit of many years.

Prayer is an exciting adventure in your spiritual life and growth. It must never be taken lightly or be allowed to stagnate. It is an experience that you share with God Almighty through Jesus Christ. Therefore, it should never become a flood of meaningless words.

God never gets tired of listening to your prayers. Therefore, your first priority must be to build your life around Him. Develop the very good habit of tuning your mind and emotions in to Him so that, when you fulfill your daily tasks, you are conscious of His divine presence all the time.

After praying to God and speaking with Him, it is of the utmost importance to discipline yourself in such a way that you will be receptive to the prompting of the Holy Spirit. In this way you will be guided to find His answers to your prayers, as He will reveal them to you in His own wonderful way.

Never take for granted that He promised to answer your prayers. At all times thank God for the assurance that, in His wisdom and grace, through the living Christ, He will meet all your needs.

God, I want to bring honor and glory to You for You are an amazing God who never tires of us. *Amen.*

The Gracious Gift of Prayer

Continue earnestly in prayer, being vigilant in it with thanks-giving.

~ COLOSSIANS 4:2

What value do you give to prayer? Do you regard it as a very special gift of grace from God, or as a burden? When some people move into the presence of God in prayer, they experience the sentiment of the hymn writer when he spoke of being "lost in wonder, love and praise".

The sad thing, however, is that the great majority of people regard prayer as an unpleasant task which needs to be done. Therefore they pretend to pray, but all they are doing in actual fact is repeating well-known phrases like a recitation.

The privilege of prayer is a very special gift of grace from God. It is God's personal invitation to you to enter into His sanctuary and to talk to Him and listen when He has something to say to you. How grateful we are when someone in a position of authority manages to take a few minutes to listen to us! Are you grateful towards the living Christ for the fact that He wants to speak with you and listen to you?

Prayer is a discipline which is more than worthwhile. However, it requires preparation and practice. Make time to become quiet in the presence of God. Focus your attention on Jesus. Make time to listen to God as well as speak to Him, thanking Him always for the gracious gift of drawing strength from the Source. This will enable you to live your life in an atmosphere of peace and trust.

Thank You for the privilege of prayer. Thank You that it allows us to talk to You in Your inner sanctuary. *Amen.*

The Challenge of True Prayer

"When you pray, you shall not be like the hypocrites. For they love to pray standing in the synagogues and on the corners of the streets, that they may be seen by men."

~ MATTHEW 6:5

When you've allowed your prayers to be nothing more than a public show, it is no longer communion with God, but one big self-glorification. Of course there are times when groups or nations come pleading before the Lord. If they are humble and lay their petitions before God in repentance, He will hear their prayer. But public show is not the same as true prayer.

Personal prayer has many facets. It is a wonderful source of comfort. Once you are aware of the tremendous power of prayer you will discover your view of life being extended. Personal prayer enables you to remain calm in the midst of life's storms.

There is, however, a facet of prayer that is overlooked very often: it is the challenge of prayer which sooner or later comes to each one of us who is used to spending time with God. I'm referring to those times when God wants to reveal to you His will and desires for your life.

Often God's expectations are in conflict with your own desires. You would much rather not listen to what God wants to say to you. If however you have the courage to persevere in prayer, not only will His will be revealed to you, but you will also develop a new program for your life – and in conjunction with that, the peace of God which guarantees you peace of mind.

Lord, Your expectations are contrary to my desires. Please help me to listen to You and follow Your will for my life. *Amen.*

Miracles through Prayer

Praise be to the LORD, for He has heard my cry for mercy. The LORD is my strength and my shield; my heart trusts in Him, and I am helped. My heart leaps for joy and I will give thanks to Him in song.

~ PSALM 28:6-7

Despite the disbelief and cynicism of the modern age, God can still perform miracles. Every time that someone is healed in answer to prayer, God has performed a small miracle. Every time we experience peace in our hearts after a time of tension and suffering, when a young couple falls in love, when our grief becomes bearable or is converted to rejoicing gladness, then a miracle has occurred.

Many people pray to God when they experience a crisis, but when the crisis passes and their worst fears do not come true, they ignore and forget the fact that they prayed in their distress.

The evidence that God hears our prayers is overwhelming. Many Christians of our time can testify that miracles still occur in answer to faithful prayer. Lives have been reformed, the sick have been healed, destructive habits have been conquered and broken human relationships have been restored.

Hand your problems over to God today and wait on Him in faith. If there is something you have to do yourself, do it without delay. Do not be overwhelmed by despair in your extreme distress. At the right time and in the right way, God will answer you.

My God and Father, I know that You are powerful and that You can do far more than I can pray for or think of, because You are the Almighty. Let this truth guide me from day to day. *Amen.*

Be Ready for Answered Prayers

When Rhoda recognized Peter's voice, she was so overjoyed she ran back without opening it and exclaimed, "Peter is at the door!"

~ ACTS 12:14

The early church was in a crisis. Their leader was in prison, believers were scattered and the authorities were involved in acts of cruel persecution. But they still prayed.

John Wesley said, "God does not do anything unless it is in answer to prayer." When Peter was in prison, "many people had gathered and were praying" (Acts 12:12) in Mary's house. When he knocked on the door and Rhoda heard his voice, she excitedly ran to convey the good news. Their reaction was one of boundless astonishment and disbelief.

How slow we are to acknowledge answered prayers. We are quick to seek all kinds of different explanations rather than to praise God and thank Him for answering our prayers.

When God is slow to answer our prayers we become impatient or we complain that He is not listening to us. We do not wait in excitement for the revelation of His omnipotence.

When we pray, we should also ask God for the ability to recognize His answers when they are given. We sometimes continue praying for things which God has already given us. Because it is sometimes not exactly as we expected it, we fail to recognize it as God's answer to our prayers.

We should develop a sensitivity to recognize our answered prayers with joy, and without skeptical surprise.

Lord, help me to wait with excitement on Your answers and to know when my prayers are answered. *Amen.*

God Can Do Anything

Jesus looked at them and said, "With man this is impossible, but with God all things are possible."

~ Matthew 19:26

Despite the disbelief and cynicism of modern times, God is still capable of miracles. Unfortunately many of the modern miracles are ascribed to coincidence. Often when prayers are said for the sick and they recover miraculously, the prayers are forgotten and no thanks or acknowledgement is given to God. Many people pray when they face a crisis, but when the crisis is past, they ignore the fact that they have prayed, or even feel embarrassed about it.

The evidence that God does answer prayer is overpowering. Lives have been unrecognizably changed; illnesses have been miraculously cured; twisted human relationships have been restored. Many people have personally discovered that God gives guidance when we ask for it.

Despite the miraculous power of prayer, God requires our co-operation for the answering of our prayers. God cannot solve your problem if you lay it before Him in prayer, but then take it back again. Hand the problem completely over to Him and do not try to solve it yourself. Allow God to handle it.

Do not succumb to extreme despair. At the right time and in the right way God will answer and you will be amazed by the result. Then you will rejoice in the fact that you did not interfere. In this way we gradually learn obedience in prayer and God increasingly works His miracles in our lives.

Not my will, Master, but Your will be done in my life. I once again place my life completely in Your hands. *Amen.*

Prayer Relieves Tension

In vain you rise early and stay up late, toiling for food to eat – for He grants sleep to those He loves.

~ PSALM 127:2

Life increasingly makes demands on all of us. If we try to control the circumstances and problems that threaten to overwhelm us, tension starts building up in our minds and hearts. Insomnia, touchiness and depression are the external symptoms.

Preventing tension is easier than healing it. In order to do this, it is necessary to develop a meaningful life of prayer. Time spent quietly with God lifts the lid off the pressure cooker and brings calmness and balance. His holy presence enriches your life and you are blessed.

The Lord leads you to oases of peace and calm. You'll find rest and renewal in prayer. From the eddying whirlpool of life which threatens to rob you of your peace of mind, God brings you to the quiet of His holy fellowship. There you will find deliverance and healing.

Do not neglect this experience simply because you believe in action and drama. Time spent in prayer and meditation is not a luxury but a definite necessity. It heals the wounds of your heart through the tender touch of His Spirit.

Then you will deal with tension like a mature disciple of Jesus Christ. Then you will understand how the Lord God gives a good night's rest to His loved ones.

I thank You, heavenly Father, that there is a place of peace and quiet in the eye of the storm. May I always find my strength and peace with You by being quiet and trusting in You. *Amen.*

When Things Go Wrong

"I revealed myself to those who did not ask for Me; I was found by those who did not seek Me. To a nation that did not call on My name, I said, 'Here am I, here am I.'"

When things go wrong, there are always those who question the existence of God. In the midst of the chaos of personal tragedy we hear their cries of distress, "If there is a God, why does He allow such things to happen?"

The brutality of war or the death of a child is used as the basis of an argument in which the love of God is denied. Time and again God stands as the accused, as if He is simply allowing the tragedy to happen. God's love is denied and the skeptics flourish by using these arguments to drive people further and further away from God's protective love.

God's immutable promise to His children has always been, and will always be, that if they only turn to Him in prayer, He will hear their voices and answer their prayers. Jesus promised, "Whoever comes to Me I will never drive away" (John 6:37). The Almighty God challenges His children and says, "Return to Me with all your heart ... Rend your heart and not your garments. Return to the Lord your God" (Joel 2:12-13).

Whatever your worries, however desperate your situation, turn in sincere prayer to God and gratefully accept the guidance that He has promised.

When I am tired and overburdened, weak and unbelieving, Lord Jesus, I turn to You in prayer so that I may receive new strength and vigor. Help me through Your Holy Spirit. *Amen.*

Persevere in Prayer

After He had dismissed them, He went up on a mountainside by himself to pray. When evening came, He was there alone.

~ MATTHEW 14:23

To our Lord prayer was an essential discipline. When He was at the peak of His popularity thousands followed Him to hear Him preach and to learn from Him. But even when He was denied by all His friends and had to endure the humiliation of seeming defeat, He found His strength and inspiration in prayer.

Unfortunately many of His modern disciples only pray when they feel like it, and they forget that prayer does not depend on your emotional state. If you only pray when you feel like it, the time will finally come when you will not pray at all.

At times all Christians experience spiritual drought, when it seems as if God is distant and remote. Consequently, their love for Him cools and their spiritual life loses its luster. During these times it is difficult to pray, but it is precisely then when prayer is crucial. Even though it might seem as if the heavens are insulated with copper, continue praying, because it is your only channel to God. Job says, "Though He slay me, yet will I hope in Him; I will surely defend my ways to His face" (Job 13:15). This is what ultimately impelled Job from his sorrow, and guided him to a renewed awareness that God's blessing rested upon him.

Discipline yourself in prayer so that you may triumph over your prayerless times, and so experience the supportive love and strength of the Master in your darkest and most vulnerable hour.

I thank and praise You, Lord my God, that I may experience the supportive power of prayer in my darkest hour. *Amen.*

An Exercise in Prayer

Be joyful in hope, patient in affliction, faithful in prayer.

~ Romans 12:12

Is your prayer life everything that you would like it to be? And everything that Christ would like it to be? Your answer can make the difference between an ineffective prayer life, or one that is filled with an awareness of the presence of God.

Your family and friends probably form part of your normal prayer pattern, and it is possible that you seldom think beyond them. Yet the whole world is pleading for prayer.

Just look at the newspaper, it is a prayer manual in itself. You can pray for the editors and those who are responsible for forming public opinion; you can pray for those who are the victims of violence, and even for those who committed the acts of violence. If you search for it, you may even be able to find something for which to thank God.

When you move out of your everyday world you will find innumerable opportunities for prayer. Give some thought in prayer to those who seem tired and disillusioned or even irritable. Rejoice together with those who are happy and thank God for their happiness. You never have to search for a reason to pray.

The great advantage of expanding your prayer base is the fact that it intensifies your own quiet time with God. While you are praying for others you will find a more intimate communion with the living Christ.

Lord Jesus, with Your disciples I want to plead: Teach me to pray! Open my eyes and heart to the needs of others. *Amen.*

Come, Let Us Pray

There on the beach we knelt to pray.

~ ACTS 21:5

One is often reminded of the saying that there is a time and a place for everything. It is also often applied to religion. In many segments of society the matter of a person's faith is regarded as a taboo topic of conversation.

Furthermore, there are also people who believe that prayer should be limited to the church or to the privacy of your inner room. They regard any form of public prayer in the run of daily life with uneasiness or even disapproval.

Prayer is as much a form of communication as conversation is. The difference is merely that conversation is a form of communication between people, while prayer is a conversation between us and our heavenly Father. There is nothing more natural than this.

There are moments in our lives when it is both essential and desirable to draw near to God. In these circumstances prayer is normal and appropriate as a form of communication.

While you should never be too shy to pray, it is also necessary to be careful and discreet in terms of the time and the place where you choose to pray. Trust in the guidance of the Holy Spirit and your prayers will at all times be a blessing to you as well as to others.

O Hearer of prayers, thank You that I may draw near to Your sacred throne at all times and under all circumstances, and know that You will always listen. *Amen.*

Do Not Treat Prayer Lightly

Is any one of you sick? He should call the elders of the church to pray over him ... And the prayer offered in faith will make the sick person well; the Lord will raise him up.

~ James 5:14-15

Never underestimate the power of prayer concerning illness. We cannot deny the fact that medical science plays an important role in curing illnesss, but we must never lose sight of the fact that miracles have been performed in the past – and are still performed today – through God's healing power brought about through intercession.

Too often prayers for the sick are mechanical and superficial. Often no attempt is even made to determine the cause of illness. Nothing is asked about the sick person's identity, or the circumstances in which he finds himself.

If you study Jesus Christ's devotional procedure, you cannot but notice how intimately He identified with the sick person seeking healing. He even felt how strength flowed from His own body when the healing process started.

True prayer for healing is not an experiment in trial and error. It requires the highest form of trust in God on the part of the person who prays and a belief that He will manifest His perfect will in the sick person. Complete involvement on the side of the intercessor, and total acceptance of God's will on the side of the patient, will lead to the greatest miracle of all healing: the peace of God, which transcends all understanding.

Eternal Father, guide me to say prayers to Your greater glorification with faith that can move mountains. *Amen.*

Be Patient in Prayer

I will stand at my watch and station myself on the ramparts; I will look to see what He will say to me, and what answer I am to give to this complaint.

~ HABAKKUK 2:1

So often people complain that their prayers remain unheard. In many instances they start losing patience with God – to such an extent that their faith weakens and they run the risk of getting lost in the wilderness of spiritual stagnation. This is one of the tragic consequences of man's misconception regarding prayer.

It is an established and irrefutable fact that God hears and answers our prayers. However, we need to know His Word to understand that His answer comes in His perfect time and in His perfect way, according to His perfect will. This is also done according to our needs – not your will and your wishes, unless they are in accordance with those of God.

Truly effective prayer often requires us to wait and watch. We must patiently wait for God to give us guidance, and we must wait willingly for a sign from Him that may manifest itself through circumstances, through another person, or even through the directions of your own heart or intuition as the Holy Spirit conveys it to you.

If you allow Christ to enter and rule your life, you will develop the ability to remain patient and calm in all circumstances. God will reveal Himself to you and show you His way. Our strength lies in being quiet and having faith.

Father, grant that in times of doubt I will turn to You, that I will hold on to You and to the certainty that I have in Jesus Christ. *Amen.*

Be Fervent and Persevere in Prayer

So He left them and went away once more and prayed the third time, saying the same thing.

~ MATTHEW 26:44

In Gethsemane, the living Christ taught us an endless amount about prayer. There are many people, including devoted Christians, who experience problems with their prayer lives in one form or another. They wonder why the discipline of persevering, fervent prayer is necessary, if God is all-seeing and omniscient. They feel guilty about the fact that they "trouble" God time and again with issues that He is already aware of.

Firstly, many things about various people are known to you as well, but you do not interfere until you are asked for help. However, when asked, you react. If you therefore feel that a particular matter deserves God's intervention, you must not hesitate to place it before Him. Remind Him of His promises and ask Him to take care of the situation.

Secondly, if you feel that something is worth praying for, it deserves more than just a passing reference before God. Your prayers should be placed before Him in all earnestness. True prayer implies honestly giving of yourself. Jesus gave Himself to such an extent that His sweat was drops of blood falling to the ground.

God will never tire of listening to you if you come to Him in the name of Christ. Learn to be sensitive to God's voice through the Holy Spirit. Prayer requires fervor and perseverance of a special quality.

In distress I call to You, O Lord, because only You can grant me peace. Thank You for hearing my prayers and for always answering my cry for help. *Amen.*

All-Inclusive Prayer

For this reason we also, since the day we heard it, do not cease to pray for you, and to ask that you may be filled with the knowledge of His will in all wisdom and spiritual understanding.

~ COLOSSIANS 1:9

Without noticing, one's life can become self-centered. Only your own needs, your family and your friends are stressed. And it is so easy to forget the spiritual needs of others.

Every person has the need to be encouraged and uplifted through prayer. There is no person on the face of the earth who can lead a committed Christian life, except through the grace of God. Nobody is infallible and we are all exposed to temptations. Through our weaknesses we can easily fall prey to Satan.

For the sake of the church of Christ, it is of the utmost importance that we will remember others in our prayers. Pray for those in the ministry and the unique temptations they face; pray for those who are serving in the mission field; members of church boards; those in special services; organists, vergers and everyone who must see to it that everything runs smoothly in a congregation. Pray for strength and guidance for those in youth ministries, or who take care of the aged, for social workers and the staff in children's homes.

In short, intercede for everyone who gives his or her time and strength to the church. Especially pray for Christians the world over that the triumphal procession of Christ may be advanced and that His holy name may be glorified.

Father, I pray for everyone who dedicates their time to the church. Bless them for their sacrifice and keep them strong in You. *Amen.*

Integrity before God

I know, my God, that You test the heart and are pleased with integrity.

~ 1 Chronicles 29:17

If you sincerely try to cultivate a positive and meaningful prayer life, you will at some time or another have experienced the problem of wandering thoughts. In the time you have set aside to be alone with your heavenly Father you may read a passage from the Bible or from an inspirational spiritual book. Then you start praying, only to discover that instead of being focused on God, your thoughts run amok and start focusing on the most irrelevant things.

If this has happened to you, take comfort in the thought that it happens to everyone who takes prayer time seriously. However, those who have persevered have ultimately succeeded in making their prayers a delightful reality and a powerful force in their lives.

When your thoughts wander, don't become upset or frustrated, because then you are playing right into the hands of the Evil One. Gently turn your thoughts back toward God, and ask the Holy Spirit to take control of your mind. You may rest assured that the problem of your wandering thoughts can be conquered, so don't allow it to spoil your relationship with the living Christ.

The wonder of Christian prayer is that when you turn to Jesus you will find that He is already waiting for you. Prayer is not one-way communication, because in this sacred practice Jesus is just as eager to meet you, His child, as you are to meet Him.

Thank You, heavenly Master, that I may experience the reality of Your living presence through prayer. For this I praise Your name. *Amen.*

Make Prayer a Way of Life

Pray continually.

~ 1 Thessalonians 5:17

The great benefit of putting aside time for prayer and quiet meditation is undeniable. Rich spiritual blessings flow forth from such times of prayer: inner peace; spiritual strength; determination and purposefulness. They form anchors in your life and are founded in those quiet moments spent alone with the Master. This gives meaning to life.

It should be clear to every Christian disciple that true prayer consists of more than a few mumbled requests. When prayer is used only as a means to satisfy God, or to prevent something unpleasant from happening to you, it is only a safety catch or a superstition.

True prayer is a relationship with life; an attitude that overshadows the nuances of everyday life. The ordinary humble tasks that have already become routine can become hallowed by regarding them as practical prayers to the glory of God.

During those moments, when your thoughts are not occupied with a specific task, it can be tuned in to the Master. He is your ever-present Traveling Companion through life. Wherever you are, know that you are in His presence and that you can talk to Him as to a friend.

The power and beauty of prayer lies in its simplicity. It is the heart-strengthening childlike prayer to God, that makes Him a living reality in your life.

I thank You, Example and Redeemer, that I can develop a living and practical prayer life that can become a way of life through the help of the Holy Spirit. *Amen.*

Pray Even When it Is Difficult

Then He spoke a parable to them, that men always ought to pray and not lose heart.

~ LUKE 18:1 (NKJV)

For many of the Lord's children, prayer is very natural and comes easy. Most of them, however, regard it as a discipline which they just never quite master. Their prayer lives today is exactly at the same level that it was many years ago.

Although they have made very little progress in their prayer lives, they continue praying. They believe that, in spite of their weakness, there is a God who really cares for them. This is one of the basic components of the practice of prayer. You should, however, never feel that God's caring love depends on your emotions. Even though you feel as if you are isolated from your heavenly Father, He is still as close to you as ever. God's love never changes and therefore your prayer life does not depend on how you feel. Faith always triumphs over feeling.

Keep on praying diligently, especially when you find it difficult. Persevere until you break through the desert of self-imposed inability, into the light of the living Christ. It is not the will of God that you should feel removed from Him. He is approachable at all times. You must only be determined to reach Him in prayer.

There are certain ways in which you can be assured of a meaningful prayer life. Seek God's forgiveness for sins of the past; discipline yourself and wait upon the Lord; develop a consciousness of the presence of Christ.

I praise and thank You that in spite of my emotions, You always love me and that love never changes, even when I fail You. *Amen.*

Disciplined Prayer

Pray continually.

~ 1 THESSALONIANS 5:17

The generally accepted thought regarding a disciplined prayer life, is that certain times of day should be put aside to be alone with God: early in the morning before the activity of the day, or at night before we go to bed. Over the years it has been proven beyond a doubt that such practice yields many blessings for man.

It is difficult enough to create a pattern of prayer in your life. It is somewhat more difficult to cultivate a sustained prayer life. Every right-minded disciple of Jesus Christ, who has endeavored to pray "continually", knows something about the feelings of guilt and the frustrations resulting from the knowledge that hours have passed without us sparing a thought for the Lord.

Continual prayer does not mean a constant repetition of the same requests, because that would be a manifestation of unbelief. To keep your prayers constantly in your thoughts could also mean that you are so obsessed with your problems that you do not really want to let go so that God can take over. The motive behind sustained prayer is to listen to God and to be sensitive to His guidance through the Holy Spirit.

Regardless of where you may find yourself, or what you may busy yourself with, you can lift your heart to God, even for a single moment and in a fleeting thought, and in doing so, experience the reality of His presence.

Thank You, Lord, for hearing my prayers of supplication and thanksgiving, and that You bless those who wait on You in prayer. *Amen.*

Be Positive in Prayer

"What do you want Me to do for you?"

~ Mark 10:51

Unfortunately, there are many people who are extremely skeptical about the value of prayer, and they deny themselves one of God's greatest gifts of mercy to mankind. They will point to everything that is going wrong in the world, to those who suffer failure upon failure, to the unfortunate victims of disease and illness, to those whose lives are in ruin. Inevitably, they will then question the value of prayer, as well as the love of a God who allows it all to happen.

When you come to God in prayer, it is essential to be clear in your requests, and that you reveal faith and trust that will enable you to entrust your petitions, or the person for whom you are praying, to God's sublime will. When you have stated your requests, you must trust in God to take them up and answer them in His time and way.

Do not be vague, half-hearted or unsure when you pray. It is a sign of lack of faith if you pray negatively, because you are subconsciously finding a loophole to hide behind if what you seek does not transpire. When you are in the presence of God, place all your fears and concerns before Him. Ask Him to guide you and allow the Holy Spirit to determine your thoughts.

If you have been honest and sincere with God, then leave the matter in His loving hands. Be filled with expectation and await His answer. He will not disappoint you.

Almighty Lord, cleanse me, make me holy and pure, so that I may draw near to Your throne. *Amen.*

Sometimes the Answer Is "No"

Answer me when I call to You, O my righteous God. Give me relief from my distress; be merciful to me and hear my prayer.

~ PSALM 4:1

We often hear people complain that God does not answer their prayers. They declare that they prayed extensively and earnestly, but nothing happened; they prayed for some or other specific thing, but did not get it; they asked for God's guidance on a particular path, but nothing came of it. The result of these prayer experiences is that many people's faith wanes because they maintain that God does not listen.

However, nothing could be further from the truth. In the Scriptures we are assured that God hears and answers the prayers of His children. But we err in forgetting that God does, upon occasion, say "no." We focus so much on asking Him for those things that we want that we lose sight of the fact that Jesus assured us that He would provide for all our needs, and no-one knows better than Christ what we need.

True prayer does not consist of telling God what you want or what you are planning to do, and then asking Him to place His stamp of approval on it. Prayer consists of opening up your life to God, laying your needs before Him and trusting Him to lead you on the right path.

Lord Jesus, You are my Guide, my Leader and my Friend. Therefore I submit obediently to Your will, even though You sometimes say "no" to me. Lead me according to Your will until the end of my pilgrimage. *Amen.*

Unshakable Principles for Prayer

"When you pray, go into your room, close the door and pray to your Father, who is unseen. Then your Father, who sees what is done in secret, will reward you."

~ MATTHEW 6:6

Prayer is not meant as a means to obtain things from God, but rather as a means to hear God's point of view. Prayer is to seek God's will, rather than to command Him to do what you want. Prayer is to give yourself to God completely and not to use God for your own selfish goals.

It is just as much "listening" to God as it is "talking" to God. Prayer is a dialogue, not a monologue.

It is patiently waiting on God and not expecting everything to be done immediately. It is not an emergency button that you press in times of crisis, but it is a way of life.

Prayer is creating joy by spending time with God; and is not a hasty ceremonial duty.

It is not a list of requests presented to God with the monotonous introduction, "Give me"; it is a total commitment that honestly asks, "Lord, what do you want me to do?"

Prayer is never "Do it now!" Rather confess, "Thy will be done." It is through mercy that God keeps us waiting, and does not always give us what we ask for.

Often we are not equipped to use the things we ask for. The main purpose of prayer is to honor God, to glorify His name, to carry out His will and to edify His Kingdom.

Our Father in heaven, hallowed be Your name, Your Kingdom come, Your will be done. *Amen.*

An Effective Prayer Life

*Do not be anxious about anything, but in everything, by prayer
and petition, with thanksgiving, present your requests to God.*
                                        ~ PHILIPPIANS 4:6

Of all the Christian doctrines, prayer is probably most common-
ly practiced and, in all likelihood, the least understood. Many
people regard prayer as a life-jacket to be used in desperate situations. Or as a method to tell God what they really wish for and to
obtain His blessing for that which they have already decided upon.
With this attitude, it is no wonder that so many people maintain
that their prayers go unanswered.

At first, as with every other relationship, a relationship of prayer
with God has to be established. Failing that, your prayer life will
never develop in a meaningful way, nor become a significant experience. You have to develop an affinity for the living Christ by
constantly acknowledging His presence in your daily life. Grow
ever closer to Him while studying His Word, and meditate in the
quiet presence of the peace of God.

Always remember to thank and praise God for the privilege of
prayer, and then cast all your cares, fears, problems and requests
upon Him and ask Him to grant you that which He deems necessary.

Then wait patiently on the Lord and be sensitive to the whisperings of the Holy Spirit that will lead you onto the path of peace.
Then God's destiny will unfold itself and the way forward will
become clear with God as your Governor and Guide.

From Your hand You grant us more than we could ever ask for. We
know that Your promises hold good. Thank You Lord. *Amen.*

Surrender Your Prayer Life to God

"Lord, teach us to pray"

~ LUKE 11:1

Most Christians are deeply aware of their own inability to pray according to the will of God. They realize that they should pray more regularly and ask the Master to grant them a more meaningful prayer life. However, they forget that having a vital and pulsating prayer life also depends upon themselves, and not only on the Master.

Christ sacrificed Himself unconditionally for all who embrace Him in faith and trust Him as their Savior and Redeemer. He gave Himself freely, but He will enrich your life only as far as you will allow Him to. The depth and quality of your devotion will be reflected in the power of your prayer life.

Superficial devotion can never yield a living and pulsating spiritual life. The truth is that if you desire complete dedication to your Master, the responsibility rests squarely on your shoulders.

If you seriously deepen your surrender to Christ, your awareness of His living presence will become an ever-increasing reality in your life. You will discover and open up channels of communication with Him that you can use anywhere at any time. If this happens, your prayers will surpass your former devotional time and will become the driving force of your everyday life.

It does not mean a thing to ask God for a meaningful and positive prayer life unless you do your share to develop it.

Lord, teach me not to fret about what tomorrow may bring. Teach me to quietly trust in You, because You are good and all-wise. *Amen.*

Talk Things through with God

Be joyful always; pray continually.

~ 1 Thessalonians 5:16-17

There are many ways to pray. Some people find liturgical prayers dignified and valuable. Prayers that are spoken in deep distress possess an urgency that does not take style and composition into consideration.

The silence of contemplative prayer is another way to move into the presence of God. The steadfast belief that God does answer your prayers is important, regardless of how you pray.

In prayer the attitude of the heart and mind is of essential importance. No fixed and predetermined method should have preference over the cry of the yearning heart that craves communication with God. At any given time or place this cry has priority over all other forms of prayer.

When you are confronted with overwhelming temptation; when the heavy burdens of life threaten to crush you; when life is comfortable and attractive ... These are all occasions that may be shared with God. Whatever your circumstances or your needs, learn to turn to God and share them with Him.

As you talk things through with God you will become sensitive to His guidance and leadership. You will also become aware of a newly found strength that inwardly fortifies you.

Eventually everything that you think or do will come under the influence of your conversation with God. And then your prayers become meaningful and significant.

Loving Master, I entreat You to grant me the gift of Your Holy Spirit so that I can pray meaningfully in all circumstances. *Amen.*

When We Pray

"When you pray, do not keep on babbling like pagans, for they think they will be heard because of their many words."

~ MATTHEW 6:7

There are many people who associate prayer with pompous eloquence. They seem to be under the impression that prayers should necessarily be long, that they should be complex and that the language of prayer should be formal and very correct.

The prayer most acceptable to Christ is in fact a childlike prayer. It should be simple, humble and sincere. The Afrikaans poet N. P. Van Wyk Louw speaks of the "honesty of deathbed words". The parable of the Pharisee and the tax collector is a classic example of this. Very often long drawn-out prayers are said more for effect than out of sincerity. The cry of distress, "Father!" which comes from a repentant heart full of love, will be heard by God.

Pay attention to the instructions of Jesus in your prayers. He placed a high premium on simplicity and childlike faith. He also taught us to pray in private which is just as important – if not more important – than praying with others.

When you pray, speak to God in simple everyday language as you would speak to a trusted friend. Jesus is your Friend after all. Pour out your worries before Him; share your anxiety and joy with Him. Wait on Him in silence. He will hear you and answer your prayer, often in the simplest and most surprising way. Truly believe this for He gave you His word.

O Holy Spirit, guide my thoughts and words when I pray. Help me when I do not quite know what to pray. *Amen.*

Dependency on God

I cry to You for help, O LORD; in the morning my prayer comes before You.

~ PSALM 88:13

In these days of sophisticated advertising, the virtues of a variety of products are proclaimed. The listening, watching and reading public is invited to "start the day in the right way" with some kind of cereal or fruit juice. Various vitamin tablets and health salts are offered as the right way to prepare yourself in order to be able to cope with the day ahead. Every remedy on offer claims to be more successful than the others.

Each one of us needs help to successfully meet the demands of each day, especially in these competitive times in which we live. Modern life emphasizes super-speed, super-excellence and super-performance, which makes life more stressful and more tense.

There is only one sure way to meet every day with its tough demands successfully, and that is to face each day with peace of mind. In order to achieve this, it is essential to start every day in the presence of God and with the living Christ. Reveal to Him your fears and place those things that concern you before Him.

Somebody said that we should start each day in prayer, so that the day would not fray at the edges. Seek Christ's help for whatever the day might bring, by asking Him to help carry your burden.

Hand over the new day, your concerns, the day itself, and yourself to Him. Then face the day, shielded by His hand, with peace in your heart. Dependency on God leads to true success!

You make everything bright. Even the darkness becomes light. You are the Morning Star to which I lift my eyes. *Amen.*

Prepare Yourself for Life

Pray continually.

~ 1 Thessalonians 5:17

Although the future is unknown there is nothing preventing you from preparing for it. The only effective way of doing this is by developing a healthy prayer life.

This means a prayer life that enables you to maintain your balance when it seems as though the world around you has been turned on its head. It will provide you with strength in moments of weakness and comfort in times of sorrow. This is not achieved overnight, but is the precious fruit of ample time spent in the presence of the Lord.

As a wise sailor does not start repairing his sails in the middle of a storm, but already ensures in the calm of the harbor that they are in good condition, the pilgrim on the spiritual path will empower himself in the practice of prayer while he can devote his attention to it, without the pressure and influence of external problems.

An effective prayer life is the result of a disciplined and creative disposition before God. If you are sincere, you will not only pray when you feel like it, but you will share each fleeting emotion and feeling with your Master. Share your joy in prayer with God while the sun shines, and there will be no panicking when the storm comes up.

How wonderful, heavenly Father, to praise and to glorify You. I wish to sing praises of Your great love and faithfulness for all to hear. *Amen.*

July

Be Encouraged

"Be strong and of good courage; do not be afraid, nor be dismayed,
for the LORD your God is with you wherever you go."

~ Joshua 1:9 (NKJV)

You may still need to grow beyond that point in your spiritual life where you believe that God is a super-examiner who finds great satisfaction in penalizing you for every mistake you make. To have such a concept of your heavenly Father, is to do Him great injustice. It also creates a serious barrier, preventing His loving encouragement from flowing into your life.

It is God's desire for you to live in intimate fellowship with Him; that you will experience His creative abilities; that you will express His wisdom in your relationship with others; that you will draw strength from Him when you are weak, courage when you are discouraged and inspiration when you are despondent. Your heavenly Father does not take pleasure in your failures, but He waits for you to ask Him to meet you at the point of your need and to enable you to become that which He expects you to be.

If you make God your partner and the consciousness of His living presence becomes a reality in your life, then your perception of God will change radically. Then you won't regard Him as One who takes pleasure in condemnation, but as the main source of encouragement and inspiration. Then He becomes your shining light of encouragement when you are downcast, or when you experience bitterness, failure and disappointment. Then He will be there to whisper to you, "Do not be afraid, nor be dismayed."

Father, Your constant encouragement and inspiration is my shining light in dark times. Thank You for that. *Amen.*

God Is Omnipresent

The steps of a good man are ordered by the LORD, and He delights in his way. Though he fall, he shall not be utterly cast down, for the LORD upholds him with His hand.

~ PSALM 37:23-24

Christians are not exempt from deep emotional experiences. Sometimes they find themselves on cloud nine, while at other times they are cast into the depths of spiritual despair. It is important to maintain a healthy balance between these two extremes and to keep your grip on your faith.

Don't convince yourself that you've disappointed or denied the Master. He knows what it means to be upset and He understands your moods. He also understands your moments of spiritual ecstasy when your spirit reaches out to God. He is the Lord of every frame of mind, because He became a man.

You must beware that your despondency is not caused by physical weakness, because it can create apathy in spiritual matters. The most common cause of despondency and depression, is disobedience to the law of God and His plan for your life. When a Christian disciple refuses to do the will of God, he experiences an inner turmoil which results in frustration and despair.

The remedy for this state of mind is a more intimate walk with God. This means more time in prayer and meditation; a disciplined quiet time and a consciousness of the presence of the living Christ. Your encouragement is that when you search for Him, He is already there to receive you.

Thank You, Father, for Your constant presence. Even if I turn away from You, You are still there waiting to receive me again. *Amen.*

God Wants to Be Your Friend

So the Lord spoke to Moses face to face, as a man speaks to his friend.

~ Exodus 33:11 (NKJV)

In their search for God many people experience only silence in His presence. They feel as if they are in a spiritual void. They try to empty their minds of all thoughts in order to be filled with a consciousness of the living God, only to find that their minds are being filled with petty and confusing thoughts.

One method of getting to know God, is to accept Him as a tried and trusted friend. Share your deepest thoughts and feelings with Him. Include Him in your everyday thoughts, and make Him an integral part of your life. The development of such familiarity will in no way decrease the respect that you have for Him. On the contrary, the development of such an intimacy enables you to enter the presence of God, thus strengthening your inner life and refreshing your spirit.

An intimate relationship with God can only be achieved through the sanctified friendship which the Master offers to His committed and dedicated disciples.

God wants to be your friend. Make Him your friend. Share with Him your deepest thoughts. Enjoy fellowship with Him constantly in the quietness of your spirit. Then you will discover those beautiful moments that are filled with His presence. The thoughts that you share with Him fill that void and make you receptive to His encouraging closeness.

Lord, I praise Your great name because even though I am not worthy, You still desire me as Your friend. *Amen.*

Protect the Oasis of My Life

"He makes me to lie down in green pastures; He leads me beside the still waters."

~ PSALM 23:2

For many people life is nothing but drudgery. Their daily routine has become so monotonous that the joy they once derived from the small, interesting things in life is now dead. They simply exist; without any purpose or expectation.

When you take a close look at these people who have lost their vision, you will find that they have neglected the oasis of their lives. They have plodded along without realizing how important it is for them to come to a standstill, refresh their spirit and determine the course they are following. Their lives have turned into a desert. If you carry on without making time for spiritual refreshment and for adapting your course, life itself loses all meaning and purpose. Then the monotony suffocates your spirit and you will not be able to appreciate the loftier things in life any more.

Cultivating an effective life is not a luxury, but a practical necessity. Life today has such a hectic pace that it is imperative for you to make time to withdraw for a while and spend time alone with God. Neglect this spiritual exercise and you can be sure that the tensions of life will overwhelm you.

You need to protect the oasis of your life with diligence and spend quiet time with God in order for you to lead a meaningful life and to ensure that you are still within His sphere of protection.

Holy Spirit of God, with Your help and Your presence, I will embrace every day with enthusiasm. *Amen.*

God Protects His Laborers

Being confident of this very thing, that He who has begun a good work in you will complete it until the day of Jesus Christ.

~ PHILIPPIANS 1:6 (NKJV)

From every generation Jesus Christ has His followers who preach His gospel and do His will. Some of them reach high positions in society; others perform the task He has assigned to them to the best of their ability. Regardless of their status they zealously love the Lord, to the extent that it challenges and motivates their fellow believers.

The spiritual giants of the Christian faith always have a vivid and unique experience with their Savior. Paul never forgot his experience on the road to Damascus; Brother Lawrence loved being in his kitchen with Christ; John Wesley felt his "heart to be strangely warmed" in a room in Aldersgate Street in London. There are also many other disciples who experience the reality of the living Christ in various ways.

One thing that the followers of Christ should understand is that the Master comes to them in their own, unique circumstances, meeting everyone at his own level and place. The ordinary disciple does not necessarily have a Damascus Road experience.

As your relationship with Jesus Christ deepens, you will be guided into constructive service. You become aware of a divine plan unfolding for your life. Such a plan might perhaps not be dramatic, but it is God's plan for you, and in executing it you will find joy and a deep satisfaction – as well as His protection.

Master, make my experience with You one that will take me to higher heights in my walk with You. *Amen.*

Have You Lost Your Way?

"I am the way."

~ John 14:6

Few things can create a feeling of dreary despair faster than discovering that you have totally lost your way. There is nothing more frustrating than walking around in circles in an effort to find your way, while you don't have the vaguest idea of where you actually are.

How much worse the frustration must be when you discover that you've lost your way spiritually, that you are stumbling and groping around in what seems to be a never-ending wilderness, in an effort to rediscover your previous relationship – a relationship which had earlier brought you much joy, but which you've now lost.

The first disciples also expressed their doubt about finding their way to God. Jesus clearly explained to them that He is the way and that nobody can come to the Father, except through Him.

And still today the situation remains the same: to reach God you need to have a personal relationship with the living Christ. It is important that you walk with Jesus along life's path and through faith have intimate fellowship with Him. To get to know Him better, you must use God's means of grace. Through faith, Bible study and meditation on the wonderful acts of God, you will walk in Christ with God. He will protect you from wandering away and the danger of getting lost.

Lord, when I go astray, help me to find my way back to You quickly. Help me also to protect myself against that. *Amen.*

Peace that Calms the Storm

"Be at peace among yourselves."

~ 1 Thessalonians 5:13 (nkjv)

As the pressures and pace of life increase, people become more tense and grim. Many people, in many spheres of life, become more and more aware of the demands of our day and age. The more modern technology is geared to meet these demands, the more hectic the treadmill of life becomes.

Inevitably this tension causes people to snap. Obvious signs are irritation, moodiness, petty jealousy, and eventually the basis of our Christian faith; love, is destroyed. Of course Satan rejoices in this because anything which makes it impossible for you to love your fellow man will make it impossible for you to love God (see 1 John 4:20).

In order for us to handle the extreme demands of modern life without losing our spiritual stability, an intimate spiritual fellowship with God is essential. Open up your heart, mind and soul to the influence of the Holy Spirit so that He may control your life and your emotions. You will find that, in His power, you are able to handle the pressure without giving in to your human weaknesses. The Holy Spirit will fill your life with the peace of Jesus Christ.

In turn you will be able to let this peace flow through to others because you are a channel of God's love and peace. This is the only way in which the storm of tension and hurry-scurry can be calmed.

Faithful Master, around me a storm is raging yet You grant me peace that surpasses all understanding. *Amen.*

The Safe Haven of Jesus' Love

The LORD is my rock, my fortress and my deliverer; my God is my rock, in whom I take refuge. He is my shield and the horn of my salvation, my stronghold.

~ PSALM 18:2

All people need shelter at some point. It may be the security of your own home, or a shelter against the wind and rain. In times of war, shelter is sought against falling bombs. But a bomb-attack, poor weather and other forms of attack are not limited to our physical being.

Our spiritual and intellectual faculties are often attacked by the storms of life. In order to seek shelter against these and to prevent devastating emotional consequences, we all need a haven in life that will be constant and safe and where we can shelter in complete faith.

Regardless of what may happen to you, and the seriousness of the situation in which you may find yourself, place your trust and faith in God at all times. Even when it seems as if everything is lost and your world collapses around you like a stack of cards, entrust yourself to the love of Jesus Christ.

God has promised never to fail you nor forsake you. With this certainty in your heart, you can face the future with confidence. With the newly-found self-confidence that the Holy Spirit grants you, you will know that, regardless of how dark the road ahead may seem, Christ is your shelter and safe haven. Where, in this whole wide world, could one feel safer?

Thank You, my Lord and my God, that I may take shelter in You and that I may be safe for time and eternity. *Amen.*

The Center of Christ's Peace

"Peace I leave with you, My peace I give to you; not as the world gives do I give to you. Let not your heart be troubled, neither let it be afraid."

~ JOHN. 14:27 (NKJV)

Few people can honestly say that they haven't longed for peace of mind and inner tranquility at some time or another. The general insecurities of life today, sickness, death, dangers and unrest, create a deep-seated uncertainty. The list is endless, yet the results are the same: unknown pressure and insecurity which border on despair.

Many of those who suffer seek professional help. The psychiatrist's couch and tranquilizers have become a common way of living. Others, who lack the willpower, indulge in drugs and liquor. Yet others give in to despair and live in a void where their lives have no quality whatsoever.

The only proven way to handle the pressures and tensions of life is through faith that is steadfastly founded on the living Christ. Your relationship with Him cannot only be a fleeting friendship or a matter of convenience. You need to permanently experience unity with Him.

Under all circumstances hold on to Him, talk to Him, regardless of how desperate your situation might be, trust that He is always with you. Even though you may find it difficult to understand His peace, you will recognize it when it flows through your mind, overcoming all your fears.

Prince of Peace, please help me to rely only on You for help. My faith in You can pull me through anything. *Amen.*

Peace that Overcomes

"The God of peace will crush Satan under your feet shortly."

~ Romans 16:20 (NKJV)

When problems clamp down on your life and you are upset and despondent, it is so easy to begin to doubt. It often seems as if one setback leads to the next and you start to wonder if you will ever be able to move through the dark tunnel of depression. That is the time when you are most vulnerable and an easy prey to Satan. He is always ready and willing to lead you away from God onto the road of despair.

It is generally accepted that you must at all times keep your quiet times with God faithfully. In doing so you will strengthen your relationship with God. This is especially valid when your faith is being tested.

When everything goes well with you it is fairly easy to maintain an intimate relationship with the Lord. However, when life's problems hit you, the tendency develops to drift away from the Master. And that is fatal.

Whatever your circumstances might be, always remember that God loves you with an unfathomable love, a love that cannot be measured and which is perfect. He truly cares for you and invites you to turn to Him with all of life's burdens (see 1 Pet. 5:7).

If you would only cling to Him, believing His promise that He will always be with you, then He will fill your life with His heavenly peace, and Satan will be defeated time and time again in your life.

Lord Jesus, You promised to be with me always. Help me to trust in that and not doubt. *Amen.*

Jesus' Steps of Peace

*So it was, while they conversed and reasoned, that Jesus Himself
drew near and went with them.*

~ LUKE 24:15 (NKJV)

You must never entertain preconceived ideas of how Jesus
Christ will come to you. If you regularly have your quiet time
and wait upon Him, these will become precious times to you during which you will become aware of His divine presence. At such
times it is almost unnecessary to say a word because you will know
that Christ is with you, and your soul is nourished.

The time comes, however, when you have to take part in the activities of life and accept life's challenges. Even though your quiet
time with God has provided you with spiritual and mental balance, the demands of your specific circumstances could make you
forget that you have spent time with Him.

The way in which to maintain contact with Jesus throughout the
course of a busy day, is by seeing Him in unexpected places. He
is not restricted to your quiet time with Him or to your personal
prayer life. He can speak to you through the voice of your fellow
man. He might look to you through the eyes of a lonely stranger,
seeking companionship. You might see His beauty in the smile of
a small child. A brief prayer for passersby in a busy street might
bring Christ very close to you.

Never be too busy to obey God. As you obey Him in seemingly
unimportant matters, He will become increasingly real to you and
you will hear His soft footsteps at unexpected places and times.

Help me to see You in unexpected places today. Give me a discerning
heart to discover You. *Amen.*

Christ's Utmost Desire

"That I may know Him and the power of His resurrection, and the fellowship of His sufferings, being conformed to His death."

~ PHILIPPIANS 3:10 (NKJV)

All Christians experience some or other deep desire, and the quality of that desire determines the strength or weakness of their spiritual lives. If inferior influences have top priority in their lives, it is only a matter of time before their lives will wane and lose all purpose, and meaning.

It is important that true Christians should have pure desires to motivate them on their spiritual pilgrimage. The highest of all desires is "to know Christ and experience the power of His resurrection". When such a sanctified desire takes hold of man, all other surrounding perspectives fall into their rightful places. Without the urgent desire to know Christ more intimately, the spiritual life loses its motivational power.

"To know Christ" is much more than an emotional experience. It is an act of faith which opens up your mind to the influence and working of His divine mind. It enables you to walk in His steps. Knowing Christ so intimately makes it impossible for someone with that knowledge not to reveal it in his everyday life.

Such a high standard of living would have been unattainable, if those who knew Christ didn't experience the power of His resurrection. It is that exact power which enables them to live according to His will. And it is also part of the unspeakable grace of the highest Majesty.

My deepest desire, O Lord, is to know You more. I want to know You intimately and deeply. *Amen.*

Quietness with God

"In that day, 'Holiness to the LORD' shall be engraved on the bells of the horses. The pots in the LORD's house shall be like the bowls before the altar."

~ ZECHARIAH 14:20 (NKJV)

Piety is a word which has mostly negative connotations. When someone is described as "pious", the impression is created that such a person is hypocritically virtuous.

Nevertheless, piety is a virtue that is very close to the heart of God. True piety is not an act to impress people. It is conduct which flows from a life that is anchored in God, a longing to give expression to His will and allowing His Spirit to take the initiative in every situation.

This means that your life will become holy. Zechariah had a vision of piety when he prophesied that the common, everyday things will be engraved with the words, "Holiness to the Lord."

Many people find that this lifestyle does not attract them at all. However, for those who seriously strive to live for God, there is a rich reward. To consciously live in God's presence sanctifies one's whole life. His guidance takes you along the paths which He has planned for you. The power which He imparts to your spirit, enables you to obey Him. The more intimately you love Him, the more you understand Him and the life He has called you to.

If you include God in every moment of your life, He will give you His peace. Then you will own a precious treasure which comes from God only.

Grant me, O Lord my God true piety. I want to constantly live in Your presence and Your peace. *Amen.*

Your Search for Peace

"'This is the rest with which You may cause the weary to rest,' and 'this is the refreshing;' yet they would not hear."

~ Isaiah 28:12 (NKJV)

In times of tension, confusion and stress people generally show signs of fatigue. This is especially true in our world where so much is made of achievements, progress and results. People of all ages, from teenagers to the elderly, struggle with tremendous pressure. The result leaves scars on the spirits and minds of people and they yearn for rest and peace.

Yet in the midst of our overly-busy lives, Christ kindly invites us, "Come to Me, all you who labor and are heavy laden, and I will give you rest" (Matt. 11:28). It is remarkable that so few people respond to this invitation. We much rather look for man-made solutions to help us cope with the pressures of life. It is incomprehensible that people hesitate to turn to Jesus Christ and accept the only true peace. It is offered to us freely and promised with much love.

Regardless of how busy you are, it is imperative that you make time to withdraw from the demands of each day and spend time in quietness at the feet of the Master. Focus all your attention on Him and His love. In the quietness, become soaked in and strengthened by His peace. Make sure you do this regularly. Regardless of how demanding your life might be, you will experience a feeling of strength, peace and tranquility while the Holy Spirit ministers His healing work in your life.

I have such a need of Your rest, Lord, I want to focus on You so that Your peace and rejuvenation can flow through me. *Amen.*

An Unfailing Ally

If God is for us, who can be against us?

~ ROMANS 8:31

Pessimism leaves a stain on man's soul. The effects are varying and far-reaching and can influence your life negatively. Your outlook on life can become narrow, growth is hampered, trust is undermined and your whole life can stagnate.

If you are experiencing any of these emotions, it is imperative that you take a very close look at your life immediately in order for you to take steps to end this condition before it is too late. Otherwise you are robbing yourself of purposefulness and energy and you are in danger of living a futile life.

In spite of the most severe attacks of pessimism, there is one tried and tested method of preventing the decay that comes through these negative influences. That is to have intimate spiritual fellowship with God. Through Jesus Christ you can walk with Him daily. He has given you His unfailing Word that He will be with you always (see Heb. 13:5). Why don't you accept this offer that is so rich in grace – thus making the living Christ your partner in each undertaking and experience of your life?

He is ready to share your success and failure with you. Allow Him to share in your sorrow and joy. Meet life on a daily basis with the sure knowledge that Jesus is closer to you than a brother. With Christ at your side you cannot help but walk through life with new confidence. This new-found assurance is established in your heart through the Holy Spirit. Face the future with that.

Lord, with You as my ally I need not be pessimistic. The joy of the Lord is my strength. *Amen.*

Messengers from Christ

"As the Father has sent Me, I am sending you."

~ JOHN 20:21

It is an overwhelming thought: Christians are called to a purposeful life. The delusion of wishful thinking that leads to the byways of life, is not our fate. You are in the service of His Majesty, the living Christ, and you have voluntarily accepted the responsibility of serving Him. This means that you accept all the disciplines of a spiritual life, so that your love for Him can increase and so that you can be His efficient messenger.

Where will you serve Him? For a privileged small number, their service will lead them to foreign countries and exciting circumstances, but for the majority of Christian believers it will mean service in an ordinary world. He sends you into the world that you know so well.

You may be in commerce or in a profession, you may hold a position of authority, or fill a humble post, you may be a homemaker; wherever you may find yourself, you are His representative. People who know about your loyalty to Him, will expect you to maintain certain standards in your speech and in your conduct, that they will not expect from the world.

If your life is filled with the love of Jesus Christ, your infectious faith will bring a message of hope and love, wherever God wishes to use you.

Here am I, Master, send me to serve You wherever You may need me. *Amen.*

When God Lives in You

You will keep in perfect peace him whose mind is steadfast, because he trusts in You.

~ Isaiah 26:3

Our thoughts are servants to us. Total control of your thoughts is possible if you do not give wrong thoughts free reign. Your thoughts influence your deeds because that which you think and believe is the cause of your circumstances. It is therefore imperative to discipline your thoughts in order to have a positive and constructive disposition towards life.

Behind every thought lies the power of desire. It is therefore important to rid yourself of destructive emotions that result in mental deterioration. Replace them with positive thoughts.

The greatest force in a healthy emotional life is allowing the Holy Spirit to take control of your thoughts. Trust in God and live in harmony with Him. If your thoughts are concentrated on God, He will enable you to approach life with trust, and your emotions will increasingly be subject to the sovereignty of the Holy Spirit.

You can, through the strength which Christ grants you, select your thoughts and, in doing so, experience the peace of God. There will be moments of disruption when evil thoughts are trying to re-establish themselves. But while you are focusing on the benevolence and grace of God, you will receive confirmation that the Master is in control of your thoughts; and then there is nothing that can destroy your peace.

You are my only Savior. Lord, protect me from the Evil One. *Amen.*

The Omnipotence of Christ

Do not conform any longer to the pattern of this world, but be transformed by the renewing of your mind.

~ ROMANS 12:2

Long before the term psychology became popular in modern-day society, the Bible taught us the necessity of being renewed by an inner strength. Man was created in the image of God. Since his fall from former glory, he has been trying to restore his unity with God.

For the renewed soul, there is an ongoing battle to become that which he instinctively feels that he should be: a child of God who is worthy of this high honor. Man has tried hard to achieve this goal, using all the means at his disposal to rediscover a meaningful relationship with God. This battle often results in frustration and disappointment. He, who does not find and embrace God outwardly, will also not discover God inwardly.

Once we have developed a positive relationship with the living Christ, our mental outlook will also be renewed. Instead of living a life filled with fear, you will face life with confidence. Instead of frustration, a sense of purpose will enter your life; your spirit is filled with joy, happiness and contentment, inspired by the Holy Spirit of God.

Such a transformation takes place because your mind has been possessed by the Spirit of God. This is what Paul is talking about when he says in Philippians 2:5, "Your attitude should be the same as that of Christ Jesus."

Living God, I humbly ask that You will renew my spiritual life through the Holy Spirit residing in me. *Amen.*

Do You Belong to God?

"You have found grace in My sight, and I know you by name."
~ Exodus 33:17

Apart from the fact that the Bible is the revealed will of God, it is also a report of the lives of very interesting personalities. Some of them were faithful servants, some rebelled against God and worked against Him, some disappointed Him very badly, but God knew them all by name.

You have a heavenly Father who delights Himself in mankind. In modern society it may seem as if names are less important than numbers, but to God you are one-of-a-kind, and He regards you as so important that He calls you His child.

If you are the kind of person who lives an extremely lonely life because you see yourself as inferior and unimportant, you have probably forgotten that your heavenly Father knows about you and loves you dearly.

The fact that God knows you by name, causes you to feel that you have some worth. This can be cultivated through prayer and spending time with Him. In your relationship with Him, the Master no longer speaks to the masses, but to you personally. He teaches you about love, righteousness, honesty, unselfishness and other wise ways about how to live your life.

The fact that He knows you personally by name is sheer grace. You can only enjoy the benefit of this relationship if you have accepted Him as your Redeemer and Savior.

Father, I thank You for the assurance that I am special and unique in Your sight. You know me by name. *Amen.*

Grace and Peace Found in God

I lay down and slept; I awoke, for the LORD sustained me.
　　　　　　　　　　　　　　　　~ PSALM 3:5 (NKJV)

Insecurity leads to uneasiness and confusion. If you are insecure about your future, if you are not sure at all about the next move of your competitor in the business world, if you are all alone in the dark of night, imagining that you've heard footsteps: all these experiences lead to the uneasy combination of anxiety, fear and confusion.

Foremost in your mind is the importance of preparation and self-defence. How do you prepare yourself to handle any situation that could arise, in order that you may be relatively sure of a peaceful and safe life?

Right through history it is apparent that those people who had an intimate walk with God, were exactly those who found hidden resources of power to overcome their setbacks. Those who have an unflinching faith in the living Christ will not waver or break under attacks. Those who put their trust in the all-surrounding love of Christ will not give in to fear.

There is no magical power in these statements. The same Christ who hushed the wind and stilled the storm when the disciples were panic-stricken, is calling out to you today, "Be strong and courageous; do not be afraid!" Put your trust in Him and experience for yourself how His love and grace cause the storms in your life to subside.

O Lord, I put my trust in You for You are a mighty God. I refuse to feel insecure or confused, because You are my God. *Amen.*

All-Surrounding Love

The LORD is my shepherd; I shall not want.

~ PSALM 23:1 (NKJV)

To the Palestinian shepherds their flocks of sheep and goats were their life source and everything depended on their well-being. These animals provided milk, meat and cheese, as well as wool and skins for clothing. Therefore the shepherd took very good care of them; he provided them with pastures and water, protected them against attacks, kept them safely on the right path and searched for the ones that went astray.

For Jesus Christ His children are also very precious. That is why we got to know Him as the Good Shepherd. He cares for you by providing for your daily needs, by protecting you, by showing you the path of righteousness and by searching for you when you go astray. Then He lovingly brings you back to the safety of the flock.

However, there is one crucial difference between the Palestinian shepherd and his relationship with his flock, and the good Shepherd and His children. And this difference is what makes the Christian faith real.

The flock were only valuable because of what they produced, but Jesus Christ, the Good Shepherd, offers you His protection and immeasurable love, and only asks that you should love Him in return. Is this a price too high to pay for a love which exceeds all other loves by far?

Good Shepherd, thank You that I am valuable to You. *Amen.*

We Are His Children

Behold what manner of love the Father has bestowed on us, that we should be called children of God!

~ 1 John. 3:1 (NKJV)

This heading is one of the great evangelical truths that causes Christians to be grateful, happy people.

God's children are to be found in every area of life. A few fill high positions and have a lot of authority, but millions spend their lives in humble obscurity. Regardless of what area of life they move in, they have the assurance that the eternal God is their heavenly Father. This knowledge brings indescribable joy and happiness into their lives – something which the non-Christian can never understand.

To accept the fatherhood of God and to rejoice in it, brings joy and beauty into your life. You become aware of the fact that God is your Guide. You remain sensitive to the prompting of the Holy Spirit. It is an exciting and satisfying adventure that creates a wonderful sense of partnership with the Father. Calling God your Father implies that you live in harmony with Him. If you co-operate with Him in unity, life unfolds for you in a wonderful way.

Regardless of what humble position you may hold in life, you can hold your head high when you realize whom you belong to. Such an attitude isn't the cause of spiritual pride. It causes a godly dignity to be added to every earthly task, because everything you do, you do as a child of God – to His glory! Life can hardly give greater joy than this to any human being.

To acknowledge You as Father, is an honor that I am not worthy of. Thank You for calling me Your child. *Amen.*

When Unbelief Increases

*O wretched man that I am! Who will deliver me from this body of
death? I thank God – through Jesus Christ our Lord!*

~ Romans 7:24 (nkjv)

Sometimes it appears as if some of the Lord's children are permanently living on spiritual heights while you aren't.

Even though your faith may fluctuate between the valley and
the mountain top, and even though there may be times when you
despair of your ability to lead a committed spiritual life, there are
certain core truths of which you should never lose sight. Even
though you might be tossed between the highest and the lowest
poles, your salvation definitely does not depend on your emotions.

Christ always remains the same (see Heb. 13:8). It is impossible
for you to sink so low that the love of Christ cannot reach you and
that His arms are not under you. You have not been saved by your
emotions, but through your faith in your Savior.

To acknowledge and receive the love of God as a gift of grace; to
plead in deep remorse for the forgiveness of your sin; to allow His
Holy Spirit into your life – these things bring unparalleled experiences into your life. Worries and affliction will still exist, but you
can always share them with your Savior.

Don't ever be ashamed, depressed or fearful when you experience times of spiritual recession. Through your fellowship with
the living Christ you will eventually rise above them and you will
even taste a more powerful experience of faith.

Thank You, Lord, that I can be sure of Your presence and love in my
life every day. *Amen.*

The Area of the Mind

"How is it you do not understand?"

~ MATTHEW 16:11 (NKJV)

Whether you have progressed a long way on the path of life or whether you are only at its beginning, eventually you come to the place where you are faced with a big question mark.

When you have reached that point, you can sink back in blissful ignorance, willing to admit that there are many things you don't know. Or you could, when confronted by a question mark, look beyond the problem and try to find an answer to the question.

Life is full of question marks and even the most brilliant scholars encounter them. The area between the mind and the spirit has not yet been clearly defined. The basic truth is that man has both a mind and a spirit. Only a privileged few have succeeded, through their training and interest, to discover the depths of the human mind. They are all single-minded, serious people who managed to make progress into the domain of the spirit. They approach the question from another angle. And this also gives you a new experience with God which gives new meaning and purpose to your daily living.

Not all of us are mentally bright and gifted, but we can all approach the area of the mind through prayer and meditation. This will bring us to a fuller understanding of life because that is exactly what is derived from an increased knowledge of God through fellowship with Him.

Thank You, Lord my God, that through daily prayer I can increase in my knowledge of You and have a deeper understanding of life. *Amen.*

Inner Beauty

Let the beauty of the LORD our God be upon us, and establish the work of our hands for us.

~ PSALM 90:17 (NKJV)

People sometimes spend large amounts of money to make themselves beautiful. Some succeed while others don't. Most people accentuate their outward beauty, but this doesn't necessarily create a strong character or inner beauty. It is in man's character that the true beauty of a person's life has its basis. Man can be beautified with artful skill, but if his heart is self-centered and malicious, it will be a hard and unattractive beauty in the eyes of the Beholder.

Others again may perhaps not be physically beautiful, but the quality of their inner lives could be so beautiful that people don't notice their outward appearance, but only the inner beauty that they emanate.

Those who accentuate the importance of outward physical beauty and perfection, miss the important inner spirit and attitude of man. The inner life can only prosper and be reflected in the physical when there is perfect harmony between man and his Creator.

True beauty does not start at the cosmetics counter, but in that sacred place where you are intimate and alone with God. Allow the beauty of your spirit to develop through your fellowship with God and then your whole life will emanate beauty.

Jesus, I pray that my life will reflect Your beauty as I strive towards imitating Your perfect example. *Amen.*

Golden Opportunities

*Very early in the morning, while it was still dark, Jesus got up, left
the house and went off to a solitary place, where He prayed.*

~ MARK 1:35

A positive and meaningful faith can be maintained only by continued fellowship with the living Christ. The best time for doing this is before the rush and responsibilities of the day. Excuses
in this regard are many, but to offer a lack of time as an excuse
while you refuse to get up half an hour earlier is unacceptable.

It is a sad fact when our comfort means more to us than our
quiet time with the Master. We are robbing ourselves of a dynamic
source of energy as our failure prevents us from experiencing an
awareness of God's living presence.

Although it is possible to pray wherever you are: in the street
or in the factory; the office or while doing your chores, nothing
can take the place of the prime time you spend with Him at the
beginning of the day. Your indifference to this critically important
meeting with Him at the start of the day is a source of great joy to
Satan. He is skilled in undermining all spiritual discipline. Soon
your time of prayer will become so neglected that it will be of no
value to you.

Make time to be alone with the Lord and try conscientiously to
keep this appointment. Then you will find increasing joy in your
growing intimacy with Him. In this way you will discover a source
of power at the beginning of every challenging day.

Loving Savior, I want to seek You early in the morning, so that I can
experience the magnificence of Your presence all day long. *Amen.*

Inspiration for Life

When he came to his senses, he said, "How many of my father's hired men have food to spare, and here I am starving to death!"

~ LUKE 15:17

Many people refuse to come to a standstill and deal with personal issues in their lives. Deep down in their hearts, however, various questions arise regularly and demand answers.

Questions which most people have asked in one or other form, are: "What is truth?"; "Is my life governed by blind fate?" and "Can I really know God?"

These and other questions of equal importance need to be answered. There are no instant answers to these questions. Many students have devoted a lifetime to searching for the answers and trying to express them.

When you reach the moment of truth in your life and admit that the questions which touch the core of life are far beyond your understanding, the wise and constructive thing to do is to place yourself under the instruction of Jesus Christ. Accept His wisdom and guidance for your life. It requires the discipline of prayer, meditation, study of the Scriptures and self-discovery. He teaches you and guides you in your daily life.

Then you will find that, though you may not discover all the answers immediately, you will develop an awareness that God is guiding you to a more complete and richer understanding of life. Then your struggle with the vital questions is not in vain.

Lord, because You control my life, I leave all the unanswered questions in Your hands. I am convinced that You will give all the answers to me in Your time and in Your way. *Amen.*

Unspoken Wishes

The Spirit Himself intercedes for us with groans that words cannot express.

~ Romans 8:26

It is a laudable desire to be skilled in prayer, but, so often, starting to pray leads to frustration. Take heart, every unspoken wish could be a prayer.

God does not expect highfalutin and learned words, fancy phrases or superficial eulogies. He asks a life that sincerely seeks Him. Your yearning for Him is an indication that your thoughts are turned to God. It is of utmost importance that you should put time aside for prayer and meditation. If you suspend your own efforts and become quiet before God, you will become aware of His nearness and presence. We must never forget that meaningful prayer is a continual exercise that may be practised at any time, anywhere.

Prayer is a practical experience of your mind and spirit that can be practised at all times and under any circumstances. Your prayers should be simple and natural. It is not irreverent to talk to God as you would to a trusted friend. Such intimacy will, without a doubt, bring joy to His paternal heart. God is not so much interested in your "style" of worship, as in the sincerity of your heart.

If you truly want to pray effectively, allow your most honorable thoughts to be the foundation of your prayer life. Then you will develop a growing intimacy with your Father and the Spirit will pray in unison with your spirit.

Father, the heart is so easily misled. Come and rule in my heart and life, Lord, to the greater glory of Your name. *Amen.*

God Hears Your Call

I call on the LORD in my distress, and He answers me.

~ PSALM 120:1

In the business world, in the workplace, on the sports field and in the family circle, problems and difficulties present themselves from time to time.

At times like these it is a great comfort to know that there is somebody to turn to.

To know that there is a friend or confidant who is willing to help, to give guidance and advice, gives you peace of mind in moments of despair and distress. Unfortunately there are people who have no friends to lean on and lead a lonely and troubled life.

It is essential for you to realize that you are never completely alone and that you are not without friends in this harsh world. Jesus, the living Christ, has undertaken never to leave nor forsake you (see Heb. 13:5). He offers you His friendship and all that He asks from you is obedience to His commandment of love. Secure in this knowledge, you have the assurance of His constant presence in your life.

In order to enjoy the benefit of this relationship, you must maintain this contact through prayer and meditation. Live in His fellowship at all times. If you do this, you will in various ways become aware of the wonderful answer to your call of distress. Through the Holy Spirit, follow the light of His guidance and you will walk a safe and fulfilling path.

You know our deepest sorrow and hear our sighs. Help us, Lord, never to forget that You alone are our salvation. *Amen.*

Stand by Your Convictions

Simon Peter answered, "You are the Christ, the Son of the living God."

~ MATTHEW 16:16

There are many people who wish for stronger faith. Many of them attend services and are active in church affairs; some have been involved with the Christian faith for many years. Notwithstanding, their spiritual lives have become lukewarm and their relationship with Christ humdrum.

There comes a time when all of us are confronted with the question that Jesus put to Simon Peter, "What about you? Who do you say I am?" This question may be put to us at a time of our lives when we do not know who to turn to for help or what we must do; it might loom before us when we are frustrated and dissatisfied with our own seemingly empty and aimless spiritual lives. This is a question that you cannot avoid; you have to answer it.

In order to get the maximum benefit from Christian experience, and to know the fullness and abundance of true life that Jesus offers us, it is essential for you to have a personal relationship with the living Christ.

This does not only mean to learn everything about Him that there is to learn; it means to know Him personally and to surrender to Him; to open your life and allow His Holy Spirit to take control. Acknowledge Christ's sovereignty and then abundant life will be yours. That is why Jesus came to this world.

Make me Your prisoner, O Lord, because only then will I be truly free. *Amen.*

Remain in the Love of Jesus Christ

"As the Father has loved Me, so have I loved you. Now remain in My love."

~ JOHN 15:9

It is a disturbing thought that you could lose your awareness of the love the Master has for you. It is a scriptural truth that the Master loves His disciples, but how often do you wake up in the morning and thank Him for that love by telling Him how much you love Him? It is an inspiration for the day to wake up and profess, "I sincerely love You, O Lord!"

The living Christ promised that when you realize your dependence on Him, you will be able to do things that are simply beyond your ability. You can never realize your full potential before you are united with Him in love. He reminds you that, without Him, you can do nothing, but by remaining in Him, your horizons are broadened and your strength increased.

It is a serious tragedy that many Christians attempt to serve the Lord without the indispensable love that they should have for Him. They are active in Christian service, but the inspiration of the love for God and their fellow man is still lacking. The Master has harsh words for these people. He says that anyone who does not remain in Him, will be separated from Him. He does not bring about the separation; they do so themselves through their lack of love.

Develop an ever-increasing love for Jesus Christ so that you will be drawn closer to Him and become aware of His living presence.

Savior and Master, let me never lose the awareness of Your love, but may it always remain fresh and sparkling. *Amen.*

August

Faith is Productive

"According to your faith will it be done to you."

~ MATTHEW 9:29

There are people who manage their faith as if it were a commercial product; something of which they either have a lot or have little, depending on the circumstances of the moment. In times of stress and tension they yearn for more faith, but don't quite know where they can acquire this.

However, the fact is that you *have* faith and that your need is not for more faith, but for a change in the quality of the faith that you already have. Perhaps you have had faith in the wrong things for too long. Perhaps you have had more faith in failure than in success; you long for inner victory but are convinced that you will fail. Your actual faith isn't really a religious question; it is what you expect life will give you. This daily expectation, which is merely another facet of faith, is what really becomes evident in your practical life.

You will agree that it is important to maintain an attitude of expectation in life: to expect only the finest and the noblest in the knowledge that what you expect will be realized in good time.

How is it possible to expect the best when standards are dropping so quickly and the outlook seems so grim? Only the person who has faith in God and His plan for the final redemption of the human race can step into the future with courage and tranquillity of spirit. This enormous truth brings a reassuring purpose in your life and enables you to go towards the future with confidence.

With steadfast faith in You, my God and Father, I step into the future with confidence and peace of mind. *Amen.*

Light from the Darkness

When all the people saw this, they fell prostrate and cried, "The LORD – He is God! The LORD – He is God!"

~ 1 KINGS 18:39

Today, as in the days of Elijah, it requires an earth-shattering experience for some people to recognize the existence and omnipotence of God. People become used to a way of life that has little or no space for the Lord: they immerse themselves in their work or their chosen lifestyle.

Regardless of this, God moves in mysterious ways to manifest His wonders. These ways may be drastic. Therefore we should not judge the Lord with our senses, but trust Him for His mercy. Behind the severe ways in which He sometimes acts lies a heart full of unfathomable love.

Perhaps you have experienced adversity or tragedy, or maybe your burden seems unbearable and your problems irresolvable. At times like these, don't throw in the towel, but turn to the living Christ in faith. He was a human being just like you. He knows all about your situation, understands your distress, and is waiting to come to your assistance.

To draw people to Him, Christ underwent the torment of crucifixion. As He did then, He who leads you out of distress still sometimes uses negative circumstances to draw you closer to His heart. Accept this assurance and live in peace under the certainty of God's love.

Blind disbelief is doomed to destruction, O Father. Everything that it does is in vain. But You, wonderful God and loving Father, have a perfect plan for my life. *Amen.*

God is in Control

Then Job replied to the LORD: "I know that You can do all things; no plan of Yours can be thwarted."

~ JOB 42:1-2

In every sphere of society and in every successive generation, you will meet hardened pessimists who find little or nothing that is right with this world. They see no hope for the future and wherever they go they create an atmosphere of gloom and dejection. This attitude finds precipitation in their personal lives and as a result they become negative.

In the midst of this atmosphere of despair it is beneficial to take a few minutes to ponder the greatness of God. Look back over the years and you will find many examples of the wonderful ways in which God has transformed despair into vivacious hope; changed sorrow into joy and allowed victory to grow from defeat.

Of all these examples the one that towers above all the others is the way in which God used Jesus' crucifixion to manifest the wonder of His forgiving love in the glory of the resurrection. To those of little faith, Golgotha was the end of a sorrowful road, but Easter Sunday ushered in the beginning of a wonderful new life: God's plan for the redemption of mankind had been completed.

When things around you appear dark and terrifying, hold on to the promises of God. Remember the mighty deeds that He has performed, and continue in confidence and with the certain knowledge that He is wholly in control.

Almighty God and loving Father, my heart's knowledge that You are in control allows me to be courageous even in dark days. Guide me on Your path and keep my faith strong. *Amen.*

Handle Your Problems

My flesh and my heart may fail, but God is the strength of my heart and my portion forever.

~ PSALM 73:26

There are a variety of factors that may cause you to feel despondent, weak and helpless. These factors cover a wide spectrum of issues, but their effect on your mental, spiritual and physical wellbeing can be very destructive, should you allow circumstances to overwhelm you.

There is no getting away from the fact that Christians must endure problems and setbacks. Indeed, Christ warned us of this, and most of His followers were severely tried when their faith was put to the test.

The joyful assurance that you receive from Christ is that He will never abandon or forsake you. In addition, He will provide you with the ability to successfully cope with your circumstances through His strength.

To some people this may sound like an unattainable and idealistic dream, but you can transform it into a glorious reality. You have the assurance that the heavenly Guide will always be with you. All that is expected of you is to accept His Word in faith, and to remain in His company. Lay your fears, worries and hopes before Him. Do this, and you will experience the peace that surpasses all understanding.

Holy Lord Jesus, my ability to handle my problems emanates solely from my unconditional faith in You. *Amen.*

Do You Feel Unsafe?

Surely God is my salvation; I will trust and not be afraid. The LORD, the LORD is my strength and my song; He has become my salvation.

~ ISAIAH 12:2

We are all under pressure sometimes. The state of the world has penetrated all of our homes and has created a fear of the future. It seems as if the world is heading for disaster, which nothing and no one can prevent. This external pressure causes internal tensions, and feelings of fear and insecurity have become an integral part of many people's lives.

God's omnipotence and redemptive power are much more than mere religious clichés. It is an experience that may be enjoyed by all who place their faith and trust in the living Christ and entrust their lives unconditionally to His care. To do this is not an act of self-denial or an unwelcome discipline that adds to the burdens of your life, but a voluntary act that gives you confidence and assuages fear.

If your faith is focused on Christ and you are guided by His principles, you not only conquer all destructive fears, but you also become aware that He equips you with spiritual power and strength. It is unnecessary to feel weak and insecure if you know that He loves you and promises you His assistance. Always remember the promise of the Scriptures: "The eternal God is your refuge, and underneath are the everlasting arms" (Deut. 33:27). Hold on to this promise – God will never disappoint you.

I put my trust in You completely, holy Father, and it fills me with confidence, which banishes all uncertainty and fear. *Amen.*

What an Amazing Thought!

We have the mind of Christ.

Even if the Christian faith was no more than a beautiful philosophy, it would still be applicable to every sphere of life, because it expresses the great human need for love and fellowship.

Imperfect people still aspire to perfection and every heart and mind contains the seeds of the quest for God. Until man has found union with the Father, he will feel incomplete and frustrated.

The Christian gospel propounds a unique way of life when it speaks of love for God and surrender to His will. In the gospel this is of much greater value than academic achievement. Such achievements are praiseworthy, and those who possess them can offer God a greater spectrum of services, but it is not essential in order to experience the fullness of the Christian faith.

To believe that God is true to His word, that He will do everything He promised, is the greatest stimulus that you can have in your spiritual life. If you have this, you become a channel of His divine love, conveying it to the world in which you live.

To allow the world of your mind to be possessed by Christ is not only a wonderful religious experience, but also a revolutionary act of faith that brings spiritual forces to the fore in every aspect of your daily life. Through the Spirit of Christ you realize the true splendor of life.

Jesus, my Lord, let Your Spirit govern my thoughts and my spirit so that I may gain a new appreciation for life. *Amen.*

Faith is the Answer

The mystery of godliness is great: He appeared in a body, was vindicated by the Spirit, was seen by angels, was preached among the nations, was believed on in the world, was taken up in glory.

~ 1 Timothy 3:16

However contradictory this statement may appear to you, it remains an indisputable fact of the Christian faith in all its complexity and simplicity. Where else would you find God assuming a human form or a King living as a simple town cabinetmaker? Kings live in palaces, and yet the Prince of peace had no place to rest His head.

Jesus stood His ground against the scholars of His time and overwhelmed them with His knowledge and intellectual abilities. And yet simple people understood Him when He explained profound truths to them in the form of parables.

The circumstances of your life often confuse and trouble you. Your peace of mind can be disturbed by fear, illness, death and so many other negative things. Your faith so easily becomes unsettled and then you start questioning God's love and the purpose of your faith.

This is the time for relying on God. He arranges everything for the benefit of those who love Him. For the faithful, good is born from evil. From the evil of Golgotha, the victory of the resurrection emerged. God has a sacred purpose for everything that happens in your life, and when the time is right this purpose will be revealed.

Thank You, Lord, that I can accept Your every act in my life because I know that everything works for the good of those who love You. *Amen.*

Ponder the Benevolence of God

How I long for the months gone by, for the days when God watched over me, when His lamp shone upon my head and by His light I walked through darkness!

~ JOB 29:2-3

There is nothing strange about people occasionally losing their spiritual way. It can easily happen after the ecstasy of a dramatic conversion has abated and you once again start living your life according to your accustomed ways, with old temptations once cropping up.

Or perhaps you are suffering from depression and despondency as a result of sorrow or illness, anxiety or fear, or setbacks and failures. It is in these circumstances that feelings of helplessness and despair may easily overwhelm you.

In times like these you need to hold on to your faith and put your trust in Christ who has promised never to forsake or abandon you. Think of the goodness of God and remind yourself of the path along which He has guided you up to now; how He has protected you and looked after you in the past.

Jesus never changes. As He has done in the past He now waits for you to turn to Him in your times of crisis. Lay all your fears and worries before Him. True to His promises, His perfect love will drive away all fear and you will be enveloped in His love.

Be still my soul, the Lord is on your side. In this knowledge I will handle my disappointments, sorrow and grief, because You grant me the strength to do so. For this I praise and thank You. *Amen.*

When Things get Tough

And who is equal to such a task?

~ 2 CORINTHIANS 2:16

We all go through times when things threaten to overwhelm us and our faith appears to be an inadequate defence. It seems as if our circumstances are continually worsening, our relationships suffer grievous blows and everything suddenly appears unmanageable.

What is actually happening is that you have allowed the challenges of the world to exceed your spiritual reserves. The demands of life have proved your faith to be insufficient. When you feel as if you have reached breaking point, you need to return to the fundamentals of your faith and assure yourself of the presence of God in your life. This will help you to restore the balance in your life.

It is definitely not God's intention to place you under so much pressure that you reach breaking point and collapse under the strain. A living and positive faith is a stabilizing influence under the most confusing circumstances. Possessing such a faith is not a spiritual luxury, but an urgent necessity if you wish to deal with the demands of life successfully.

Realizing the necessity of faith is the first step to possessing it. If you are unaware of your need, how will you be able to fulfill it? When you tell the Lord that you need His help and trust Him unconditionally you will know that He will carry you through, because you love and trust in Him.

Lord Jesus, through Your wisdom and strength I am able to cope with all the demands of life. Keep me close to Your heart. *Amen.*

Light in the Darkness

To those who have been called, who are loved by God the Father and
kept by Jesus Christ: mercy, peace and love be yours in abundance.
~ JUDE 1-2

For as long as one can recall it has seemed as if the world has been in a state of chaos. Apart from dozens of lesser confrontations between nations and people, humanity has also experienced two world wars in the past century. Lawlessness and violence have lately been increasing steadily. The cost of living continues to climb and people live lives of fear and insecurity. What is the solution to this sad state of affairs?

There can be only one answer and this is to fearlessly place your faith and trust in Jesus Christ. He has conquered a dark and hostile world and replaced fear with love. He has restored hope where circumstances appeared to be hopeless. To those who believe in Him He has given the blessing of His peace that transcends all understanding.

This is your answer to the dismal confusion and fear of our time. Believe in Jesus Christ and His promises; place your trust in Him unconditionally and He will lead you from the darkness into the light of His unfathomable love for mankind. If you do this you will no longer worry about the future because you will always be protected by the peace of God.

Thank You, Lord my God, that You grant perfect peace to Your children in this dark world. Thank You that I may experience this inner peace because I trust in You. *Amen.*

Faith Requires Trust

"Master, we've worked hard all night and haven't caught anything. But because You say so, I will let down the nets."

~ LUKE 5:5

To many people true faith is nothing more than an unattainable dream. They will sometimes admit with reservation that other people's faith is rewarded, but they seriously doubt whether faith will work in their own lives.

The Bible provides us with ample proof of the reality and the rewards of faith in the lives of ordinary people. One of the great misconceptions about true faith is that you can simply ask what you want from God and then sit back and wait for it to be realized.

The disciples once labored hard throughout the night without catching any fish. They were experienced fishermen and knew that under the circumstances that prevailed there would be no fish to catch. Regardless of this, as well as the risk of appearing foolish in front of their colleagues, they let down the nets once more. According to the Scriptures they caught so much fish that the nets almost tore. In this way their faith was rewarded.

When you lay a matter before God you should trust Him so much that you are willing to accept His will and be obedient to the suggestions of His Spirit. Forget about what others will think or say. Trust God unconditionally and He will reward your faith.

I place my trust in You completely, Lord Jesus, in the knowledge that You will never disappoint me. Help me not to disappoint You through unbelief. *Amen.*

Your Divine Support

Immediately Jesus reached out His hand and caught him. "You of little faith," He said, "why did you doubt?"

~ Matthew 14:31

There are times in all of our lives when our problems threaten to overcome us, and we feel that we are in danger of drowning in the waves of doubt and despair. One moment we are completely sure of our faith, and the next we are overwhelmed by a tidal wave of fear and unbelief. This is especially true when we have experienced Jesus' peace in our personal time with Him, and then suddenly lost our faith when we had to cope with difficult situations.

Peter had exactly this kind of experience. He was overcome with joy when he saw Jesus walking on the water towards them. In his excitement he left the safety of the boat and walked across the water towards Jesus. Then he was suddenly overwhelmed by fear when he saw the wind and the waves. His faith failed him, and Peter started sinking.

When the storms of life threaten, there is only one thing to do, and that is to follow Peter's example and to call on Jesus to rescue you. He will take your hand and lead you safely through. Place your trust in Him, because He will never disappoint you. Even though you may not be aware of it, Jesus is at your side at this exact moment, ready to help you, should you call on Him.

My Savior Jesus, grant that I will retain my faith in You through the work of the Holy Spirit, even in the most trying circumstances. *Amen.*

Seek God's Countenance

"I revealed Myself to those who did not ask for Me; I was found by those who did not seek Me. To a nation that did not call on My name, I said, 'Here am I, here am I.'"

~ Isaiah 65:1

When disaster suddenly strikes, the cry is often heard, "Why has God allowed this to happen?" Whether it is a personal tragedy or a national disaster, there are always those who are ready to blame God or even question His existence. They base their misleading argument on the false premise that, if there is indeed a God, He would not have allowed something like this to happen.

If we take a closer look at the tragedies and disasters that occur, we will find, time and again, that the human element is always present. Look carefully and honestly at every situation, and you will find ample evidence of indifference, greed, neglect, a search for status and influence, combined with all the other elements that collaborate to create the ingredients of disastrous situations that so often hit us.

Especially in these turbulent times, there is a desperate need to turn to God in prayer, to seek His will and guidance for ourselves, as well as for our country. It is necessary that we should listen to the voice of God as a matter of urgency, and obey that voice, so that, by staying within His will, we can live our lives in "the peace of God, which transcends all understanding". It is by seeking God in sincerity – not by blaming Him – that we will do our share to make this world a better place to live in.

Heavenly Father, hear my prayers, and assist me to abide by Your commandments and glorify Your name forever. *Amen.*

God Is Your Helper

Cast all your anxiety on Him because He cares for you.

~ 1 PETER 5:7

Sometimes incessant worries about things beyond your control prey upon your mind. You may be concerned about your job or your co-workers, about an increase in taxes or rent, or about the conduct of a loved one. You only see gloom and premonitions attesting to an unsure future. When your life is ruled by paralyzing fear, you cannot experience the freedom and joy of those who love God and trust in Him.

If you are anxious and worried about a personal matter, you must remember that your God is greater than all the circumstances and situations that could befall you. For a moment, you might have allowed clouds of anxiety, fear and uncertainty about the future to obscure your image of God. However, He is forever constant and He desires to share the deepest experiences of your life with you.

In a spirit of thanksgiving, take your anxieties, fears and worries and share them with your merciful God. Give these things over to Him unreservedly. You will experience an untold feeling of deliverance. This could be brought about by a single episode of prayer in your life.

Accept the challenge to follow God's plan of action. God's omnipotence will sweep away all petty thoughts, and all uncertainty will disappear. The true greatness of God is not only revealed in His majestic universe, but also in His measureless love and concern for people like you and me.

Your works are perfect, Lord, and even when I drink from the cup of bitterness, You will never forsake me. *Amen.*

I Know for Certain!

He makes me lie down in green pastures, He leads me beside quiet waters.

~ PSALM 23:2

It is a blessed assurance to know that you are guided, from day to day, by an omnipotent and loving God. The Lord does not promise that all the pastures will always be green: sometimes they are barren and desolate. He has also not promised that the waters will always be tranquil: sometimes the waves break over us and the sky above is covered with ominous storm clouds.

But the promise is that He, in His time, will bring us to green pastures and quiet waters. If we put our trust in Him, we may rest assured in the knowledge that He will guide us.

We cannot be guided by someone who is far away and detached. We must stay close to the Shepherd in order to be guided by Him. Often we experience difficult and incomprehensible times, sometimes even storms and stress. However, if we stay close to the Lord, we will become aware of the tranquility surrounding us.

Regardless of how stormy and unpredictable the circumstances of our lives may be, our spirit will be quiet and peaceful if we allow Him to be our Governor. Then we can state with assurance, "He makes me lie down in green pastures, He leads me beside quiet waters." I know for certain: He is my Shepherd, my Friend, my Governor and my Guide. Praise the Lord, O my soul; all my inmost being, praise His holy name!

Lord Jesus, Shepherd of my life, thank You that I may be safe and secure in Your care. Help me to accept Your guidance. *Amen.*

God Our Guide

I will counsel you and watch over you.

~ PSALM 32:8

The psalmist is so joyful about being forgiven by God's love, that he wants to teach people how to receive it too. He pleads, "Do not be as foolish as a stubborn mule that has to be controlled by a bit and bridle! Trust in the Lord, confess your sins to Him, because everyone who does so, is enfolded in His love."

What a comforting and blessed promise to take with you on your pilgrimage through life. This encourages and supports us, especially if we are confused and uncertain about the right road to follow. There are many people who wish to give us advice and who recommend some kind of action. Often it is useful and professional advice, but we still remain unsure whether it is really the advice that we need.

There is one Friend who not only promised to be our Counselor, but who will do it. He will always watch over us for our good. We only need to ask His advice: He knows the road from beginning to end and He knows what is best for us. Then we will never have to live with uncertainty.

Let us ask His guidance from day to day, and believe without a doubt that He *will* advise us and that He *will* watch over us.

Governor and Lord, thank You that You keep watch over me. In the darkest hour it is a comfort and encouragement to me. *Amen.*

Walk with God

Then the disciple whom Jesus loved said to Peter, "It is the Lord!"
~ JOHN 21:7

When the disciples beached at dawn, following a night of fishing, they recognized Jesus on the beach. He had prepared a meal for them. Jesus was the host for this meal. This tells us of the Lord's care who, even after His resurrection, stayed close to His followers and His church. He will care for His children and His congregation. Much of our anxiety and stress will be prevented if we accept that He is by our side under all circumstances.

If we persist on our own path, without asking for His guidance and presence, we cannot say that the Lord caused some accidents and disasters to happen. The Lord could allow these things to happen so that we will once again turn to Him and ask Him to be our Guide on our pilgrimage.

When we walk in fellowship with Christ, looking to Him for guidance, we receive the strength to accept His holy will, regardless of our circumstances. Then our hearts are strengthened by the consoling knowledge, "It is the Lord!" Then we find peace and rest. We know that He guides us on our path with that which is best for us. If we meet Jesus with unfailing certainty every day on our path through life, we are amongst the most fortunate of all people on earth.

I praise and glorify You, Lord Jesus, because I see Your hand in every situation in my life and I know for certain that You will never leave nor forsake me. *Amen.*

The God of the Temple

For this God is our God for ever and ever; He will be our guide even to the end.

~ PSALM 48:14

This Psalm of the Sons of Korah is about the temple and the God of the temple. The God of the temple is more important than the temple itself. This should be true of us as well.

We must worship the Lord in such a way that people notice *Him* rather than beautiful clothes, expensive church buildings or lofty prayers. Then our lives will also have the quality of Jerusalem, the city that points to God and displays the glory of God.

We all like to say, "That is mine!" or "It is my own!" The joy of possession is strong in most of us. Here is something that each of God's true children can say with certainty, "For this God is our God for ever and ever." What an overwhelming thought. The Almighty God of the universe, the God of the fathers of old; He is also my God! Do we ever pause to reflect upon this truth?

"He will be our guide even to the end." We so often need a reliable guide who can show us the right path and warn us against the pot-holes and stumbling blocks on our path. Could there ever be a more reliable guide than God? Let us then exult and rejoice with trust and confidence, "For this God is our God for ever and ever." He will lead us through life, through the valley of death and into the Father's house. What more could we ask of life; and of God! With Him as our guide, we are sheltered against all dangers on our uncertain pilgrimage.

Eternal and Unchanging God, thank You that You are also my God and that You will guide me safely into the House of the Father. *Amen.*

God's Guiding Hand

He led them by a straight way.

~ PSALM 107:7

This Psalm describes the various phases in God's guidance of His people to the Promised Land. Today's section refers to those who came through the desert. Those were people who suffered, got lost, and were hungry, thirsty and exhausted.

They represent people who get lost in a spiritual desert. Whether literal or figurative, these lost people could pray, and that made all the difference. The Lord saved them and gave them abundance and put them back on track.

Does it seem as if you are following a strange road? Are the problems that you encounter on the road causing a trace of doubt in your heart? Never doubt the Lord's guidance. If you allow Him, He will surely and safely lead you down the right road, just as He has done through the ages with all His children.

He knows every step of the way and we can follow His lead with absolute trust, while we remember the words of the psalmist, "He led them by a straight way."

He is, indeed, the way that we must follow, the truth that we must know and the life that we must live (see John. 14:6). If He led His people safely in days gone by, we can trust in His guiding hand to lead us, even through dark depths.

We simply have to trust in His wisdom and know for certain that His loving hand will always hold onto our unsteady hands.

God of the pilgrim, thank You that I have Your Spirit to accompany me on my journey to the house of the Father. *Amen.*

Let God Be Your Counselor

"I am the vine; you are the branches. If a man remains in Me and I in him, he will bear much fruit; apart from Me you can do nothing."

~ JOHN 15:5

People often express disappointment when well-thought plans come to nothing. Much time and energy are invested in planning, only to see dreams and hopes turn into failure. What makes it even more difficult, is that, in the minds of the people who did the planning, their objectives were noble. Some people become disillusioned and withdraw from further action.

Regardless of how commendable the cause to which you aspire, or how much effort you put into something, it is essential – should you strive towards the very best – that you take your aspirations and hopes in prayer to the Lord and seek His guidance. Remember, Jesus said that He was the vine – the life-giving support – and that you, as a branch, are totally dependent upon Him for everything. This is especially true of your spiritual growth.

Whatever you undertake in life is important to your Master. He cares for and takes care of you. For this reason it is essential to turn to Him for guidance before deciding on a specific plan of action.

God knows what is best for you and He knows the future. Put your trust in Him for guidance and surrender your hope and expectations to Him. Wait for His guidance and then act according to His will, and you will not be disappointed.

Not my will or my choice, loving Counselor, in matters great or small. Be my guide, my strength, my wisdom, and my all. *Amen.*

Faith and Wishful Thinking

Then He touched their eyes and said, "According to your faith will it be done to you."

~ MATTHEW 9:29

There is a fundamental difference between true faith and wishful thinking. Many people never learn this distinction which results in spiritual impoverishment. Such people desire something passionately, but in their heart of hearts they believe that it is unattainable, unless they are lucky. This creates conflict in their innermost being and they become ineffectual people without spiritual strength.

Sincere faith is convinced that every hallowed wish is possible and waiting to be claimed in the name of the Almighty. You do not yearn for the unattainable in your own strength; it only happens when God's omnipotence is revealed in your life every day.

Faith which wants to show results should always have God as its inspiration and source. If we expect great things from God, we will receive great things from Him and do great deeds in His name. As was the case with the two blind people of whom we read.

If your spiritual life has God as its source, you will become a channel through which His mighty deeds are done. Then a new life of powerful energy will open up to you. You will no longer limit His omnipotence by lack of faith, disbelief or wishful thinking. Through your surrender and commitment to Him, what you long for in faith becomes a glorious reality.

Almighty and merciful God, thank You for what I am able to do through faith in You. Strengthen me constantly through the power of Jesus Christ, my Redeemer and Savior. *Amen.*

Less Effort and More Faith

Commit your way to the LORD; trust in Him and He will do this.

~ PSALM 37:5

Most of the time we create the problems we experience in our Christian lives ourselves. We build dividing walls where they do not exist; we feel we are far from God while He is close to us; we debate the characteristics of faith, but seldom try to apply them in practice.

It is exciting to prove that faith in God is an attainable proposition. For a while, you may have struggled with a problem. You may have tried every possible solution and as a last resort, you started praying. This prayer was different from all the others. When you prayed before, you were already planning in your mind how to find solutions in your own strength. You prescribed to God how matters should progress. Now you are saying the prayers of a desperate, drowning person. All supports have been removed and you are fully dependent on the Lord.

The action of total surrender to God in complete faith, will give you a feeling of relief and deliverance. You will now have a new spirit of expectation. You will wait on God to act when you have become deeply conscious of your own inability.

To be able to wait during this period – be it long or short – you should joyfully subject yourself to the perfect will of God. Remember that God always acts in your best interests.

Just let go – and let God!

Savior, I joyfully surrender my life to You completely. I ask that only Your perfect will be done in my life. *Amen.*

2 CHRONICLES 20:18-30

When Faith Becomes Confusing

Have faith in the LORD your God and you will be upheld.

~ 2 CHRONICLES 20:20

We live in a period of spiritual awakening and the Spirit of God is working across the entire world. Although this does not always seem to be true, humankind is becoming increasingly aware of spiritual values. There is a search for God and for truth seldom observed in previous generations.

This desire for spiritual values has resulted in various interpretations of the doctrines of Christ. There are many sectarian teachings that create confusion in non-Christian communities and even among Christians of established churches.

What you say in defense of your faith is important. But still more importantly, is the place that you give to Christ in your life. You should love Him more than the doctrines and theories about Him. The core of our Christian belief is after all based on the love we have for Christ.

Outraged propagandists may argue and perhaps confuse you about what you should believe. Unless their testimony is inspired by the love of Christ, they should not be trusted.

When you are confused by strange and new doctrines, keep your spiritual eye on Jesus, your Guide. Allow Him to renew and strengthen your faith through the Holy Spirit.

Your faith then rests in Christ and His Spirit will protect you against confusion in your spiritual life.

Savior and Friend, You captured me through love and You are the foundation of my faith. I praise Your glorious name. *Amen.*

Victorious through Faith

Now faith is being sure of what we hope for and certain of what we do not see.

~ HEBREWS 11:1

To many people faith is a mystic, almost foggy belief that is totally removed from practical everyday life. People desire more faith, yet they are sadly lacking the ability to believe every-day spiritual things. They beg God continuously for more faith but their testimony remains ineffective.

We must realize that faith is an integral part of humankind's make-up. Every person practices some kind of faith. The tragedy is that so many people experience it wrongly. It is not a question of more faith, but of correctly using what we already have.

When Jesus commands His disciples to have faith in God, He is educating them to a positive and constructive way of life. Every-one can believe in someone or something, but without faith in Christ, no person can be a Christian or please God.

Faith is essential for victory in our spiritual lives. Without it, we can have no fellowship with God; we cannot tackle the struggles of life; we cannot work through our own grief and problems. Faith means to trust God and His actions in our lives. Faith flourishes on what it brings forth.

The glorious fruit of Christian faith is the certainty of God's presence and the unshakable knowledge that He loves you uncon-ditionally. With this, everything that happens in your life falls into place in a meaningful way.

Thank You, Father, for knowing that the Holy Spirit works in my heart and assures me of Your love for me. *Amen.*

Faith and Practice

"Men of Galilee," they said, "why do you stand here looking into the sky?"

~ ACTS 1:11

There are pious, sensitive Christians who only have an interest in spiritual matters. They would like to have wings to fly from this life straight into heaven. However, forgetting the earthly because of the heavenly is just as wrong as forgetting heaven because of earth. You must find the middle ground.

The indispensable and the perfect is above! But there are also things here below that may claim the dedication of our hearts and the strength of our hands. Our faith must not turn us into impractical dreamers who neglect responsibilities.

The life of labor on earth is an apprenticeship for eternal life. The Bible calls us time and again to perform our daily tasks faithfully. The light of our divine calling should, however, shine on it. We dare not exalt ourselves spiritually and stuff ourselves with heavenly pleasures, while neglecting our daily duty. Even if we are not of this world, we are living in the world.

There are rich blessings in looking up at heaven. Mount of Olives hours are essential because they empower you for the good struggle. But you should always return to reality, your hand more firmly on the plough. The results of a Mount of Olives experience must become visible in your service to the Master. He will return as He left. May He find you ready when He comes.

I thank You that Your Holy Spirit enables me to maintain a true balance between faith and speech, my Redeemer and Lord. *Amen.*

Christ's Self-Image

Though an army besiege me, my heart will not fear.

~ PSALM 27:3

Nurturing feelings of inferiority and incompetence can paralyze you spiritually. You know that these negative feelings are contrary to the wishes of the indwelling Spirit of God for your life, but you feel incompetent to do anything about them. The only antidote for a poor self-image, insecurity and feeling inferior, is a positive attitude towards God, "The Lord is my light and my salvation – whom shall I fear?" (Ps. 27:1).

To achieve and maintain religious confidence, you must allow Christ into your life and dedicate yourself to Him completely. Then He will live in you and His power will be expressed through you.

You can rid your life of these negative and detrimental attitudes if God works in you through Christ, enabling you to lead a life of faith, trust and victory. The more you cultivate an awareness of the presence and omnipotence of Christ in your life, the stronger your faith and trust in Him will become.

Through this, you will conquer your feelings of insecurity and inferiority, and you will be able to lead a fruitful and satisfying life. Nothing is impossible if we are anchored in the power of Jesus Christ, "If you remain in Me and My words remain in you, ask whatever you wish, and it will be given you" (John 15:7).

The treasury of God is wide open to those who want to enter into a life of fruitfulness and victory through Jesus Christ.

Eternal God and Father, dwell in me through Your Holy Spirit so that I will never be saddled with feelings of insecurity and inferiority. *Amen.*

Anchor in the Storm

Without faith it is impossible to please God, because anyone who comes to Him must believe that He exists and that He rewards those who earnestly seek Him.

~ HEBREWS 11:6

In today's uncertain world a living faith is absolutely essential. We should firmly believe that this is still God's world and in the words of Psalm 24:1 we should fearlessly say, "The earth is the Lord's, and everything in it, the world and all who live in it."

In these chaotic days we live in, many people wonder what the future holds for humankind. Evil is rampant and nothing is done to stop it. The destructive forces make the powers of justice appear small and insignificant. But do not allow appearances to deceive you. This is still God's world!

Across the world people are longing for the knowledge that God cares and that He is in control. This longing and desire has sidetracked many people. Without faith in an omniscient God who holds the future of nations and individuals in His hand, we are lost. Jesus Christ did not come to this world to establish a new theology or to teach a new doctrine, but to bring His children abundant life so that they can live purposefully and victoriously, even in the most confusing circumstances.

With faith in Jesus Christ, you can meet the future with confidence and know for certain that He is your Guide and Leader in these worrying and confusing days.

Almighty God and heavenly Father, I thank You that I know through faith that I can share Your peace in the midst of the hurricane of events in this world. *Amen.*

Faith, Love, Actions

The only thing that counts is faith expressing itself through love.
~ GALATIANS 5:6

There is a form of faith that involves theological speculation and wishful thinking. It does not lead to actions of love and is therefore not fruitful but often useless. If my faith does not lead to a deeper experience of God, it is an illusionary faith and it will serve no permanent purpose in my life.

Loving Jesus Christ so much that His presence is a living reality in your life is such an inspiration for your faith that you are urged by His love to do His will. A steadfast faith and trust in the glorified and living Redeemer is the foundation of all pure Christian teaching.

Faith can only be alive and meaningful if it is supported by love. Without love your faith is twisted and it will never achieve the height, depth, length or breadth of its many possibilities.

To be pleasing to God and to achieve your highest purpose, faith should be confirmed, inspired and supported by love.

If your faith finds expression in love, your beliefs become an everyday, practical reality. Then you look away from yourself and your own problems and you see the world in distress. Then you hear the Master say, "Whatever you did for one of the least of these brothers of Mine, you did for Me" (Matt. 25:40).

Then your faith is no longer only speculation and pious words, but it becomes love in action.

God of love, through our love for You we have learned to serve our fellow man in love. May we continue doing so by the grace of Your Son. *Amen.*

Enthusiasm or Faith?

*In the same way, faith by itself, if it is not accompanied by action,
is dead.*

~ JAMES 2:17

There are few things in life as encouraging as an enthusiastic Christian whose faith is practical and alive. When the winds of unbelief start raging around him, when darkness envelops his soul, he remains steadfast, clinging to the essence of his faith.

The Christian who relies on the emotional boost he receives from a loaded church service and who cannot survive on his own inner strength, lacks the firm foundation that is required to remain standing in stormy weather. Enthusiasm without a living faith is insufficient. Nevertheless, positive, practical faith supplies real enthusiasm, enabling the believer to reflect his faith with joy.

Faith, not emotions, determines the quality of your Christian life. Faith in the living Christ always brings about new life and growth, a constructive and consistent goal in life, and love for God that makes obedience to Him a joy and a privilege.

Living faith fills every void that may exist in your life with the wonderful assurance that your heavenly Father desires to be totally and completely united with you. Through Christ He revealed how this unity is possible.

Emotion is always secondary to your faith in Christ Jesus your Redeemer. Once you have accepted Him as your Savior, your emotions will also fall into place.

Creator, please bring balance into my life between faith and emotions so that my enthusiasm can develop into practical faith. *Amen.*

Allow Faith to Dispel Fear

He said to His disciples, "Why are you so afraid? Do you still have no faith?"

~ MARK 4:40

There are few people who do not harbor fear in one form or another. It might be concealed in the complexity of their personality and they cannot explain it all that well. However, it reveals itself in a discomfort which they cannot control and which robs their lives of peace and stability.

It is a strange fact that many people cannot explain the fear that haunts them. It affects the deepest stirrings of a person's spirit, refuses to be analyzed, but is nevertheless a burning presence.

There is but one sure cure for a life that is dominated by fear, and that is a living faith in Jesus Christ. Fear and faith cannot co-exist in the same life. Should people try to accommodate both, conflict is created which undermines their peace of mind and eventually destroys them.

Faith nurtures faith and fear nurtures fear. Put your trust in God. At first, in the little things in your life His love and wisdom will be revealed and confirmed and, in time, the bigger things in your life will be under His control. Put God to the test, even if it is only in the little things, and you will soon find that He is actively working on the big issues in your life.

When this happens, fear will subside until your whole life is free from destructive anxiety. You will increasingly be controlled by a positive faith and will taste success above fear.

As Your child, I know where to find veritable peace. Dispel fear and selfishness from my heart, so that I may serve You faithfully. *Amen.*

An Experience with Christ

For to me, to live is Christ.

~ PHILIPPIANS 1:21

Christian faith is a spiritual experience based on your relationship with the living Christ. However you experience Jesus, He only becomes meaningful when you know Him as your personal Savior and Redeemer. This is an encounter in the first person with Christ who is alive. This alone makes your faith alive.

Unfortunately your faith might fluctuate according to your moods. One day you might be in the clouds, determined to live your spiritual life to the full. The next day you might be so downcast that you can hardly pray and you feel that the assurance of Christ's presence has sadly disappeared.

Whether the light of your faith is burning brightly or not, the glorious truth is that God's love for you is strong and powerful, unchanging like God Himself. It never fluctuates. God is close to you when you are close to Him, but also when you are drifting away from Him. His sustaining love is unfailing and eternal. This makes the reality of Christian love something which does not belong to yesterday or tomorrow, but it is here and now and has indescribable meaning.

Once you realize that the Christian experience does not only have meaning for the past or future, but also for the present, it becomes relevant to modern life as well. Christ is with His disciples wherever they are. Remember it is He who said, "And surely I am with you always, to the very end of the age" (Matt. 28:20).

I praise You, heavenly Master, because You are Lord of the past, present and future. *Amen.*

September

Scriptural Religion

"Why do you call Me, 'Lord, Lord,' and do not do what I say?"

~ Luke 6:46

Why is it that so many good, churchgoing people in our time experience a sense of disappointment and failure that borders on despair? They have faithfully attended church throughout their entire lives and honestly feel that they truly love God in their own way. Yet there is something important lacking in their spiritual experience.

The answer may lie precisely in the fact that they love God in their own way, instead of in the scriptural way. They have created a form of Christianity that fits neatly into their lifestyle. This private and personal version of Christianity turns them into masters of compromise. They find excuses not to forgive; they are selective in who they want to love; their business negotiations are controlled by whatever suits them at that moment and not by scriptural principles.

Scriptural Christianity starts with an act of repentance and confession. This implies a complete turn-around and an awareness of the presence of the living Christ. Scriptural Christianity means complete obedience to God and to the standards set out by Christ in the New Testament which He commands and equips us to keep.

When we are empowered in this way, Jesus Christ guides us into the fullness of life.

Thank You, Lord Jesus, that You came so that we may have abundant life. Keep me from seeking my spiritual salvation outside the Scriptures. *Amen.*

Who Controls Your Life?

You, however, are controlled not by the sinful nature but by the Spirit, if the Spirit of God lives in you.

~ Romans 8:9

Are you in control of your own life, or are you controlled by changing circumstances, variable moods and other forces beyond your comprehension or control? It may be possible that you say and do things that are not true to your nature. Paul says, "When I want to do good, evil is right there with me" (Rom. 7:21). This is a very common human experience. You therefore need an external force that is larger than yourself to control you when you cannot control yourself.

The nature and temperament that you have inherited is often a slave to destructive habits, and when you are constrained by such bonds, your whole spirit is in slavery. Even though your spirit tries to assert itself, it finds that it cannot enjoy the freedom which it intuitively knows to be its birthright. However, here is a wonderful truth of Christian principles and experience: Now the Lord is the spirit, and where the Spirit of the Lord is, there is freedom (2 Cor. 3:17).

When the Holy Spirit of God takes possession of your life and expresses Himself through your spirit, you will discover that your life gains new meaning and significance and is filled with spiritual strength that enables you to grow to maturity in Him.

Thank You, Lord Jesus, my Redeemer and Savior, that when Your Holy Spirit fills my life I am governed and guided by Him. *Amen.*

Live for Christ

His divine power has given us everything we need for life and god-liness through our knowledge of Him who called us by His own glory and goodness.

~ 2 Peter 1:3

In this month we once again hear the call to live a Christian life, but some of us are so overwhelmed by the immensity of the task that our faith falters.

We tell ourselves that in our human weakness it is impossible to meet the standards that God expects of us. The sad consequences of such an attitude is that you lose courage and refuse to even try. In this way God is robbed of yet another disciple and you deny yourself the joy of serving the Master.

The mistake that you make is to rely on your own abilities to serve Christ, when you should actually from the outset devote yourself to Christ with absolute faith in your heart, and trust Him to enable you to walk His path.

On your Christian pilgrimage you must remember that Christ will not call you to any form of service without equipping you for it. He has set the example, and all that He expects of you is to follow Him. If you dedicate yourself to Him and place your trust in Him completely, He will provide you with everything that you need to truly live.

Heavenly Father, I dedicate myself to Your service anew, in the certain knowledge that You will provide everything that I need to live for You. *Amen.*

Spiritual Hunger

My soul yearns, even faints, for the courts of the LORD; my heart and my flesh cry out for the living God.

~ PSALM 84:2

Spiritual hunger is not that easily recognizable and therefore many people deny its existence. They think that it is a religious term that has no bearing on everyday life. However, its symptoms are apparent to anyone who is willing to look.

Most people experience a profound longing for inner satisfaction. They want to reach that point where they no longer have to strive after the seemingly unattainable. If they don't experience feelings of satisfaction, they embark on a restless quest to fill the void.

This restlessness manifests itself in different ways. Life is lived at a pace and with a passion never intended by God. Time is devoted to, and energy wasted on, things that are of little or no significance. When this restlessness takes possession of your spirit, life becomes a cruel cycle of frustrated ideals and broken dreams.

A person who spends quality time with God is never spiritually hungry and is better able to live a balanced life and avoid foolish mistakes. Spend time with your heavenly Father and note the effect that it has on your life. Spending time in His presence will fulfill all the desires of your heart and His peace will satisfy all your spiritual hunger.

Living Christ, through my communion with You I experience the deep and peaceful fulfillment of all my needs. *Amen.*

Get the Most from Your Faith

"Whoever has will be given more ... Whoever does not have, even what he has will be taken from him."

~ MATTHEW 13:12

There are many people who are deeply dissatisfied with their faith. They have no yearning to walk more intimately with God. The inevitable result of this unhappy state of affairs is that their discipleship weakens and becomes ineffectual.

To receive everything that faith offers you, you should regard it as a full-time task and a dedicated way of life, and not as an addendum only to be used whenever convenient. A dedicated Christian must also be a scripturally-bound Christian. Refusal to use the Scriptures as a code of moral conduct may cause your faith to become emotionally unbalanced. And then the message of the gospel becomes distorted to suit your own personal conviction and ideology. Eventually all the power of faith disappears in wishful thinking and unscriptural argumentation.

The church and the world currently have a serious need for disciplined Christianity that will affirm and proclaim the ideas of Jesus. The one truth that embraces all others is so simple that people have turned away from it. Jesus said, "As I have loved you, so you must love one another" (John 13:34).

The dedication that is required to live a life of Christian love demands a strength that can only be acquired from the Holy Spirit. This attitude is kept alive through prayer and contemplation and a constant yearning for a more profound experience with God.

I plead with You, O living Jesus, for the gift of Your Holy Spirit so that I may experience my faith to its fullest potential. *Amen.*

Feelings of Guilt

Like newborn babies, crave pure spiritual milk, so that by it you may grow up in your salvation.

~ 1 PETER 2:2

Many Christians have a fundamental guilt complex. They blame themselves because their commitment to the Master is half-hearted; their prayer life is insufficient or their study of God's Word is fragmentary.

Often this feeling of guilt can be ascribed to a spiritual laziness which leads to a feeling of spiritual inadequacy. Another reason for feelings of guilt among Christians is the fact that they have stopped growing spiritually. When Christ's love shone on their lives for the first time, they were filled with joy and a quiet determination to learn even more about their newly-found Lord.

For a while their love for Christ was their most precious possession. But slowly their faith became mere routine and other things started claiming their interest and loyalty.

Without growth, the most beautiful spiritual experiences die. When you accepted Jesus Christ as Lord and Redeemer, He occupied the center of your life. If you have relegated Him to second place, you will experience intense feelings of guilt.

It is not necessary to overburden your life with guilty feelings of this nature. Renew your relationship with Christ every day and practice your loving loyalty to Him. Through prayer, Bible study and an application of His holy will in your life, you will regain the glory of faith and peace in your heart.

Lord my God, I long for solid spiritual food so that I may grow to complete salvation, delivered from all feelings of guilt. *Amen.*

Mature Christianity

Grow in the grace and knowledge of our Lord and Savior Jesus Christ.

~ 2 Peter 3:18

Spiritual immaturity is a self-imposed characteristic. When you become a Christian you accept Jesus Christ as your personal Savior and Redeemer. From that moment on, you start a way of life which requires you to commit yourself daily to the Master. Without a daily commitment you can never significantly come to maturity. You cannot have a meaningful experience on a part-time basis.

When you confirm your faith in Him, the living Christ accepts you as His disciple. He keeps all His promises. The responsibility to develop a vigorous faith, however, rests with you. You may have a desire for a richer prayer life, but unless you devote time to deepen and improve your prayer life, even God cannot give you your heart's desire.

You may long for greater and stronger faith, but if you do not use the little faith you already have, you will not receive more faith. A sincerely developing Christian never stops striving for conformity to His Lord. This may seem like a high ideal, but no child of the Lord struggles on his own. The Master is always there to encourage, to inspire and to strengthen you, especially in times of weakness and frustration.

The Christian life is a continuing process of growth to maturity. If you stop working on it, your spiritual life will stagnate and eventually stop existing.

Enabling Master, I plead that Your Holy Spirit would stir me in moments of spiritual laziness. *Amen.*

Growth through Truth

Instead, speaking the truth in love, we will in all things grow up into Him who is the Head, that is, Christ.

~ EPHESIANS 4:15

If you think growth unnecessary or unimportant, it will not be long before your spiritual experience will be shipwrecked on the stormy seas of life. There must be growth and development, or else your spiritual life will diminish and die.

There are many resources that God has made available to us to improve our spiritual growth. But we should take care that the aids don't become goals in themselves. Fellowship with believers is necessary, but fellowship that is not centered around Christ serves no constructive purpose.

A study of the Bible will be a source of continuous inspiration and guidance, but the purpose should always be to point the disciple to Christ and to glorify Him. Good deeds and charitable work for the underprivileged undoubtedly find favor with God, but these are only the results of our acquaintance with Jesus Christ and can never take the place of our faith in Him.

There can only be spiritual growth if your main objective is to reflect the image of Christ more and more. It should be the heart's desire of every believing Christian disciple. In this way your spiritual life becomes more than emotion and it demands of you your very best for the Most High.

My Lord and Redeemer, let Your Holy Spirit take possession of me in such a way that I will live solely for Your glory. *Amen.*

Reflected Glory

Do you not know that your body is a temple of the Holy Spirit? You are not your own; you were bought at a price. Therefore honor God with your body.

~ 1 Corinthians 6:19-20

The core of your life is not the doctrines that you support or on which you base your life but the glorious reality that God's Holy Spirit has come to live in you. The recognition and acceptance of this truth place a great responsibility on you.

You may never slight your body, but rather approach it with the respect that one of God's most wonderful creations deserve. Show moderation in eating and drinking, ensure that you get enough sleep and relaxation. Don't poison your body with nicotine or other drugs. If you do these things you show a destructive attitude towards what God created.

Your body is a temple of God created to worship Him. Committing your body to God should never be a burden to you, it should create a healthy spiritual and intellectual view of life.

Since God's Spirit is living in you, your thoughts must be purified and approved by Him before any of them are released in your life. As you become increasingly aware of His indwelling presence, your outlook on life will not only be purified but also broadened.

You will become more aware of the greatness and worthiness of His omnipotence. The path to spiritual greatness is to allow the Holy Spirit to work through you. This requires obedience at all times.

Almighty God, I open my life to the inflow of Your Holy Spirit and pray humbly that my life will reflect something of Your glory. *Amen.*

Spiritual Decline

Hardship does not spring from the soil, nor does trouble sprout from the ground.

~ JOB 5:6

You may be surrounded by difficulties and think there is no way out. Your faith may have reached rock-bottom and you may even doubt the love and mercy of God. But remember God has only good intentions for you.

To lose the assurance of Christ's living presence that was so real to you once, is a painful experience caused by uncertainty and despair. Knowing what God intended you to be and realizing what you are, leads to a heart-searching challenge. Where did your spiritual life go off the track? Why do you experience defeat and frustration instead of a life of growth and victory?

This unhappy situation does not arise without cause. God's love for us is eternal and undying. Therefore the fault lies with us and not with God.

We should never take our spiritual condition for granted. We should never think that we've reached our destination and that we have a guarantee that we'll not revert to our old way of life. The spiritual path is a never-ending pilgrimage that leads to an increasingly pure love for and understanding of God.

The only way to stop your spiritual decline is through serious prayer and meditation, until you experience the presence of the living Christ in your heart again. You will find the strength to live in the land of victory and know the joy of true peace of mind.

O Holy Spirit of God, I praise You because You established growth and enthusiasm in my life. *Amen.*

Growth Is Essential

Grow in the grace and knowledge of our Lord and Savior Jesus Christ.

~ 2 PETER 3:18

The Christian's spiritual life should never be stagnant. If you are not continuously growing towards a more intimate relationship with Christ, you are allowing your love for Him to cool down and your communion with Him to fade.

Do you know Christ better now than a year ago? An honest answer to this question will indicate the direction that you are moving in spiritually.

Peter encouraged the disciples of the early church to grow in the grace and knowledge of Jesus Christ. Grace is a gift bestowed on us by the Holy Spirit. As your experience of the risen Lord deepens and grows richer, His nature is reflected in your life and is directly linked to your commitment to God.

A disciple who lives according to Christ's example is never too conscious of this development taking place in his life. On the contrary, he will deny this since he is very much aware of his own shortcomings. Nevertheless, denying this can be proof of his spiritual growth.

Growing in the knowledge of Christ can be understood only in view of the knowledge God gives His disciple through the Holy Spirit and through His Holy Word. The Christian reacts to this knowledge and grows in his resemblance to his Perfect Example, Jesus Christ.

Help me, my Redeemer and Example, to grow through grace in such a way that the world will see something of You in me. *Amen.*

Growth through Pain

He cuts off every branch in me that bears no fruit, while every branch that does bear fruit He prunes so that it will be even more fruitful.

~ JOHN 15:2

God often uses pain and sorrow to teach His children important lessons. By doing so He gives us the opportunity to grow spiritually. Sorrow is a fruit and God does not allow this fruit to grow on branches that are too weak to carry it.

Christ tells us that God is the great Gardener who lovingly prunes His children. The right pruning methods result in vines, shrubs and trees growing better and bearing more fruit.

In our lives, there are many infertile shoots: bad habits; wrong thoughts and sinful inclinations. Therefore, the pruning-shears of God are sometimes required. Christina Rossetti said, "Although today He prunes my twigs with pain, yet doth His blood nourish and warm my root; tomorrow I shall put forth buds again and clothe myself with fruit."

Our heavenly Father is a Master Pruner. He knows all about our shortcomings. His pruning promises growth and abundant fruit. Under the tender care of the Gardener, the wounds heal and new life breaks out everywhere.

He who has learnt to carry his cross will find peace. You will be a conqueror and you will stand strong in this world. Christ did not come to make all pain disappear, but to teach us to bear it with dignity and to glorify Him through it.

Father of abundant grace, help me to accept the pain in my life as part of Your loving pruning, so that I can bear abundant fruit. *Amen.*

Ensure Your Spiritual Growth

So then, dear friends, since you are looking forward to this, make every effort to be found spotless, blameless and at peace with Him.
~ 2 Peter 3:14

The point of departure for our spiritual lives is unconditional surrender to the love of Christ. However, afterwards it is essential that we grow. Growth is the goal and purpose for most people. Children wish to become adults; short people want to be taller; a weak person longs for a powerful and muscled body. Gardeners and farmers sow seeds so that flowers, vegetables and fruit will grow. The best methods are accurately followed to ensure maximum growth.

This is similar to our spiritual lives. If we do not work at it in a dedicated, committed way, no spiritual growth will occur. A life starving for spiritual food will never develop to its full potential; it will be handicapped in its development and lack spiritual quality.

Just as you would care for your body or a cherished plant, you should care for your spiritual life conscientiously by nourishing it with the Word of God.

Thus, you create a sturdy foundation for spiritual growth. In addition you should be aware of the presence of the living Christ. This must happen every day so that He can accompany and guide your growth. His Holy Spirit must reveal to you the true meaning of His eternal Word.

Pay serious attention to it and you will be surprised to discover that you are developing your full spiritual potential.

Master, help me through Your good Spirit to nourish my spiritual life so that I will grow to reveal Your nature in my life. *Amen.*

Growth in Christ

Instead, speaking the truth in love, we will in all things grow up into Him who is the Head, that is, Christ.

~ EPHESIANS 4:15

Christianity without spiritual growth can never bring deep and true joy and satisfaction. When you accepted Christ into your life, you promised eternal faithfulness to Him. The strength or weakness of that faith depends on your relationship with the risen Savior.

The strength of any human relationship depends on communication. Through the interaction of shared hopes, fears and ideals, people develop a clearer knowledge of each other. Without communication, friendship dies.

In the Christian life the Master knows you better than you know yourself. You, however, can only understand Him better if you share your life with Him unconditionally.

You will grow in Christ only when you start focusing on God and others, and not on yourself. Your own interests, ambitions and desires will be moved to the background for the sake of others who need help.

Growing in Christ is not meant as an exercise to create a comfortable religious feeling which is far removed from the hard realities of life. It is supposed to motivate the spirit to positive action. Renew your life of prayer and rediscover the Spirit of Christ in the Scriptures. Discover that growth in Christ leads to new dimensions of life.

Lord Jesus, strengthen my faith through the renewal of my prayer life. Give me abundant spiritual growth. *Amen.*

Misfortune as a Means of Growth

Consider it pure joy, my brothers, whenever you face trials of many kinds, because you know that the testing of your faith develops perseverance.

~ JAMES 1:2-3

If the Christian faith could have guaranteed deliverance from all temptations and suffering from the moment it was accepted, everyone would want to be a Christian. However, Christ never makes this promise in His pronouncements. On the contrary, although Christ offers His followers a new relationship with God, He guarantees them that they will be tempted and will experience times of suffering and problems.

One of the inspiring themes of the New Testament is that by carrying a burden, a disciple will grow in grace and to a deeper understanding of and identification with his Master. The Christian is urged to rejoice when the road becomes difficult, because in every misfortune it is possible to prove that God is all-sufficient and that faith in Him can carry us through.

Handling every situation without self-pity requires a positive faith in the eventual purpose of God and in His goodness and love. This again requires faith in the risen Christ, a faith which rises above fear for the unknown.

It is definitely true that you can grow as a Christian through suffering and temptations. If you deal with your misfortune in a positive and constructive way, you will gradually develop a deeper understanding and love for your Father and Lord.

In Your power and strength, holy Master, I can transform defeat into victory. I praise Your holy name with thanksgiving. *Amen.*

Spiritual Growth Is a Process

You are still worldly. For since there is jealousy and quarreling among you, are you not worldly? Are you not acting like mere men?

~ 1 Corinthians 3:3

There are many people who believe that God is great, yet they approach life narrow-mindedly. They know that He promises His strength to all who serve Him sincerely, and yet they remain weak. They say that they believe in God, but they have never experienced His transforming presence in their lives.

Tragically these people remain spiritually immature. They might perhaps be active in rendering Christian and religious service, but as soon as matters go against their wishes, they refuse to cooperate. If they cannot be the leaders, they refuse to follow. Their characters reveal their spiritual immaturity.

The example of Christ and His actions is a source of enrichment to His followers. It broadens their views on life and their understanding of the actions of other people. While the process of growth and maturity continues in their lives, they develop a greater understanding of their fellow man and an increasing love is reflected in their lives.

If the love of Jesus Christ controls your life through the Holy Spirit, there will be no room for jealousy or bitterness. These emotions and attitudes will fall like dry leaves from branches when spring arrives. Only God's immeasurable love can make this happen.

Lord, make me a channel of Your love and an instrument of Your peace. *Amen.*

From Never Land to Reality

When I was a child, I talked like a child, I thought like a child, I reasoned like a child. When I became a man, I put childish ways behind me.

~ 1 CORINTHIANS 13:11

When we were children we played games of make-believe and we lived in a world of fantasy. When we became adults, our childish ideas were replaced by dreams. Some dreams inspire us to make them come true. Yet others remain illusions since they lack driving force. They deprive life of the joy born from real achievement.

For most people there is a time of awakening. They begin to distinguish between fantasy and reality. Some people discard their unrealistic dreams and concentrate on the art of living. Others however, remain in a world of fantasy and make-believe until the end of their lives.

When you accept Christ's challenge, you come face-to-face with the realities of life. With Him, you have no illusions about vain greatness, since you see yourself as God sees you and that is a humbling experience. Meeting reality drives away all fantasy and enables you to struggle with life under the guidance and strength of the Holy Spirit.

God's reality is a greater inspiration than all the games of make-believe, in your life. God reveals to you what you can become and He gives you the inner strength to achieve it. Then you become mature in Christ and children's games will be a thing of the past.

Lord, guide me in the reality of a new life in You. *Amen.*

Reach a Spiritual Maturity

When I was a child, I talked like a child, I thought like a child, I reasoned like a child. When I became a man, I put childish ways behind me.

~ 1 Corinthians 13:11

Little children are wonderful creatures and they give us much joy and pleasure. However, it is tragic when little children remain little children. Many people have a spiritual rocking-horse existence: there is a lot of movement, but little progress. The grudges of yesterday are transferred to today, poisoning their attitude and confusing their thoughts.

We must forget the insults and grudges that we have nurtured over the years. To state that a grudge can't be forgotten, is to aggravate and perpetuate the poisoning. It could cause untold harm to your spirit. It is merely another way of saying that you will never forgive and forget. The most damage is done to the life that harbors the grudge.

The quality of your Christlikeness should enable you to overcome insults, grudges and vexations that hamper your spiritual growth. Today you have an opportunity to grow by God's grace, to put the negative behind you and to reach for a future of exuberant spiritual growth. If you open your spirit to the influence of the Holy Spirit and allow Him to find expression in you, a new lifestyle will open to you. One aspect of this growth in your spiritual life is that it enables you to forgive and forget. Then you can concentrate on those things that contribute to your spiritual maturity.

Lord, I cannot do anything without You. Fill me with Your Spirit so that my life may grow and I may experience fulfillment in You. *Amen.*

Assess Yourself

Do not think of yourself more highly than you ought.

~ Romans 12:3

Many people have a poor opinion of themselves and their abilities. When asked to perform a modest task, they refuse because they are not sure if they can manage it. They refuse invitations because they have no self-confidence. Such people lead unhappy and frustrated lives, because what you believe of yourself is inevitably reflected in how you live.

As a Christian disciple, you must, sooner or later, assess yourself in the light of God's Holy Spirit. You will then see yourself as you really are: with pettiness, superficial self-pity and self-delusion. It could be an uncomfortable and humbling moment in your life. If you accept God's forgiveness for that which you had been in your own eyes, you will begin to see who you could become through His strength, wisdom and inspiration. The point of departure for success is: know yourself.

Stop disparaging yourself and convincing yourself that you will never achieve anything worthwhile. This leads to inner conflict, frustration and unhappiness. The fundamental truth is that you were created in the image of God and in His eyes you are invaluable. If you embrace this truth, the honest assessment of your life is about to begin. Instead of always expecting failure, start to live successfully, especially in your spiritual life. Despair is then replaced by hope. Your goal in life is then equal to God's assessment of your life. If you seek success, start here.

Jesus Christ, I am endlessly grateful to have been redeemed by Your blood. Through You I can inherit eternal life. *Amen.*

Your Thoughts Are Crucial

"The good man brings good things out of the good stored up in his heart, and the evil man brings evil things out of the evil stored up in his heart. For out of the overflow of his heart his mouth speaks."

~ Luke 6:45

Be grateful that God gave you a brain. Your brain may be bright, it may be slow or mediocre, but if you are a healthy person, you have the ability to think. This gives you the power and responsibility to decide what you are going to allow into your thoughts.

Many people do not take the trouble to make decisions and they just drift through life, driven by the feelings that rule their lives and not their minds.

As a disciple of the living Christ, you are controlled by your love for Him and therefore your thoughts should be controlled by Him. This implies a follower of whom high standards of devotion are required. It requires the cultivation of a spiritual life that grows continually; to learn to linger in the presence of the Master – not out of duty but because it is considered a joy and a privilege – so that your life may be gradually filled with His Holy Spirit.

Such a high standard of spiritual life is overwhelming and the prospective disciple may well ask with Paul: Who is equal to such a task? (2 Cor. 2:16). To follow Christ's doctrines and live in awareness of His holy Presence, cannot be achieved by our own strength. However, He has promised us His Holy Spirit. If you are united in faith with Christ, you will find that He controls your thoughts and you will start thinking creatively and successfully.

Holy Jesus, hear my prayer and strengthen my heart. Mold me to Your image so that my life will be to Your greater glory. *Amen.*

Always Be Your Best

I urge you to live a life worthy of the calling you have received.
~ EPHESIANS 4:1

People are inclined to display a personality in the workplace that is different to who they really are. They wear a mask. A Christian must be himself and strive to be the best he can be – to be the person God intended him to be!

Some people feel it serves no purpose to live as a Christian. For a long time you have endeavored to maintain the appearance of Christlikeness. You sinned, pleaded for forgiveness and sinned again, until it degenerated into such a routine that you made a mockery out of God's forgiveness. You know who you should be through the mercy and power of Christ, and you also know who you really are. This is so discouraging that you feel inclined to put an end to all efforts to be the Christian that you should be.

However, there are also many good reasons to persevere and to keep on trying. Jesus loves you and wants to be your Friend. The love He has for you is greater than the ebb and flow of your emotional experiences. His love is steadfast and constant. In contrast to your weakness, He puts His strength at your disposal and asks you to draw this strength into your life through prayer, meditation, Bible study and positive thinking (see 2 Cor. 12:9).

As the love of Christ becomes an increasing reality in your life, your faith will grow and become powerful and creative. Do not be discouraged: the Master believes in you. He will strengthen and comfort you at all times.

Lord, shape my heart. Let everything I do, bear testimony of Your presence. *Amen.*

Know Yourself

So if the Son sets you free, you will be free indeed.

~ JOHN 8:36

It is surprising how many people are strangers to themselves. They act without being able to account for their behavior. They say things they do not really mean, and dislike how they treat others. It sometimes seems as though these people have been separated from themselves.

Unless you are completely honest, you cannot discover the truth about yourself. This honesty is not easy to attain, because man is a master of self-deception. By trying to justify these realities, they deceive themselves: Dishonesty and theft are labelled "borrowing", and sin is referred to as a "weakness". Beautiful names conceal ugly characteristics and situations.

Honesty towards yourself requires conviction and guidance by the Holy Spirit; not as you desire others to see you, but as you really are. Your weaknesses, flaws and sins are exposed and you must face them and deal with them. Some Christians abandon the challenge rather than accept the harsh reality about themselves.

As you become increasingly aware of the true "you", the picture need not only be dark and discouraging. The Holy Spirit grants you insight into what you can become through Christ. While you grow in the Holy Spirit in the knowledge of yourself, your weaknesses and shortcomings will fall away through His grace and you will be able to live with confidence, freed from all the bonds that restricted your personality. Free indeed, because Christ has set you free.

Your miraculous love redeems even the worst sinner. Thank You that we may live with You in truth as Your children. *Amen.*

When Your Past Haunts You

One thing I do: Forgetting what is behind and straining towards what is ahead.

~ PHILIPPIANS 3:13

If you are haunted by thoughts about "what could have been", you cannot experience the freedom of spirit that is your spiritual heritage. The words, "confession" and "remorse", mean to "turn around", to be converted, to mend your old ways and to choose a new path and a new life.

Conscious of what you were, you see a vision of what you could become through the merciful atonement of Christ. The past might cause you to feel burning shame, but the shining halo of the future supersedes the past. That which you once thought to be totally impossible, suddenly becomes gloriously possible.

When confronted by the challenge of the living Christ and when you take the reality of your confession seriously, a new life opens before you. Revelation 21:5 states, "I am making everything new!" Former flaws and sins no longer have any hold or control over your life. By embracing salvation through Jesus Christ, His Spirit fills your spirit with peace, even with regard to the past.

When this transformation takes place in your life, you are looking ahead to a "vivacious", sparkling future in God's presence. This means that you start every day with God, undisturbed by negative thoughts about failures and flaws of the past, and visibly aware of the restored future awaiting you. Then you enter the future in the presence of God.

We cannot cease praising You for Your goodness. Through Your mercy even Your weakest child is redeemed. *Amen.*

Don't Get Impatient with Yourself

Patience is better than pride.

~ ECCLESIASTES 7:8

Too many of the Master's disciples get impatient with themselves. They instinctively feel that they should make better progress in their spiritual life, and they lament the poverty of their prayer life and their lack of knowledge of the Scriptures.

They yearn to get to know God better and do not realize that this yearning in itself is a prayer that is acceptable to the Father. He understands only too well your desire for deeper and more intimate fellowship with Him, which is expressed in your impatience with yourself.

Anything that is worth achieving takes time to obtain. As an infant you crawled before you could walk. If you play a musical instrument, it took time before you mastered it. It is the same with your spiritual life. Sanctification does not happen in a moment. It is the result of a life lived in harmony with Christ and embracing a disciplined spiritual life.

You can measure your progress from time to time. Spend some quiet time in the presence of God. Allow His Spirit to reveal Himself to you. Is Jesus Christ a greater reality today than a few years ago? Is there greater depth in your prayer life? Does the Word of the Lord play an ever-increasing role in your life? These questions will inevitably present themselves to you. Do not get impatient with yourself because your progress on the road of spiritual growth is slow. Walk daily with Christ and leave the rest to Him.

Teach me to walk with You in faith and to please You. I know that those who follow You are one with You. *Amen.*

Born Again to Grow in Grace

"You must be born again."

~ JOHN 3:7

Grow in the grace and knowledge of our Lord and Savior Jesus Christ.

~ 2 PETER 3:18

Spiritual rebirth is a scriptural truth and a vital experience for those who embrace Christ as their Savior and allow their lives to be controlled by His Holy Spirit. However, many born-again Christians do not understand that this wonderful relationship with the Savior could be experienced in various ways: through gospel revival services, or in private quiet time with God.

The living Christ is not bound by stereotyped methods. If a hungry, searching soul searches for God, He will meet that person wherever he may be. The important fact is not the method used, but whether you are truly born again and know Jesus as your Lord and Savior.

In your spiritual life, you *must* grow "in grace and knowledge". As you grow in the Spirit of Christ, you may sometimes look back to a point where everything began, but do not try to cling to that moment. If you do not grow, you will decline spiritually.

To grow spiritually, to cultivate an increasingly profound love for God and your fellow man, is as important as the experience of a new birth. May both be blessed experiences for you.

Lord Jesus, through the guidance and edification of the Holy Spirit, help me to grow in grace and knowledge so that I may experience spring in my life. *Amen.*

Do You Truly Wish to Change?

If anyone is in Christ, he is a new creation; the old has gone, the new has come!

~ 2 Corinthians 5:17

It seems as though everyone is focused on doing something "one day" in the future: the schoolboy thinks of playing for a national team, the young clerk dreams of the day when he will become company manager, the shop assistant lives for the day when he will have his own business. We all have the right to dream, but the tragedy is that so many dreams remain only dreams and never become reality.

As it is in daily life, so is it in spiritual life as well. Christianity is filled with people who will live a more devoted life "one day", who will practice a more meaningful and more profound prayer life, who will make a thorough study of the Word of God, who will strive to be a better Christian "one day". Unfortunately, that "one day" seldom arrives.

One of the challenges that you will have to face, is whether you truly wish to change or not! There is a world of difference between a desire to change "one day" and to really do so. The Lord never changes a person against his will. Before change can take place, there must be cooperation with the living Christ. He asks you to submit to His will before He can put new life into your old, rigid life. The moment when you sincerely desire to change, the transformation begins – and what you once regarded as impossible, becomes possible through Christ's strength.

I praise and thank You, heavenly Father, for the new life that You granted me through Jesus Christ, my Savior. *Amen.*

Cultivate an Inner Life

"Remain in Me, and I will remain in you. No branch can bear fruit by itself; it must remain in the vine. Neither can you bear fruit unless you remain in Me."

~ JOHN 15:4

Hard work in spring time holds the promise of a rich harvest in summer. Cultivating a dynamic inner life is imperative if you wish to become mature in Christ. To really know Him is the most rewarding experience of your life.

Unfortunately there are those people who boast about their spiritual maturity. They have sadly lost touch with the reality of life the way "ordinary" people experience it every day. In their efforts to take hold of God's hand, they let go of life's realities altogether. When this happens, their faith repels those who do not know God because they regard these people as haughty and loveless.

The life of Jesus Christ on earth was characterized by a great love and true concern for the most humble person. In this He was very practical: He not only taught deep spiritual truths, but also took care of people's physical needs. He taught His followers that it is impossible to love God without loving your neighbor and that love is not real unless you give of yourself.

Along the path of spiritual growth there needs to be the practical expression of inspired service. What value does your spirituality have for God or your fellow man if it is not coupled with the practical expression of love? Reflect your love for Christ in creative service so that ordinary men and women will praise God that you are a living branch grafted onto the True Vine!

Lord, let Your beauty fill my life so that it reflects You. *Amen.*

Water Is Life

*He turned the desert into pools of water and the parched ground
into flowing springs.*

~ Psalm 107:35

Water is absolutely crucial for survival. Man, plants and animals suffering from drought will pine away and eventually
die. The severe droughts that have been experienced in many parts
of the world are living proof of this fact. Water is crucial to man's
prosperity and survival.

Your spiritual life can suffer in the same way, unless you drink
of the water that Jesus offers you. There is no human substitute
for that. Christ offers you something which only God can give,
and through that He changes the barren desert of your life into a
fertile paradise, and the burning sand into bubbling springs – an
unmistakable sign that God has touched your life.

If you want your life to have purpose, take deep draughts from
the fountain of living water that Christ offers you, "Whoever
drinks the water I give him will never thirst" (John 4:14).

Get to know Christ through the revelation of His character in
Scripture; through the dedication of your life to Him; through
daily conversation with Him in prayer and by submitting yourself
to His authority.

Keep in touch with the Source through prayer and meditation.
Then you will grow spiritually. He invites you, "If anyone is thirsty,
let him come to Me and drink" (John 7:37). Where there is water,
there is life!

My soul thirsts after You, O God. Thank You for the life-giving water
in Jesus Christ that quenches my thirst. *Amen.*

A Desire to Grow Spiritually

He satisfies the thirsty and fills the hungry with good things.

~ Psalm 107:9

A feeling of spiritual discontent can be a blessing in disguise. It is only when a person becomes discontented with himself that he can or wants to improve. Only then can he become the person God intended him to be.

Spiritual discontent can lead to a greater understanding of God as well as a more intimate relationship with Him. You might have been satisfied with your spiritual state for a long time, but now something has happened to make you aware of the poor state of your spiritual life.

You suddenly become deeply aware of a desire for a more realistic experience with God. There is a deep hunger in your heart to know God more intimately.

When you become aware of this desire, it is your responsibility to do something about it. God has already done everything possible from His side by giving Himself in the person of Jesus Christ.

The first step to satisfy your spiritual hunger and to set your spirit free is to return to the basic elements of your faith. You have to set aside all the unnecessary frills that suffocate your faith or force you into a rut. When you do that, you regain a simple childlike faith in Christ.

When He is the source of your life, your spirit is nourished and you become inspired by a divine power that knows no spiritual hunger or thirst.

Source of abundance, I praise Your name because You satisfy my hunger and thirst daily through Jesus Christ, my living Redeemer. *Amen.*

The Courage of Your Convictions

It is written: "I believed; therefore I have spoken." With that same spirit of faith we also believe and therefore speak.

~ 2 Corinthians 4:13

If people lived their lives according to what they confessed, the world would indeed be a better place. There are many people whose lives contradict their confessions.

Our lives should complement our confessions of faith in a meaningful way otherwise we are destroying our own testimony.

Some people say that they believe in God, yet they always worry. Others say they are members of a certain congregation, yet they seldom attend services. Then there are those who say they believe in the power of prayer; yet they never pray.

Superficial faith can never grow into a strong conviction. To live a successful Christian life, there are certain convictions that you must regard as inviolable as life itself. This means that you hold on to Christian principles even when the winds of adversity rage around you.

What then are the basic principles of such a steadfast conviction? Every disciple of the Master should cling to the fact that, "God was reconciling the world to Himself in Christ" (2 Cor. 5:19).

This truth is non-negotiable to any Christian. It is the foundation of his faith, because it testifies of his submission to the divinity of Jesus Christ. If this message is your honest conviction, you will spread the news and convince others because your life will confirm your testimony.

Lord, my God, help me to have the courage of my convictions without becoming petty or fanatical. *Amen.*

October

What Makes a Christian Different?

As God's chosen people, holy and dearly loved, clothe yourselves
with compassion, kindness, humility, gentleness and patience.

~ COLOSSIANS 3:12

Because you are a Christian, people expect an honorable code of conduct from you. This is a challenge, and yet also a disturbing thought. It is a challenge in that it calls you to be Christlike, but also disturbing because it invariably brings with it the realization that you have failed to achieve the spiritual goals that Christ has set for you.

Whatever your reaction to the world's expectations of you, the fact remains that you have to be different because you are a Christian. Your value system is determined by the Master; your code of conduct gives precedence to others above yourself; you have a constructive approach to life and therefore you are slow to judge and quick to forgive. When you are confronted with destructive antagonism, you have the ability to demonstrate love in the face of hatred. Above all, because you are a disciple of Jesus Christ, you possess His Spirit. Make no mistake: you are different and it is his immanent Spirit that makes you different.

If this truth overwhelms you and causes you to feel inadequate in your spiritual experience, thank God that His Word gives you this guarantee, "My grace is sufficient for you, for My power is made perfect in weakness" (2 Cor. 12:9). It is precisely your inadequacy that may be transformed into constructive purposefulness if you relinquish it to the Master. As a Christian you possess something very special, because the Spirit of Christ lives in you.

In Your strength, I can become what You intended for me. *Amen.*

To Identify with Christ

"The life I live in the body, I live by faith in the Son of God, who loved me and gave Himself for me."

~ GALATIANS 2:20

This is one of the most inspiring and yet also challenging texts in the entire New Testament. It transcends theological argument and penetrates into the sphere of true spiritual experience where the fullness of God saturates one's life as far as it is allowed to. The love, peace, strength and other attributes of the living Christ become a glorious reality to those who accept Him and who are obedient to His will.

However, no human being can, in himself, accomplish such an intimate identification with the living Christ. It is only through God's goodness and grace that we can experience the reality of Christ's Spirit. Identifying with Christ means to walk as close to Him as is possible for a mortal man.

This privilege also encompasses weighty responsibilities. It means experiencing some of the pain that He suffers as a result of the depravity of mankind and it means to be compassionate and generous; to love others in His Spirit and with His love.

To identify with Christ you need to surrender and commit yourself completely to Him. Your attitudes, behavior, motives and lifestyle should be the expression of the Spirit of Christ in you. Identification with Christ means to grow towards being increasingly more like the Master.

Thank You, heavenly Teacher, that I may grow in the grace and wisdom of my Redeemer, Jesus Christ. For this I thank and praise You. *Amen.*

Your Reputation Is Invaluable

They loved praise from men more than praise from God.

~ JOHN 12:43

Your good reputation is of inestimable worth. Your worthiness depends on society's opinion of you. It cannot be gained overnight, nor can it be bought by favors with hidden agendas. It can only be earned by living a noble life.

Standards that are founded on essential values ought not to be influenced by the opinions of other people. Your standards should not be of the world, but rather of God. If you allow your reputation to be shaped by other people's opinions and expectations of you, your life will be governed by ever-changing values. People have differing value systems and you cannot comply with all of them.

When you live to please God alone, you accept principles that create a strong character and a good reputation. Your word becomes your bond; your candor is tempered with love; honesty becomes an integral part of your being; and, because you are aware of your own vulnerability, you refrain from harsh criticism.

Living to please God has a powerful formative influence on your life. If you honor God and allow Him to govern your life, you will have the respect of those who maintain God's standards.

Holy Lord Jesus, help me to live to please You alone. May Your values always be manifested in my life. *Amen.*

Your Calling to Be Christlike

"On that day you will realize that I am in My Father, and you are in Me, and I am in you."

~ JOHN 14:20

The life and teachings of Jesus Christ pose the greatest challenge that anyone can accept. Many people who accept Him as their Perfect Example try to follow Him by committing themselves to good works. They make great sacrifices in the hope that this will help them to become like Him.

While all disciples should have a sincere desire to be like Jesus, all the effort and toil in the world will not help them to achieve this goal. Being Christlike must have its origins in the heart and mind.

It is only here; where the awareness of the presence of the living Christ is to be found; where He becomes the Source of the strength, that enables them to grow spiritually in strength, beauty and truth. Unless the presence of Christ is a living reality in their hearts, it is impossible to reflect His personality in their lives.

The challenge and call to be more Christlike is intensely personal. It is a challenge to a deeper and more intimate relationship with the Master, in which you allow Him to reveal Himself through your life.

Holy Master, through Your great grace and immanent presence I grow every day to become more like You. *Amen.*

Imitating Christ

We who are alive are always being given over to death for Jesus'
sake, so that His life may be revealed in our mortal body.

~ 2 CORINTHIANS 4:11

Regarding certain questions of doctrine, Christianity is unyielding even though there may be widely divergent theological points of views and various forms of worship.

Such differences are unavoidable since people are so complex and different. But despite differences in Christian thinking, the final aim of all Christian doctrine is to cultivate lives which are, as far as possible, expressions of the example of our Lord and Master.

Such a goal may intimidate those people who refuse to surrender their lives to Him completely. They admire the doctrine of Christ and find joy in His calling to discipleship, but they never answer His calling as though it is a holy calling, because they think that He expects more of them than they can give.

If it is your sincere desire to lead a life that follows in the footsteps of Jesus, then there are certain unavoidable requirements which are put to you. Since you have accepted Christ as your Deliverer and Savior and have pledged your loyalty to Him, you will welcome His Holy Spirit into your life in faith.

To have the gift of the Holy Spirit and to allow Him to reveal Himself in you, is such a privilege. It does not only bring peace, a sense of purpose and spiritual power, but you will joyously become aware of the presence of the living Christ in your life. Then you are living in imitation of Christ.

Perfect Lord, the recognition of Your kingship in my life means that I am inspired daily by the power of the Holy Spirit. *Amen.*

Blueprint for Christlikeness

He has showed you, O man, what is good. And what does the Lᴏʀᴅ *require of you? To act justly and to love mercy and to walk humbly with your God.*

~ Mɪcᴀʜ 6:8

In the midst of all the theological and doctrinal arguments and discussions which are so common today, the question that is yet again asked is: "What is a Christian?"

All possible knowledge of the Scriptures does not necessarily make someone a Christian. There are many people who are experts in theology, but who are nevertheless not Christians. In the same way, good deeds alone will not make you a Christian.

The core of our Christian belief is the acceptance of Jesus Christ as our Redeemer and Savior and the placing of our faith in Him. Added to this is our readiness to open our lives to Him so that His Holy Spirit can work in and through us to His honor and glory.

When Jesus explained this truth to His disciples, He said, "Not everyone who says to Me 'Lord, Lord' will enter the kingdom of heaven, but only he who does the will of My Father who is in heaven" (Matt. 7:21).

To do God's will means steadfast obedience to the demands of God. We must obey the instructions that He has given us. We must follow Him and love Him and serve our neighbor in love as long as we may live . Then we will begin to understand what Christian discipleship really means.

Heavenly Father, through Your strength and mercy I will follow the example of Christ, my Lord and Master, and in this way bring honor and glory to Your holy name. *Amen.*

The Christian Businessman

Never be lacking in zeal, but keep your spiritual fervor, serving the Lord.

~ ROMANS 12:11

Many people make the mistake of thinking that Christianity and business are irreconcilable. However, the fact that there are prominent business people who confess their trust in God openly despite a strongly competitive business world, show that this school of thought is totally incorrect.

The failure of Christians to apply their religion to the business world is not due to the fact that they find Christ's doctrine impractical. The cause is the lack of commitment to Christ.

It can be very difficult to satisfy both God and an indifferent and aloof employer, especially if the latter is hostile to everything a Christian regards as precious. However, if the employee lives and works to honor God and carries out his task to the best of his ability, he can confidently leave the result in God's hands.

In the business environment, God is not impressed by profits but by the service rendered. The Christian businessman, in imitation of the holy Managing Director, should not seek to be served but to serve others. Although this point of view may sound idealistic, it is in fact good business acumen. More and more firms focus all their energy on service to their clients.

It is not a question of being either a businessman or a Christian. If one understands the principles of faith, one can be a Christian businessman to the honor of God.

Spirit of God, help me to demonstrate my faith in all my business activities. May I work faithfully to serve You and my fellow man. *Amen.*

Half-Hearted Christians

"I know your deeds, that you are neither cold nor hot. I wish you were either one or the other!"

~ REVELATION 3:15

There are people who expect more from Christianity than they deserve. When they pray, they expect an immediate answer. They expect guidance without any intention of obeying God. They are disappointed when they do not experience the presence of God in their quiet time, even when they neglect becoming quiet before Him.

God gives His gifts of mercy and grace to those disciples who are sincere in their commitment and dedication to Him. They are people who are willing to sacrifice time for the sake of their spiritual growth and development.

A fulfilling relationship can only be experienced when you have surrendered to God totally; when you have cheerfully given to Him everything you are and everything you have. If you sacrifice anything less to Christ, you limit His influence in your life and you deprive yourself of the reward of true Christian discipleship that can be yours.

Many Christians are half-hearted in their commitment to Christ. They are willing to serve Him, if His demands do not clash with their own plans, or do not require any personal sacrifice. Placing the living Christ first and in the center of your life means complete surrender to Him. It deserves your highest commitment and best effort. Do this and the rewards will be breathtaking.

Living Lord and Savior, I commit myself to You again. Make my faith and love dynamic and alive through Your Holy Spirit. *Amen.*

Life Partners

"I no longer call you servants, because a servant does not know his master's business. Instead, I have called you friends, for everything that I learned from My Father I have made known to you."

~ JOHN 15:15

It is only when you have earnestly requested the risen Christ to become your life partner that you realize the full impact and implications of your Christian faith. A partnership implies the shared responsibility to achieve a common goal. When Christ is in control, your life undergoes a change and transformation as a result of the partnership in which you now find yourself.

The purpose of the ministry of Christ is to unify you with the Father. He asks for your cooperation to achieve this, by acknowledging His sovereignty and His redemptive power in your life. If you do, you will experience a growing awareness of His presence in your daily life because you are following the path that Christ has mapped out for you.

Such a wonderful partnership, which is connected to such a magnificent goal, may sound idealistic, but it is the pinnacle of wisdom. To live your life in partnership with God, and with a focus on spiritual matters, brings balance to your life.

With Christ managing and controlling your life, you possess a code of conduct inspired by the Holy Spirit. You will not be a sleeping partner, but will be eager to manifest the partnership in your life at all times. It is your essential part in this wonderful partnership.

My Lord and Master, in partnership with You I will live and work in victory. I thank You for Your love and grace. *Amen.*

Decisions, Decisions, Decisions

So whether you eat or drink or whatever you do, do it all for the glory of God.

~ 1 Corinthians 10:31

To make a decision can be a cumbersome task because it often goes hand-in-hand with great responsibility. What you decide can, and often does, have far-reaching consequences for your own life as well as for the lives of other people – especially those who are dependent on you. It is precisely for this reason that so many people try and circumvent their responsibilities. On the other hand, there are also those who make decisions recklessly or with only their own best interests at heart.

To ensure that you do not become ensnared in these traps, you should take all your concerns in prayer to God. Lay your problems, doubts and fears before His feet and talk to Him about your plans and thoughts regarding the future. Leave the matter to Him and ask Him to lead you in every decision that you have to make, so that you may remain within His will.

This may seem very impractical to you, but provided that you are willing to trust the Lord unconditionally, you will find that He will open doors for you in His own wonderful time and way, and will guide you on the path that He has chosen for you.

Remain in the presence of Christ and the Holy Spirit, and continually aspire to please God. In so doing you will find that you make the right decisions because God will lovingly guide you.

Holy Lord Jesus, I want to lay every decision that I have to make before You in profound dependence. Grant me the guidance of Your Holy Spirit so that I may live and make decisions within Your will. *Amen.*

Find Inspiration in Christ

"Were not our hearts burning within us while He talked with us on the road and opened the Scriptures to us?"

~ Luke 24:32

Jesus' disciples were devastated. The humiliation and crucifixion of their Master destroyed all their hopes and aspirations. Their lives had become meaningless. Their dreams of a new era being ushered in by the Messiah were dashed to the ground. They were reduced to a small group of uncertain people consumed by fear. Then Jesus appeared once more and their lives gained a new and meaningful dimension.

Let this inspire you during every negative situation in your life. When you are afraid or worried; when your plans fail; when you experience setbacks or disappointments: you can either give up hope and be overwhelmed by despondency, or you can turn to the risen Savior and receive new inspiration from Him. The choice is yours, as it was for the disciples.

The friends and followers of the Master developed such an intimate relationship with Him during His lifetime that when He rose from death they were newly inspired by His presence, and hope flowed through them once more.

This can be your experience too, despite the disappointments of life, if you open your life and heart to the living Christ. You too will experience His influence and inspiration that will urge you towards a better and more confident life in His name.

All my hope and trust is anchored in You, risen and glorified Savior and Lord. Thank You that You inspire me time and again when I find myself in the darkest depths. *Amen.*

You Can't Serve Two Masters

If you are returning to the Lord with all your hearts, then rid your-selves of the foreign gods and the Ashtoreths and commit yourselves to the Lord and serve Him only.

~ 1 Samuel 7:3

Many people claim that they are seeking God and that they are trying to establish a more intimate relationship with Him. Few of them would admit that idols hold sway in their lives and exercise a significant amount of control over them.

In their search for a new life in Christ, people stream to gatherings, seminars and retreats; they study the Bible and other Christian literature; they attend Sunday services as well as prayer and study groups. Despite all this, their enthusiasm is often disappointed and their search appears fruitless. Consequently they begin to question the promises of Christ.

If you are seeking a meaningful relationship with the risen Lord, you may be certain that the Redeemer is waiting for you to invite Him into your life so that He may be in charge of it. However, before He will do this, you are expected to banish every non-Christian matter from your life.

Jesus has to be the focus of your existence if you expect Him to fill your life with His joy and fullness. You have to give preference to Him above all the habits and ways of life that you have become accustomed to. Do this, serve only the Lord, and you will experience His peace and joy in your life.

Lord Jesus, I dedicate my life to You anew, in the knowledge that You will give me life in abundance. *Amen.*

The Test of True Discipleship

"By this all men will know that you are My disciples, if you love one another."

~ JOHN 13:35

The majority of Christians are attached to some kind of discipline or credo. This is essential, because without such anchors they become drifters without a safe harbor.

The weakness of these different convictions becomes clear when every association or church believes that it is the only one that is right, and that all the others are wrong. Then an "anti"-spirit becomes prevalent, antagonism reigns supreme and discipleship becomes ineffective.

The Christian faith must center around and in the living Christ. By accepting Him as your Redeemer, you pledge your faith to Him and submit yourself to His demands. It involves every aspect of your daily life and requires a high quality of dedication. Love is the most important sign of discipleship and without it no one can be His follower. Therefore the litmus test of true discipleship is not which theological conviction you believe in, but whether you lead a life of true Christian love.

This truth may cause some people to hesitate to accept the challenge and responsibility of discipleship, because who can love when surrounded by bitterness and hatred? The demand of love that Christ places on us is impossible for mere humans to obey, but if His Spirit fills your life, the impossible becomes possible. Then love becomes the main ingredient in your life and enables you to become a true disciple.

Lord Jesus, let love become the motivating force in my life. *Amen.*

Inner Conflict

What I do is not the good I want to do; no, the evil I do not want to do – this I keep on doing.

~ ROMANS 7:19

To a greater or lesser extent, everyone is familiar with the inner conflict of a divided personality. There are times when you are possessed by an overwhelming desire to live an honorable and uncompromising life. In these times spiritual matters have a strong appeal for you. You are confident that you will harbor no mean or unworthy thoughts, and you experience God as a reality.

It may be precisely while you are experiencing these feelings of ecstasy that your spiritual defences start to relax, and religious pride and conceit start to undermine your faith in your heavenly Father. You start to weaken spiritually and no longer enjoy the spiritual strength you once experienced.

Under such circumstances it is difficult to maintain your spiritual enthusiasm. You know what you have to do, but you find it impossible to do it. Your baser nature is engaged in a struggle with your mind. An endless battle between right and wrong may ensue in your spirit, and it will only be settled if Christ is in complete control of your life.

Once you have completely surrendered to Him and live in the assurance that His living presence belongs to you, His unifying and triumphant power will be at your disposal, and you will become a fully integrated personality.

Lord Jesus, through the guidance and inspiration of Your Holy Spirit I become a completely integrated personality. *Amen.*

Let Christ Remain Central

*Let us examine our ways and test them, and let us return to the
LORD.*

~ LAMENTATIONS 3:40

One of the wonderful facts of the Christian life is that the Lord knows our backgrounds and personalities, and yet still loves us. Sometimes His challenges to us are so direct that we want to avoid them if we can, but at other times He calls us to Him with a tenderness from which we cannot turn away, because we know of His eternal love for us.

No one can say how God will work within a particular person, or in what way He will choose to call someone to His service. He has His own methods of doing this, and a wise disciple will never try to enforce his own will on another person.

To know that the living Christ works in different ways with different people deepens our understanding, expands our view, improves our sympathy and enriches our communion with the Master. If your heart is filled with love towards your neighbor, there can be no space for the meanness that embitters your spirit and deprives it of the wealth and beauty of God's grace. By realizing that God uses different methods for different people, you will intensify your understanding of the Master and add to your love for Him in a marvelous manner.

Be continually mindful of the way in which the Lord handles people. This will not only strengthen your faith, but also make life interesting and exciting.

Lord, grant me an immeasurable love for my fellow man so that I may serve others more effectively. *Amen.*

Simplicity of Jesus Christ

I am writing you a new command; its truth is seen in Him and you, because the darkness is passing and the true light is already shining.

~ 1 John 2:8

Religion has always been a controversial subject. Since the beginning of time people have argued about doctrinal issues and much blood has been shed in the name of the Prince of Peace. The thought of this is distressing and confusing to ordinary people whose only desire is to experience the reality and the abundance of Christ in their lives.

Too many dedicated Christians are dogmatically oriented instead of being Christ-centered. They argue so seriously about a dogmatic detail that they become isolated from their fellow Christians. Their love for Christ is not big enough to include someone who differs from them theologically. Unknowingly they become trapped in a haze of religious narrow-mindedness.

If you are experiencing a phase of mental and spiritual confusion and feel inclined to abandon all faith, briefly take a step back from all your doubts and uncertainties and again experience a vision of the holy simplicity of the living Savior.

Despite His greatness and uniqueness, Jesus lived a simple life. He was at home among people and they were able to identify with Him. He reduced a complicated religious code to a simple, practical proposition that was intelligible to everyone. His commandment to love God and one's neighbor was all-important. Let this command be the motivating force for a more effective faith.

Beloved Savior, focus my faith in You alone. *Amen.*

With Whom Do You Identify?

Does not He who guards your life know it? Will He not repay each person according to what he has done?

~ PROVERBS 24:12

You cannot go through life without certain elements having an effect on you. If you were born in circumstances dominated by hate, your character and your perspective on life will constantly be threatened by hatred. If you grew up poor, later you will feel its influence in some way or another. These are influences over which you have little or no control.

While growing up you also willingly identified yourself with certain forces that had a formational influence on your life. Many of these influences would have been positive and progressive, while others would have had a destructive effect on your character and life.

It is unquestionably true that you eventually become like the company you keep. There are many young Christians who try to maintain connections with their former friends after their conversion, and then find that the influence of the past is too strong. Consequently they start straying from their faith. Where circumstances exist that may favor the re-forging of old friendships, the situation must be prevented by cultivating strong Christian friendships. It is true that the love in your heart is that which you identify with.

If you identify yourself with the living Christ His influence will rapidly become visible in your life. Your perspective, attitude, hope and ambition all fall under His control and you continually grow in His image. Then your life will assume a purposeful course.

Come live in my heart, Lord Jesus, and make me what You are. *Amen.*

In Partnership with God

Now let the fear of the Lord be upon you. Judge carefully, for with the Lord our God there is no injustice or partiality or bribery.

~ 2 Chronicles 19:7

There are those who believe that religion and business should be kept separate. Some people accept this idea on the basis that the two matters simply do not mix, while others become uncomfortable when they consider their business practices in the light of Christian principles.

God unequivocally has a place in your business practices and in your social life, just as He does in your spiritual life, and you cannot eliminate Him from one of these spheres without inflicting damage on yourself.

Your entire life is ruled by Christian principles and you should bear witness to your Christianity, regardless of the sphere of life that you are moving in – both in your worship and in your activities outside of the church.

Integrity is one of the most important qualities in this respect. The surest way to reflect integrity in all your interactions is to make the living Christ your business partner. Whatever you do, scrutinize it through the eyes of Jesus; ask yourself how He would react and what He would do in your circumstances.

Follow Christ's example and you will be assured of a virtuous life that will earn you the respect of everyone you interact with.

Lord Jesus, I am not ashamed to acknowledge You as the Lord of my life, or to profess Your name under all circumstances. *Amen.*

Walk with Jesus

As they talked and discussed these things with each other, Jesus Himself came up and walked along with them.

~ LUKE 24:15

Tragic events paralyzed Jesus' first disciples. Their spiritual perception was unable to see beyond the darkness of the crucifixion and therefore they could not remember Jesus' promises. Consequently, the road to Emmaus was shrouded in despondent darkness for the disciples.

Jesus joined them on this journey, but they did not even recognize Him. Initially He was only a stranger who astonished them with His ignorance of recent events. But when He started to explain the Scriptures, He became a Prophet to them, and they listened to Him with interest. Only after they had invited Him to spend the night with them, did they recognize Him as the Master they loved.

The events on the road to Emmaus are not unique in Christian experience. Many have walked this path in His company without recognizing Him. He showered His blessings on them and they did not respond to His love. They may even claim to have been converted, and yet the joy and reality of true faith has escaped them.

The wonderful truth is that the Master is with you every step of the way. Even when He is regarded as a stranger, He remains your Friend; even when His blessings aren't recognized, He keeps giving; and if you listen to His Word He reveals Himself to you. The living Christ wants to walk the road with you; do you want to walk the road with Him?

Powerful Redeemer, I no longer want to treat You as a stranger, but I accept You completely as my Savior and Redeemer. *Amen.*

Cope with Wounded Feelings

You will increase my honor and comfort me once again.

~ PSALM 71:21

Many people claim to believe in an Almighty God, but their lives do not reflect this faith. They see the wonders of creation or try to fathom the mysteries of their own personalities, and feel that this knowledge is out of their reach. The greatness of God in nature and in wisdom overwhelms them and they recoil into the pettiness of their own personalities. Consequently their perspectives become confused and narrow-minded.

If your concept of God is large enough, there can be no space for pettiness or narrow-mindedness. If someone hurts you with a snide remark or an unfriendly gesture, you can either take revenge or accept it in the spirit of God's forgiveness. If you take it personally and nurse a grudge, your life will become miserable. However, if you simply accept these incidents against the background of God's omnipotence, they will become inconsequential and you will grow spiritually.

You can only experience mental and spiritual greatness if God is the center of your life. It is only when you accept everything that comes your way in the spirit of Him who lives inside you, that nothing can undermine your spiritual stature. In this case God becomes of greater importance than your feelings or desires. If God comes first in your life and you aim to please Him alone, what other people say and think will be of little importance to you.

I praise and thank You, holy Master, that I am able to handle even my injured feelings constructively and positively through the grace that You grant me. *Amen.*

True Christianity

Examine yourselves to see whether you are in the faith; test your-selves. Do you not realize that Christ Jesus is in you?

~ 2 CORINTHIANS 13:5

Many people perceive Christians to be generally weak, pro-saic and ineffective. Christians are often regarded as a spe-cies living in an isolated world of their own, removed from the realities of life. They are seen to be banding together in excluding the world while spending their time in prayer and Bible study. Of course, this is a complete misconception of the Christian faith.

There was nothing weak, prosaic or ineffective about Jesus Christ. The Scriptures, and especially the Gospels, are witness to His humanity and His divinity; to His firmness and His tenderness; to His courage as well as His humility; and above all, to His love, even when He was subjected to bitter hatred and barbaric torture and death.

This is the example that our Leader set for all Christians to follow if we wish to be faithful to our highest calling as Christians. It is an accepted fact that you cannot accomplish it in your own strength. Therefore God granted us the Holy Spirit, and if you give Him complete control of your life, the transformation that He brings about will undoubtedly reveal you as a true Christian to the world.

Thank You, heavenly Father, that we are more than conquerors in Your Son and through Your Holy Spirit. *Amen.*

Your Heavenly Leader

"You must serve faithfully and wholeheartedly in the fear of the LORD."

~ 2 CHRONICLES 19:9

It is a great source of frustration when your careful planning goes awry. You are deeply disappointed when your best attempts come to nothing and all your hopes are dashed. Often you become disillusioned as a result of this kind of experience, and sometimes you become so discouraged that you threaten to give it all up. You are convinced that everything you undertake is doomed to fail.

It is scant consolation to say that you are not alone in going through this kind of experience. However, the solution to your problem does not lie in accepting your failure, but rather in finding the reasons for it. And then it is a good time to ask yourself, "Where does God fit into my planning?"

When you embark on a venture, however minor or insignificant it may appear, always seek the will of the Lord before proceeding. He knows what is best for you, and though it may initially seem as if His will does not fit in with your plans, you have to realize that His perspective on your life is eternal. Therefore He is able to lead you into a future that may be unknown to you, but is perfectly clear to Him.

Make Jesus your partner and your leader in everything that you undertake. If you do, you can be assured that you will ultimately achieve success.

Heavenly Leader, in the past I have tried to choose my own path, but now I seek Your guidance in my life every day. *Amen.*

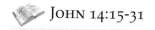

Serve Christ Joyfully

"If you love Me, you will obey what I command."

~ John 14:15

Many people regard their surrender to Christ as a strict discipline that adds an unbearable burden to their lives. They feel that the cost of being a disciple is too high a price to pay. As the demands of their faith increase, their grip on Christ weakens until they completely lose it and relapse. They consequently lead an unsatisfying spiritual life that lacks fulfillment.

You must never regard your attachment to the cause of Christ as a burden. Your life in Christ should be joyful, and as you grow in Christ, your joy should increase. If you are truly devoted to Christ, your highest desire will be to get to know Him better and serve Him more effectively. As you grow in faith you will constantly strive towards ways of serving Him better because you want to, not because you have to.

To reach this point in your pilgrimage, you have to get to know Him increasingly better through Bible study and wholesome Christian literature. However, you also have to know the living Christ personally by conversing with Him through prayer. Strive to be with Christ, and the more He becomes an inseparable part of your life, the more joy you will experience in His service.

I rejoice in Your service, O Lord, and thank You for this wonderful privilege. *Amen.*

Spiritual Pride

The Pharisee stood up and prayed about himself: "God, I thank You that I am not like other men."

~ LUKE 18:11

Spiritual growth often goes unnoticed by those in whom it is taking place. When a disciple attempts to determine his spiritual quality by comparing it to the spiritual development of other people, he is in danger of becoming self-centered.

The religious leaders in the time of Christ suffered from this ailment; they thought that they were spiritually superior and consequently they opened themselves up to the judgment of Christ.

Be careful not to become self-centered and smug, irrespective of how faithful you are to God. Sincere humility will keep you from becoming conceited over your own spiritual importance. If Christ is in you it is testimony of your true spirituality.

The most important testimony you as a Christian can show to the world, is to be filled by Christ to such an extent that you are no longer aware of the self. This means that your thoughts must be inspired by the Holy Spirit and that all your deeds must be done to the glory of God and in the service of others.

To live a Christ-centered life is to forget yourself in the reality of Jesus Christ. The more you elevate Him in your life, the more you will discover the true meaning of life.

Keep me, merciful God, from exulting in anything but the cross, especially not in my own humility. *Amen.*

Is There Room for Jesus?

"In my Father's house are many rooms; if it were not so, I would have told you. I am going there to prepare a place for you."

~ JOHN 14:2

She gave birth to her firstborn, a Son. She wrapped Him in cloths and placed Him in a manger, because there was no room for them in the inn.

~ LUKE 2:7

Had the people of Bethlehem known who these visitors were, they would probably have tried to "make" room for them. Mary would become the mother of the Messiah generations of Israel had been waiting for. Every devout Israelite would have been honored to give up his own room for Him. But God did not come to this world in greatness and splendor. He came in the shape of a servant and was placed in a manger.

Is there space for the Lord in your life? If not, your guilt is bigger than that of the people of Bethlehem. After all, we know that He is the Christ, the Savior. We dare not be Christians who have no room for Christ.

The wonder of God's grace is that He does not repay us according to our sins. Although there was no place for Him on earth, He went to prepare a place in heaven for every repentant sinner. A "no vacancy" sign is never posted.

Make room for Christ in your heart. Then you too may take your place at the feast of the Lamb. Hallelujah! Praise the Lord!

I want to make room for You in all spheres of my life, Lord Jesus. I thank You for the room You make for me now and for eternity. *Amen.*

God's Way

Good and upright is the LORD; therefore He instructs sinners in His ways.

~ PSALM 25:8

In today's world it is especially easy to lose one's spiritual way. The pressure exerted by the sinful world is felt by the young as much as the old; temptations are plentiful and offered on a silver platter; the variety of detours make it extremely difficult to follow the right path. In an era that constantly questions standards and morality, there is always a fundamental danger that our principles may be compromised, however innocent and harmless the first step may seem at the time.

There is only one way to live your life and that is to keep to God's ways. In His commandments He set out the basic rules for a pious and devout life. In addition to this, Christ became a living example that demonstrated to us how such a life ought to be lived.

Even though centuries have passed, nothing has changed with regard to the way of life that is acceptable and pleasing to God. Christ is still the way, the truth and the life, and the path of righteousness is still that of obedience to God in all things.

If you open your heart and life to the immanent Holy Spirit, you will become increasingly aware of His influence and suggestions. Follow His guidance and you will know that the path you are following is the way of God.

Search me, O God, and know my heart; test me and know my anxious thoughts. See if there is any offensive way in me, and lead me in the way everlasting (Ps. 139:23-24). *Amen.*

Put Christ First

So I say, live by the Spirit, and you will not gratify the desires of the sinful nature.

~ GALATIANS 5:16

If we were truly honest with ourselves, very few of us would be able to deny that it is extremely difficult to live a good Christian life and to act in the way that Jesus expects. As a matter of fact, it is written in the Gospels that our Master Himself said this. He never promised that it would be easy to follow Him, in fact, He explicitly warned us about the problems, dangers and opposition that His disciples would encounter.

One of the greatest obstacles on the Christian path is our human nature with its desires, accepted practices, presumptions and many other things that monopolize our time and attention. These things sneak into our lives, and whether we realize it or not, they relegate Christ to an inferior place in our lives.

It is needless to point out that this is an unacceptable state of affairs, and no person who bears the title of Christian can allow it. And yet, in his own deceptive and cunning way Satan continues to tempt us to follow our own desires – to the detriment of our faith.

To resist temptation it is essential to open up your entire life to the influence of the Holy Spirit. Deliberately invite Him to take control of your life. He will undoubtedly assist you in overcoming all evil, and help you to live the Christian life to which you have been called.

Lord Jesus, from experience we know that if we wait prayerfully for You, Your Holy Spirit will give us the strength to resist every temptation. For this we thank and praise Your holy name. *Amen.*

Work with God

As for me, it is good to be near God.

~ PSALM 73:28

Every one of us desires what is best for us. We feel that we have a vested right to receive that which belongs to us. Unfortunately so many of us have never tried to define exactly what it is that we regard as our "right," and as a result we are often unhappy and complain throughout our pilgrimage through life.

This inner desire that seems to be so unattainable, and the awareness that there is something that we seek but cannot define, unconsciously makes us lower our expectations of life, especially regarding that which is our "right". "I have the right to happiness," and "I have the right to financial independence" are but two of the rights claimed.

Often these demands are made without stopping to think about how they may be achieved through personal involvement. Many people demand happiness, without giving it; others demand financial independence, without being careful in their financial transactions. In the fulfillment of our expectations and demands, God surely has the right to our cooperation.

When God occupies the first place in our lives and His laws govern our daily lives, the demands of our lives become of secondary importance. Then it is no longer a question of what you demand from life, but rather what you can contribute to the fulfillment of His holy will in your life. Then you will experience a life of profound joy and true satisfaction.

While I seek Your gifts with a yearning heart, O Father, I offer You my humble and willing cooperation in the fulfillment thereof. *Amen.*

Live in Fellowship with Christ

God, who has called you into fellowship with His Son Jesus Christ our Lord, is faithful.

~ 1 CORINTHIANS 1:9

God has given you a wonderful privilege. He has called you to share in the life of Jesus Christ. When the full meaning of this divine gift dawns on you, the implications are almost too great to envision.

To share in the life of Jesus Christ implies unlimited possibilities, but also great responsibilities. Connected to so much omnipotence and wisdom, your understanding of God is deepened, your vision of what your life can be is expanded and you become aware of the enduring presence of Christ. The quality of your life has to be in accordance with the expression of your faith. The characteristics of God must be reflected in your life through love, complete honesty, unselfishness and purity of purpose.

To express the Spirit of Christ to the best of your ability, you should develop a vision of what you can achieve for the Master. You are no longer restricted by secret fears and uncertainties, but can move confidently forward in the empowering strength of the living Christ.

Christ offers Himself to you so that you may share your life with Him. But this offer only becomes a reality when you accept it in faith. You may have the knowledge of this glorious truth, but until you have made it your own you will not experience the strength and joy of the presence of Christ in your life.

Lord Jesus, I invite You anew to come into my life and to do Your work on earth through me. I now open my heart and life to You. *Amen.*

Followers of Christ

Do not conform any longer to the pattern of this world, but be transformed by the renewing of your mind.

~ ROMANS 12:2

The difficulties and problems of this world have a marked influence on our lives. But people are also influenced by times of prosperity and peace. In times of war or economic depression people tend to become pessimistic and depressed. In good times they are light-hearted and cheerful.

As a responsible citizen you should feel at least partially responsible for world conditions. However, there is always the danger of being tempted to allow circumstances to affect your judgment on events in your own life as well as in the lives of those who depend on you. If you depend on world conditions for your decisions in your domestic, spiritual and business life, you are looking for trouble.

To be able to live a well-balanced life and evaluate every situation calmly and sensibly, you require clarity of vision and mind. Surrender your life to God unconditionally, and allow His Holy Spirit to guide you in everything in which you are involved. If you do this, you will live your life according to God's perfect will for you and not according to the standards of the world.

Glorified Lord Jesus, I want to be Your follower every day and under all circumstances. I open my life to You and Your Holy Spirit. *Amen.*

Don't Miss Out on the Best

"Earnestly desire the best gifts."

~ 1 CORINTHIANS 12:31 (NKJV)

It is a natural inclination of man to desire only the best which life has to offer. However, it is of the utmost importance to know what is best and not subconsciously accept that which is second best. It is disturbing that many people strive towards a goal because they believe it to be the best, while their aim should actually be higher.

Unfortunately this mistake is made because people have a distorted understanding of values. They regard financial riches to be of greater importance than an honorable character, they believe it is better to receive than to give, that the means justify the end and that only a fool will help someone else free of charge.

In order for you to know what is best for you, it is necessary to take stock of what you are and what you do. It takes courage to acknowledge your mistakes, to understand your weaknesses and to be committed to doing something positive about your goals.

Such courage requires standards against which it can be measured and the highest available standards are those given to man by God. They are the old crystallized values of love, honesty, unselfishness and purity. When you allow these God-given principles to govern your conscience, you will become aware of their challenge and impact upon your life. If you carry on living according to these divine standards, God's best for you will far outshine any plans you made for yourself.

Grant me wisdom, O divine Master, to measure my goals against Your standards of love, honesty, unselfishness and purity. *Amen.*

November

Discovering God's Will

*"Remain in Me, and I will remain in you. No branch can bear fruit
by itself; it must remain in the vine. Neither can you bear fruit unless you remain in Me."*

~ JOHN 15:4

You worship a God that performs miracles. In times of stress
and tension you can call on Him. With God you will always
receive what you need, because He is the Giver of every perfect
gift and you are the fortunate receiver.

Whenever you wish to respond to the benevolence of God you
usually start by looking around you for some or other good deed
that you can perform to please the heart of God. You then start
doing it with enthusiasm and dedication. But are you sure that this
is what He wants you to do?

Discovering God's will for your life can be an exciting adventure.
You may try out various directions before you finally discover the
path on which He wishes to lead you. But when you know that
you are within God's holy will, you will discover that you are no
longer working for Him, but that He is working through you.

When this happens the road ahead opens up miraculously.
Problems suddenly become opportunities and your faith becomes
practical, alive and dynamic. You realize that by working with
God you become an effective instrument in His hand. You will
never discover your full potential in the service of Christ until you
realize what God can accomplish through you.

Holy Father, help me through Your guidance to become an instrument in Your hand so that You may work through me. *Amen.*

The Will of God Alone

"By Myself I can do nothing; I judge only as I hear, and My judg-
ment is just, for I seek not to please Myself but Him who sent Me."
~ John 5:30

There are few people who have not at some point experienced the frustration of plans going wrong or expectations that are not met. In many cases it goes much further than mere disappointment because of failure. The consequences of failure can take on immeasurable proportions. When this happens, many people ascribe it to fate, or economic circumstances beyond their control, or chance, or bad luck, or any of a host of other reasons. Few people will admit that the fault lies within them, because they refuse to live according to the will of God.

God's sacred plan for your life is one of perfection. Because you are His child and He loves you, He wishes only the very best for you. For this reason everything that happens in your life is intended to ultimately give you the very best, even though it may not appear so to you at the time.

To achieve this goal with as little trouble as possible, it is your responsibility to live and work within God's will. Submit your ideas and plans to Him and faithfully seek His guidance. The closer you live to your Master, the easier you will find it to know His will for your life. Never embark on any endeavor that falls outside the will of God, and you will experience peace of mind and tranquility, as well as the assurance that Jesus will be with you in all your endeavors.

Eternal and loving God, I surrender myself to You completely. Lead me according to Your will from day to day. *Amen.*

God's Standards

"A man can receive only what is given him from heaven."

~ John 3:27

In today's world material possessions play an important role in most people's lives. Things that used to be regarded as luxuries have become necessities in people's attempts to keep up with their neighbors.

Indeed, over the years things have changed radically, but it would be a foolish mistake to say that life ought to continue at the same pace as previous centuries. Progress simply does not allow for this, however much we long for "the good old days".

If we accept that things have changed and will continue changing, we will also have to accept that we now have a new way of life. However, we dare not allow our value system to change. Despite modern progress and changes in lifestyle, the age-old truth remains steadfast and sure: any worthwhile undertaking must have the blessing of God, otherwise it is doomed to failure.

When you are challenged to change your lifestyle, or when you are guided towards a new path of life, you should humble yourself before God before making a final decision. Pray that His way, the only true way, will be made known to you.

Eternal and immutable God, in this changing world I hold on to You in the knowledge that You are God from eternity to eternity. *Amen.*

Living in God's will

Then the LORD said, "Look, I am setting a plumb line among My people Israel; I will spare them no longer."
~ Amos 7:8

Most of us are just so good at making excuses. When we are challenged, we will usually find some excuse for what we have said or done. How often do we hear: "I didn't mean it like that" or "I was told to do it"; "You probably misunderstood me" or "I thought you wanted me to do it like that." These are but a few of the well-known excuses.

In your Christian faith there is no room for excuses not to do what God has called you to do. He always specifies exactly what He wants you to do. Just as He, through His prophet, set a plumb line among His people, from which there could be no deviation, so God gave humanity the living example of Jesus Christ to show us the kind of life that every Christian should live. His doctrine is clear and leaves us with no doubt about the standards that He has set for us.

Through His great grace and understanding God goes even further. Because He is aware of human fallibility, He gives us the Holy Spirit to equip us for leading this life. Without this assistance we would never be able to succeed, but in the strength of the Holy Spirit we can accomplish anything. Therefore, follow God's path and enjoy a life of abundance in Christ.

Grant me the ability and the will, beloved Father, to live as You wish me to live. *Amen.*

Discover God's Will for Your Life

To each one the manifestation of the Spirit is given for the common good.

~ 1 Corinthians 12:7

Sometimes it feels as if you are drifting aimlessly through life and that it doesn't really matter whether you are here or not. Day after day passes without accomplishing anything worthwhile. The sparkle seems to have disappeared from your life. This unfortunate state of affairs by no means comes about through any fault of God.

To prevent it, you should, firstly, relive the glory of your spiritual experience. Then seek God's plan for your life so that you may strive towards a positive goal in your life. When the living Christ takes control of your life and reveals Himself through you, you will cease drifting aimlessly, and become a positive and inspired Christian disciple.

A renewal of your spiritual experience with Christ occurs when you invite the Holy Spirit in and allow Him to take complete control of your life. You will discover that while you are living in harmony with the Spirit, new avenues of service open up to you, and you are guided towards infinite greatness.

When you sense that God is busy guiding you, you should confirm it through continual prayer. Dare to trust God unconditionally. To discover God's will for your life not only requires faith, but also positive actions.

With renewed faith and fervor, O Master, I step into the future with the confidence that only You can give me. *Amen.*

The Road to Love and Life

Teach me Your way, O LORD, and I will walk in Your truth; give me an undivided heart.

~ PSALM 86:11

Most of us have the human tendency to want to lead our own lives, and then still expect God's blessing. When things go wrong, we wonder how God could have allowed it.

The problem is that we did not seek God's approval or blessing for the plans that we made in the first place. We rush along the paths that we plan for ourselves with our own blind hearts and then wonder why things go so horribly wrong.

As God's child you must learn to accept His discipline, knowing that without it no spiritual growth or blessing is possible. God's discipline is never arbitrary and He does not punish some and excuse others – although it sometimes seems as if He does. The discipline that you experience is often self-inflicted reproof.

When you purposely break His law and foolishly think you can sidestep the results, don't rebel when it seems as if things have turned against you. Whatever you sow, you will reap. If you sow the wind, you will reap a storm!

God is not calling us to a lifestyle beyond our reach, neither does He set goals that cannot be attained. Never be shortsighted and think that your own methods and ways are infallible.

God's way to true life and love requires us to sacrifice every impure desire. Because His way is always the right one, it is the only safe way for the follower of Christ.

Risen Lord, I worship You as the Way, the Truth and the Life. Help me to obediently walk on the path of life and love. *Amen.*

You Cannot Do It on Your Own

"Remain in Me, and I will remain in you. No branch can bear fruit by itself; it must remain in the vine. Neither can you bear fruit unless you remain in Me."

~ JOHN 15:4

It is a painful experience for you as a Christian to discover that all your efforts have been in vain. You have been working faithfully, yet the result is unsatisfactory.

If you are experiencing such a time right now, there are a few questions that you should ask yourself regarding the areas where you have failed: Did you follow your own selfish heart or did you honestly seek the will of God before you started? Did you make time for prayer, asking God if that was really what He expected of you – or did it merely fit in with your own plans?

If you practice intimate fellowship with God on a daily basis, submitting all your plans and ideas to Him for approval and guidance, you will experience how the Holy Spirit takes over and guides you in the way that you should go. The more profoundly you are tuned in to God's will, the more certain you will be about God's will for your life. Then you will not foolishly rush into projects and ideas generated by your own shortsighted will.

Obedience is a sure sign of a committed life. Your greatest joy then will be to live in the center of God's will. If you obey God to His glory alone, every effort of yours will be crowned with success. If not, no matter how worthy your intentions, everything will fail. Always remember that He, the True Vine, warned us by saying, "Apart from Me, you can do nothing" (John 15:5).

Lord, I realize that I am weak. Draw me ever closer to You. *Amen.*

Grant Me Patience

Be still before the LORD and wait patiently for Him.

~ PSALM 37:7

How often do we rush into a situation only to be disappointed when things don't go according to plan? The only comfort we have is that we are not the only ones who are foolish. Many people pay a high price for being impetuous. As a result they become despondent and lose their self-confidence. Naturally their enthusiasm is dampened and the pendulum of their emotional lives swings from one extreme to another.

The main reason for this is because they neglect to lay their plans or problems before God and wait patiently for His guidance. It has been proved repeatedly that God's methods and timing are always perfect. His concept of life is total and eternal. We, on the other hand, can only handle what we perceive in the here and now. That is why we should learn to practice patience.

Before you make an important decision; before you move into any specific direction; before making a vital change in your life, bring the matter before the Lord in prayer and ask for the guidance of the Holy Spirit. Then wait patiently on the Lord and be willing to be led by Him.

Above all, be sensitive to the voice of the Holy Spirit because that is the way in which God will guide you. Then continue in faith, being certain of the fact that, "In all things God works for the good of those who love Him, who have been called according to His purpose" (Rom. 8:28).

Heavenly Father, You are my Guarantee and Security and that is why I can approach each day confidently. *Amen.*

Stubborn Obstinacy

Who can discern his errors? Forgive my hidden faults. Keep Your servant also from willful sins; may they not rule over me.

~ PSALM 19:12-13

Sometimes you decide to do something your own way and according to your own will, regardless of how other people's lives or feelings are influenced by it. The stronger the opposition the more adamant you become to have it your way.

If you are certain that your way is without a doubt the right one, you will be influenced by the well-meant opinions of others. The person whose stubbornness is caused by a feeling of insecurity refuses to take advice from others or listen to their viewpoints.

One of the most difficult things to develop in life is the ability not to be prejudiced. Religious enthusiasm can blind you to a deeper understanding of spiritual truths. Your social background might cause you to be ignorant about the rights and desires of other groups of people. You develop tunnel vision and refuse to consider – let alone accept – anything other than your own narrow-minded opinion.

The danger of this situation is that when God wants to lead you into a deeper understanding of Himself, you choose to follow your own way.

It is impossible to lead a positive, meaningful Christian life if you always wish to choose and follow your own way and refuse to put God first in your life. Kneel before God and clear this matter today.

Guide and Lord, I do not always desire Your guidance. I want to control my life. Please lead me now. *Amen.*

The Master Potter

"You must follow Me."

~JOHN 21:22

It will be worthwhile to meditate today on the marvelous way in which the Master Potter changed the life of Peter!

Outwardly Peter was a great success. He was well-built, had a sound knowledge of the sea and fishing, and had great influence amongst the fishermen of Capernaum.

But in the school of the Master he had to learn that inner strength was of greater importance than physical power.

Peter also had to learn that he could not fix his own broken life in the way that he fixed torn fishing nets. Only the great Artist of Life could mend his life. His leadership qualities and pride had to be changed and he had to learn to wash others' feet. Peter used to be a leader but he had to become a follower.

Despite his great physical strength, Peter was actually a man of great inner weakness. When Christ mentioned pain, suffering and death, Peter recoiled. When he wanted to walk on the water, his faith deserted him and the Lord had to save him. Then at the gate of Gethsemane he fled with the other disciples and denied Jesus three times.

Therefore, take courage poor sinner! God anticipated great possibilities for Peter. After confessing his love for the Lord Jesus he received the command, "Follow Me." Hesitantly, but obediently, he started walking the path of true discipleship and God's purpose for his life. What about you and me? How are we going to react?

Thank You, gracious Lord, that You are holding my hand. I will follow You through the guidance of Your Holy Spirit. *Amen.*

How Do I Discern God's Will?

"What shall I do, Lord?" I asked.

~ Acts 22:10

God no longer appears to us in the middle of the night to reveal His will like in Samuel's case. Neither does He send the angels from heaven with a message of what He expects from us. How can I possibly know what God's will is?

First of all your heart must be in a condition where it knows no will of its own in any matter. When we are willing to obey God's will, we have already solved nine-tenths of the problem. Once you have reached that stage, you are not very far from finding out what God wants you to do. You don't allow yourself to be led by your feelings or emotions because you know it is easy to be deceived.

Search the Scriptures to find God's will because the Spirit and the Word must work closely together in this process. If you listen only to the Spirit and disregard the Word, you are deceiving yourself. When the Holy Spirit leads and guides you, He always does so according to the Scripture – never anything contrary to this!

You must be sensitive to God's guidance in all circumstances. Kneel down and ask God to reveal His perfect will to you. Through prayer and the study of God's Word, through meditation and the guidance of the Holy Spirit you will be able to make a decision which, to the best of your knowledge, will be God's will for you.

When you have peace of mind and heart, continue to pray. When the conviction grows that you are acting according to God's will, move forward in faith.

Father, thank You for enabling me to discern Your will through the Holy Spirit, Your Word and prayer. Make me willing to obey. *Amen.*

God's Will for My Life

"I will instruct you and teach you in the way you should go; I will counsel you and watch over you."

~ Psalm 32:8

It is not always easy to recognize the will of God for your life. Most of us often hesitate and involuntarily ask, "What is God's will for me in this situation?"

To experience God's guidance so that you can do His will requires a special relationship with your Redeemer. Within this fellowship you develop a sensitivity towards obedience. Every time you want to do something that is contrary to His will, a feeling of discomfort and guilt arises in your heart. Then you know without any doubt that you are acting in disobedience.

Living close to God so that you can clearly distinguish His will means that you should love His Word and study it, since in it you will find His revealed will for your life. It contains God's answers to your deepest human problems. An intimate knowledge of the holy Scriptures makes it easier to understand the principles of God's Kingdom as they apply to your personal life.

Continuously living in fellowship with Christ and in obedience to His Word ensures that you will be guided by the prompting of the Holy Spirit. Then you achieve that ideal situation to which a child of God aspires and longs for – that everything you are and do will be acceptable to God. Then you live within the framework of His advice and under His loving eye.

Loving Teacher, through fellowship with You and the knowledge of Your Word, I am deeply aware of Your will for my life and Your merciful guidance from day to day. *Amen.*

Vocation and Loyalty

"My food," said Jesus, "is to do the will of Him who sent Me and to finish His work."

~ John 4:34

People without purpose achieve little in life. To constructively pursue a particular purpose is the secret of a successful life, but only if the purpose is true to the most noble ideals of your heart.

Many people know that they will experience the joy of fulfilment and success only in the realization of that aim. Nevertheless, because this pursuit requires commitment and hard work, and possibly also great sacrifice, they satisfy themselves with second best. This does not happen because they are incompetent, but because they are too lazy to fulfill their calling in faithfulness.

In whichever part of society you move and work, you have a responsibility to God and to yourself to give only your best at all times. You dare not be satisfied with a second-rate life, but you should live with decisiveness to the maximum of your God-given abilities. This means that you will have an aim that is noble and large enough to lift you from mediocrity; an aim that will inspire and impel you to be and to do that which God has intended.

Your calling and duty to God are not foreign to the reality of life, but consists of a way of life that includes God in every thought and deed of your existence. Then He becomes your holy inspiration through Jesus Christ, and His will becomes your calling and mission in life. It guarantees a fulfillment and inner satisfaction that cannot be put into words.

Master, knowing and doing Your will gives me a positive calling and mission in life, and this gives sense and meaning to my life. *Amen.*

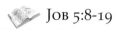

Can Discipline Bring Happiness?

Blessed is the man whom God corrects; so do not despise the discipline of the Almighty.

~ Job 5:17

Sometimes an idea may appear to be a contradiction that contains an untruth or an impossibility. Yet when we examine it carefully and test it against life, we find it to be true indeed.

Some people are an affliction to themselves. They complain continuously and the theme of all their conversations is their own disappointments, struggles and missed opportunities.

To avoid this crippling sickness of the spirit, you should make peace with yourself and remember that your attitude towards life is of the utmost importance. It may be that you are experiencing difficult times and that you feel that you are on your own, that even God has forgotten you.

If, however, you shake off your self-pity and ask what God wants to teach you in these circumstances, you will find perspective in the chaos.

Believe with conviction that God has a plan for your life and that everything that befalls you is part of this plan. When God corrects you, it always results in healing – if it is accepted with the right attitude.

Trust Him step by step and it will bring a feeling of safety and peace to you. In this way you become a co-worker of God in facilitating your own happiness in life. Then even when you are reprimanded and corrected, you can still experience joy.

God, even though I do not understand Your ways, help me through Your Holy Spirit to be a joyful person because I follow You. *Amen.*

God Can Do It

Jesus looked at them and said, "With man this is impossible, but with God all things are possible."

~ MATTHEW 19:26

Despite the disbelief and cynicism of modern times, God is still capable of miracles. Unfortunately many of the modern miracles are ascribed to coincidence. Many people pray when they face a crisis, but when the crisis is past and their worst fears have not materialized, they ignore the fact that they have prayed, or even feel embarrassed about it.

The evidence that God does answer prayer is overpowering. Many modern Christians can bear testimony of miracles that occurred in answer to prayer. Lives have been unrecognizably changed; illnesses have been miraculously cured; twisted human relationships have been restored.

Despite the miraculous power of prayer, God requires our co-operation for the answering of our prayers. God cannot solve your problem if you lay it before Him in prayer, but then take it back again. Hand the problem completely over to Him and do not try to solve it yourself. Let it rest there and allow God to handle it.

Do not despair. At the right time and in the right way God will answer and you will be amazed by the result. Then you will rejoice in the fact that you did not interfere. In this way we gradually learn obedience in prayer and God increasingly works His miracles in our lives.

Not my will, Master, but Your will be done in my life. I once again place my life completely in Your hands. *Amen.*

What You Are Meant to Be

What a wretched man I am! Who will rescue me from this body of death? Thanks be to God – through Jesus Christ our Lord!

~ ROMANS 7:24-25

There are many disciples who have become satisfied with substandard Christianity. Perhaps for some time they experienced a powerful Christian life but then the experience started to fade until only a memory remained. The glory of their faith deteriorated into something insignificant.

Nevertheless, even when their faith was ineffective, they knew instinctively that this was not God's will for them. God's will for His people is only the best. God wants to strengthen us so that we can live triumphantly and live a balanced and positive life.

God is willing to give us this and many other spiritual gifts from His treasury, if our commitment to Him is absolute.

God does not remove Himself from you. Your deep desire for spiritual growth is just an inspired restlessness that God gives. He is calling you back to Him, so that you can become what He meant for you to be.

You know what you can be through the power of Christ. God does not call you to an unfulfilled life. That is why He is calling you to renew your commitment today, so that you can regain the fullness of your faith. By doing that you will experience the glory of the power of the living Christ in your spirit and life.

O Master, through my total commitment to You, I rediscover the glory of my faith. Continue to guide me through Your Holy Spirit to a deeper life of complete commitment and obedience. *Amen.*

Gethsemane – Olive Press!

Then Jesus went with His disciples to a place called Gethsemane.
~ MATTHEW 26:36

The word "Gethsemane" is filled with a holy awareness. Even in the vocabulary of the faithless world, it is used to describe utmost anguish. When we enter this garden, we find ourselves on holy ground. Let us take off our shoes and bend our heads in deep adoration: Jesus, the Man of Sorrows was here.

Jesus came here to find strength and comfort in prayer. He prayed His High Priestly prayer for others. Then He prayed for Himself to be prepared for His sacrifice; to make the impossible possible; to bear the unbearable. Although Golgotha was the crucible of His physical suffering, Gethsemane was the crucible of His anguish. The message of Gethsemane is one of obedience to God's will.

It is a message for our times; a time in which licentiousness is called "freedom"; in which the word "obedience" has become a mockery of everything that is holy. Gethsemane speaks of absolute obedience. When Jesus taught His disciples how to pray, He taught them to say, "Your will be done!" In Gethsemane He demonstrates this to His disciples and to all people through the ages.

Christ embraced sinful humanity to save us from eternal death. However, He knew that this embrace had to conclude in His being forsaken by God. His sinless soul shrunk in this knowledge. We so easily sing, "Do only Your will, Lord, Your will with me." This is easy when we walk in sunshine, but when the dark shadows of Gethsemane close around us, what then?

Shepherd of my life, You suffered in Gethsemane so that I will never have to endure the same suffering. Thank You for that, Lord. *Amen.*

Quiet Time with God

Those who hope in the LORD will renew their strength. They will soar on wings like eagles; they will run and not grow weary, they will walk and not be faint.

~ Isaiah 40:31

In every conceivable level of life people have to take a breather from time to time in order to refresh themselves and to avoid burnout. The Christian worker also needs a respite from his labors if he wants to play an effective role in the service of his Master.

We read in the Bible how often Jesus isolated Himself from the masses so that He could be alone with His Father. It is much more necessary for us to spend time with our heavenly Father.

It is in these precious moments, when you spend quiet time with God in prayer, Bible study and meditation, that you will discover the benevolent work of the Holy Spirit in your life. He once again fills the empty reservoirs of your life so that you may be better equipped for service to the Master.

If you become aware that you are entering barren spots in your work, or if you know that your spiritual life is losing its sparkle, break away from all routine so that you can devote your entire being to becoming quiet in the presence of God.

Draw strength from the means of grace that He places at your disposal: Bible study, prayer, meditation, spiritual conversation, and so forth. Then return to the world, fresh and refreshed, bearing testimony of Him with the new strength and energy that you have drawn from the Source.

Lord, fill me with Your Spirit. I plead with You for comfort, strength and guidance – all to Your glory. *Amen.*

"Now" and "Then"

Now we see but a poor reflection as in a mirror; then we shall see face to face.

~ 1 CORINTHIANS 13:12

"Now" and "then" are two little words with profound meaning. They conjure images of glaring contrast. When we study them closely, we might discover the wisdom of some of the events in our lives. If we look ahead to "then", it might be easier for us to accept the "now" and to make peace with our circumstances.

While we are in this life "now", we are called upon to contend with many situations. For the moment, they look dark and problematic to us. Time and again things happen to us that we cannot understand, and these patches of shadow and trepidation can disturb and sour our happiness, as well as our fellowship with our Lord. But how blessed and happy will we be when we remember both sides of His promise: "now" is a mirror and a poor reflection, but "then" I will see face to face – in all the glory that God has prepared for His children.

Even if the image is now a poor reflection and lacks clarity, we have the glorious comfort that one day we will come face to face with our Lord. When we see Him then, we will discover how often His love and grace shielded us from disasters and dangers. I can know for certain that what we will experience "then" will be so much better than "now".

I thank You, my Lord and my God, that You have ordained my life in such a wonderful way and that Your love and grace guide me from day to day. With this blessed assurance I praise and glorify You. *Amen.*

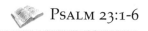

Rest Assured

He makes me lie down in green pastures, He leads me beside quiet waters.

~ PSALM 23:2

It is a blessed assurance to know that you are guided, from day to day, by an omnipotent and loving God. The Lord does not promise that all the pastures will always be green: sometimes they are barren and sterile and desolate. He has also not promised that the waters will always be tranquil: sometimes the waves break turbulently over us and the sky above is covered with ominous storm clouds. But the promise is that He, in His time, will bring us to green pastures and quiet waters. If we put our childlike and unconditional trust in Him, we may rest assured in the knowledge that He will guide us in our everyday lives.

We cannot be guided by someone who is far away and detached. We must stay close to the Shepherd in order to be guided by Him. Often we experience difficult and incomprehensible times, sometimes even storms and stress. However, if we stay close to the Lord, we will become aware of the tranquility surrounding us.

Regardless of how stormy and unpredictable the circumstances of our lives may be, our spirit will be quiet and peaceful if we allow Him to be our Governor. Then we can state with assurance, "He makes me lie down in green pastures, He leads me beside quiet waters." I know for certain: He is my Shepherd, my Friend, my Governor and my Guide. Praise the Lord, O my soul; all my inmost being, praise His Holy name!

Lord Jesus, Shepherd of my life, thank You that I may be safe and secure in Your care. Help me to accept Your guidance at all times. *Amen.*

Let Your Will Be Done

"Yet not My will, but Yours be done."

~ Luke 22:42

It is a privilege and an untold blessing to be able to say like our Master, "Yet not my will, but Yours be done." There are so many things that could happen to us, many disappointments come upon us unexpectedly, many ordeals cross our path in life. Often we cannot see the sense or meaning in them. Sometimes these are major troubles and sometimes minor irritations. However, we must confront and handle them all.

The Lord's love for us is endlessly tender and positive. His thoughts for us are always to our ultimate benefit. He wants us to trust where we cannot see. It is not a reckless leap in the dark, but sincere trust and faith that says, "I know for certain that God's will is best for me." This kind of faith leaves the choice up to God, with the words that His Son taught us, "Your will be done!" Then we will experience the blessed reality of His peace flowing through us and touching our innermost being, so that we will spread joy around us and to others.

Our faithful prayer every day must simply be, "Your will be done!" This is the only way to experience His peace here on earth. We must trust in Him through grace, until we meet Him face to face. Then we will understand how His perfect will functions: always for our own good and to our benefit, even though it does not immediately appear so. It is a wonderful privilege to be able to testify that our will is subject to God's perfect will.

Eternal God, thank You for sending Your Son to teach me what it means to let Your will be done. *Amen.*

Danger in Popularity

*No, in all these things we are more than conquerors through Him
who loved us.*

~ ROMANS 8:37

Paul maintains that one of the ways to experience peace with
God, is by realizing that, together with Christ, you are a conqueror. His words forcefully declare: God is for you! This turns
the faithful into more than conquerors. Paul turns this into a song
of triumph and a creed. He reveals our debt before God, Christ's
payment of that debt and our pardon through faith in Jesus Christ.
This is a positive point of departure: God is for me!

The children of the Lord desire to live a life of victory in which
sin and weakness are conquered. But all too often we have to
confess with Paul, "When I want to do good evil is right there with
me" (see Rom. 7:21). Then we humbly confess to God that we are
not conquerors, but that our circumstances have conquered us.

That is not what the Master wants for His followers. He desires
that we live a life of victory and triumph in everything. His Word
declares that it is through Him who loves us that we not only
become conquerors, but more than conquerors!

To experience this wondrous promise fully, we must meet with
Him every day to receive new strength from Him. We will never be
denied that. Whatever happens, whatever afflictions and problems
may surface, you must remember that "in all things" He grants
us victory. Then we will be overcomers through the strength of
Somebody who loves us and who always fulfills His promises.

I praise and thank You, Lord my Savior, that in Your strength I may be
a conqueror. Let me never live as though I am conquered. *Amen.*

What's the Purpose of Life

Knowledge puffs up, but love builds up.

~ 1 Corinthians 8:1

Love ... does not boast.

~ 1 Corinthians 13:4

Time and again Paul reminded the Corinthians that their knowledge drove them to boasting and that is a negative form of love which we call self-love.

True love is selfless. It would rather confess unworthiness than boast of its own achievements. Some people give their love as though they were bestowing an honor on the receiver. That is not love; that is conceit. The one who truly loves cannot stop marveling at the fact that there is someone who loves him. Love is kept humble in the knowledge that it could never make a sufficiently worthy sacrifice for the one he loves.

This also applies to our spiritual life. We dare not accept God's love as a matter of course as though we deserved it. Such pride robs us of the blessing and spiritual growth that God has in mind for us. If people's knowledge of the Scriptures drives them to arrogance, then they are studying the Bible in vain. If we pray to be seen and heard by people, the petticoat of our arrogance is showing. If we go to church for any other personal motive than to glorify God, our church-attendance will bring us no blessing.

Spirit of Love, keep me humble in my love, so that it does not become the cause of pride and arrogance. *Amen.*

Christ of Today

I have learned to be content whatever the circumstances.

~ PHILIPPIANS 4:11

The Greek word for *perseveres* can also be translated as "endure" or "bear". The spirit does not remain passive and endure things without being moved. It is the characteristic of a great spirit to endure adversity and conquer. Your only support in this victory is love.

George Matheson, the author of a number of famous hymns, lost his sight and also experienced disappointment in love. In one of his prayers, he writes that he prays to accept God's will, not only in silent surrender, but with holy joy; not only with the absence of a complaint, but with a song of praise. Love can endure anything, not with passive sullenness, but with triumphant tolerance because God is Love and the Father's hand will never be responsible for a single tear that falls from the eye of His child.

Paul accepts the Philippians' contribution to support him financially because they gave in the spirit of love and because he sees God's care in it. However, he has learnt to be content whatever the circumstances. That was because he experienced God's love in his life and that enabled him to endure all things.

We must trust in God and He will provide for all our needs in a way that He knows is best. We only need to learn to persevere in love, regardless of what may cross our path.

Holy God, let me accept Your will in joyous obedience and not with muttering dissatisfaction. *Amen.*

A Time to Speak

"As the Father has loved Me, so have I loved you. Now remain in My love."

~ JOHN 15:9

It is a disturbing thought that you could lose your awareness of the love the Master has for you. It is a scriptural truth that the Master loves His disciples, but how often do you wake up in the morning and thank Him for that love by telling Him how much you love Him? It is an inspiration for the day to wake up and profess, "I sincerely love You, O Lord!"

The living Christ promised that when you realize your dependence on Him, you would be able to do things that are simply beyond your ability. You can never realize your full potential before you are united with Him in love. He reminds you that, without Him, you can do nothing, but by remaining in Him, your horizons are broadened and your strength is increased.

It is a serious tragedy that many Christians attempt to serve the Lord without the indispensable love that they should have for Him. They are active in Christian service, but the inspiration of the love for God and their fellow man is still lacking. The Master has harsh words for these people. He says that anyone that does not remain in Him, will be separated from Him. He does not bring about the separation; they do so themselves through their lack of love.

Develop an ever-increasing love for Jesus Christ so that you will be drawn closer to Him and become aware of His living presence.

Savior and Master, let me never lose the awareness of Your love, but may it always remain fresh and sparkling. *Amen.*

The Art of Living

"As a shepherd seeks out his flock on the day he is among his scattered sheep, so will I seek out My sheep and deliver them from all the places where they were scattered on a cloudy and dark day."
~ EZEKIEL 34:12 (NKJV)

When watching people's behavior patterns, you will find many instances where, in some way, they act like sheep. In the same way that sheep sometimes follow one another, so people are inclined to follow the masses or public opinion.

Just like sheep huddle together, so people look for comfort and safety in a time of crisis. In the same way that a sudden shock causes sheep to scatter, so people are driven apart in circumstances of shock and confusion. This kind of behavior does not contribute to a stable lifestyle. The uncertainty leads to insecurity.

Many people will conclude that that is the way they were created and there is nothing they can do about it. That is not true. You don't have to maintain an unstable way of life. This certainly is not the life that Jesus Christ is offering you. This is also not why He came to dwell with us.

He is with you in every situation of life through the spirit of the living Christ to protect you. He is omniscient, omnipotent and all-knowing – a Father who watches over His children. He is always there, waiting for you to open the door of your life for Him, so that He can take over and lead you along His perfect way (see Rev. 3:20). At all times keep contact with the Master and you will be guaranteed a life of tranquility and peace of mind.

Lord, with You I shelter, because You watch over me always and lead me along Your perfect way. *Amen.*

God Has a Plan for You

Do not therefore be grieved or angry with yourselves because you sold me here; for God sent me before you to preserve life.

~ GENESIS 45:5 (NKJV)

It is often difficult to understand or to accept that God is busy fulfilling His plan in your life, especially when you are going through difficult or taxing times. When Joseph was sold into slavery, when an unscrupulous woman robbed him of his freedom, and when his friends forgot about him, it seemed unlikely that he would discern the hand of God in all those happenings. Nevertheless when, after many years, he looked back upon the road he had traveled, he did see the hand of God in his life.

If you are in deep waters of affliction right now, if you are experiencing problems and sorrow – remember that it might be part of God's tapestry. He determines the pattern of your life. In your darkest hour, hold on steadfastly to the belief that, in spite of the appearance of things, God is still in control.

Don't ever, in your imperfect and negative mind, confuse that which seems like an inevitable disaster to you, with the divine will of God. Rather discover that God can give purpose and meaning to Joseph's slavery, Moses' depression, Jeremiah's lamentations – and yes, even to Jesus' death on the cross. Life's darkest moments can be a testimony of God's perfect purpose for your life.

No matter how difficult your circumstances might be, you have to hold on to the assurance that God is busy working out His perfect plan for your life.

Faithful Guide, I will trust You in every predicament. I will hold on to You through every trouble. *Amen.*

You Are God's Child!

Behold what manner of love the Father has bestowed on us, that we should be called children of God!

~ 1 John 3:1 (NKJV)

When the truth of this Scripture verse becomes a personal experience in your life, a transformation occurs which brings meaning and glory into your daily life.

Perhaps you are feeling totally alone and lonely at this moment. You approach the future without any self-confidence and you make decisions about which you are completely unsure. Your salvation through Jesus Christ needs to transform this negative attitude into a positive approach to life. Because, by grace, you now call God your Father, and because you love and obey Him, it is your responsibility to make your life what God intended it to be. He requires of you total commitment so that His glory may be reflected in your life.

If the Lord's will is revealed through your life, a very intimate bond will develop between you and Him. You will have the glorious assurance that He is really your Father and that you are irrevocably His child. This intimate relationship makes it so much easier to be obedient to the Father. The closer you live to Him, the more sensitive you become to what He expects from you.

Therefore, live to strengthen these close ties with your heavenly Father. Do this through commitment and obedience. Thus the grace of God is established in your life every day, to His glory and honor and to your immeasurable benefit and joy.

Thank You, Lord Jesus, for the joy of life. I want to live my life in the fullness of all You intended for me. *Amen.*

God Loves You

"We know that all things work together for good to those who love God, to those who are called according to His purpose."

~ ROMANS 8:28 (NKJV)

Often in the face of tribulation and setbacks people cannot understand why such things happened to them. In many cases God is blamed and called to justice. Every setback in life is then ascribed to Him.

One of the basic components of Christianity is steadfast faith in the love of God. This love has been proven undeniably in the gift of His Son to a lost world. That is why, in every situation of life, you need to put your trust in the wisdom and goodness of a loving Father. His knowledge spans your whole life, temporal and eternal – not only the temporal and predictable present.

No person can fully comprehend the magnitude of God's deed of love as expressed on the cross on Golgotha. The extent of His love towards sinners is unfathomable and incomprehensible. But without the gruesome events at the scene of the cross, we would never have shared in God's pure love, and we would never have experienced redemption and deliverance. Through the death and resurrection of Jesus Christ, God has demonstrated His love to us in a crystal clear manner.

When you find yourself facing problems or setbacks, remember that your times and fate are in God's almighty hands. Because of His great love for you, everything that happens to you in life has a purpose. In His own time it will be revealed to you. Your duty is to believe in God under all circumstances, to trust and obey Him.

Jesus, in the darkest moments I will have steadfast faith in You. *Amen.*

Your Life Is in Loving Hands

As for me, I trust in You, O Lord; I say, "You are my God." My times are in Your hand.

~ Psalm 31:14-15 (nkjv)

Some people are more sensitive to certain situations than others. They examine a situation and then act immediately. Others need more time to consider the circumstances before they decide on any plan of action. This is the case in every area of life, and the spiritual life is no exception.

There are people whose spiritual intuition is very sensitive, thus enabling them to distinguish the truth and to act on it at once. Others, gradually come to an understanding of the truth, but their reaction to it is no less sincere.

It is important to remember that your times are being determined by God's perfect timing. If you find it very natural to establish God's will, then you need to make sure that you don't unconsciously move faster than God intended you to. If you are more gradual in establishing God's will for your life, then you must watch that it doesn't become a smoke-screen for laziness or lethargy.

It is possible to be in perfect harmony with God's timing for your life. You will receive proof of this when you place your times in His hand, because His timing is always perfect. If you trust God unconditionally, there will be order in your life, instead of chaos.

That is why it is so important to spend time with God in prayer as it will cause the tempo of your life to come into perfect harmony with God's timing.

Father, please guide me so that I will be in perfect harmony with Your timing for my life. *Amen.*

December

The Gospel in a Nutshell

"For God so loved the world that He gave His one and only Son, that whoever believes in Him shall not perish but have eternal life."

~ JOHN 3:16

Jesus Christ had an exceptional ability to express the gospel in the simplest terms possible so that even the simplest person could understand it, and yet, the profound nature of the message was never lost. The main topic of His message was always the eternal and constant love of God: God is love. Whoever lives in love lives in God, and God in him (1 John. 4:16).

In order to be allowed to share in this love, we must first open our hearts to Him, "If anyone loves Me, he will obey My teaching. My Father will love him, and we will come to him and make our home with him" (John 14:23). Love for God presupposes obedience to Him, and allows His Spirit to reign over each aspect of your life and to be central to your thoughts and deeds.

To declare, "God is love!" is much more than a simple, and possibly sentimental, confession of faith: it requires a particular way of life which has to be a confirmation of that unspoken faith in the immeasurable love of God that was confirmed by the coming of Jesus Christ.

Consequently we must once again ponder the birth of our Savior during every Advent-time; we must purify our festivities so that it will truly be a Christ-feast, and we must once again devote ourselves to the Child of Bethlehem.

Holy Father, I want to joyfully experience this Christ-feast in the knowledge that You are my Savior and Redeemer. May this impart a special character to my Christmas joy. *Amen.*

Close to God through Jesus Christ

You who once were far away have been brought near through the blood of Christ.

~ EPHESIANS 2:13

Christmastime is Advent-time! The term "advent" derives from the Latin word *adventuske*, which means "arrival" or "appearance". In the terminology of the church it is used to refer to the four weeks preceding Christmas: the joyous time when we commemorate the coming of Christ to this world of humanity.

The Light Christ became "flesh", but without sin. We are also flesh, but in our case the word carries the blemish of our "sinful nature". From the Word – and from experience – we know that the flesh is in a constant battle with the Spirit. Paul says in Romans 8:7 that the mind set on the flesh is hostile to God.

For Christ, however, the blemish of sin falls away. As a human being He was without sin, but still human and in the tarnished form of a servant. He became our equal in everything except in sin. This is the glorious message of Christmas: Immanuel! God with us! God visits man personally. He descended from heaven in the form of His Son to prepare the way for humankind to be restored in the favour of the Father. He came to be the Redeemer of a lost world.

First it was God above, *God far from us*, then it became, in Christ, *God with us*, and then, through the Holy Spirit, *God in us.*

May the time of Advent truly be a feast of Christ for you.

Heavenly Father, my mind reels before the mystery of the incarnation in the flesh of Your Son, my Savior, Jesus Christ. *Amen.*

The Promise of New Life

A shoot will come up from the stump of Jesse; from his roots a Branch will bear fruit.

~ ISAIAH 11:1

A long time ago the royal house of David stood in the center of the entire country like a proud tree-trunk with a high top. But all this beauty was felled in the fullness of time. The house of David was dilapidated and its glory had waned. All that remained was to be found in Mary, in whose veins the ancient, noble blood still flowed, but who was reduced to such a state of humiliation in the world that she could not believe that God would esteem her enough to make her the mother of His Son.

And yet, through God's omnipotence and mercy, a shoot came up from the meager remains of the once powerful house of David. This "shoot" that Isaiah prophesies of is none other than Jesus Christ. This humble shoot became an ineradicable and mighty trunk which spread out its branches to the ends of the earth. The Child in the manger grew up to become the way, the truth and the life. He brandishes the scepter over the entire earth and His reign knows no bounds.

With the approaching Christ-feast we must once again assess our personal relationship with Christ and confess our sins before the Lord. From the stump of Jesse He brought forth new life, a new dispensation, a new period of spiritual growth for those who had slid back – He who was seated on the throne said, "I am making everything new!" (Rev. 21:5).

Lord God, in these days bring forth new life from the half-withered stump of my spiritual life, to Your glory. *Amen.*

Live Like Royal Children

For you did not receive a spirit that makes you a slave again to fear, but you received the Spirit of sonship. And by Him we cry, "Abba, Father."

~ ROMANS 8:15

There is a world of difference between confessing that you are a child of God and living a life as a child of God. Many people profess faith and yet live in constant fear.

They suffer from a destructive sense of inferiority and they are unable to deal with life's problems. There is such a gap between what they should be and what they really are that they tend to become despondent and abandon their principles.

When God called you to become His child and when you reacted to His call with joy, a new life began for you. Your sins were forgiven and since then you have stood in a new relationship to the King. Through His grace you become part of His kingdom. Because His Spirit now lives and works in you, your behavior towards people and your total way of life has been revolutionized.

The Advent-time reminds you once again that you should face life with conviction and without fear. Your Father is the King of all kings. Knowing that He loves you and cares about you should give you inner peace.

The steadfast faith that He will guide you safely if you obey Him and return His love should be your comfort in life. Through Jesus Christ He invites you to call Him "Father".

Father, thank You for the indescribable grace of being allowed to talk to You, which Jesus Christ obtained for me. *Amen.*

Your Salvation Is Here!

The LORD has made proclamation to the ends of the earth: "Say to the Daughter of Zion, 'See, your Savior comes!'"

~ ISAIAH 62:11

During the Advent-time we commemorate the coming of Christ. However, we must never forget about the coming of Christ to our souls and into our hearts. His appearance in the flesh was not everything. We must never be content simply to testify that He came to take the curse of our sins upon Himself as Lamb of God. It is a glorious testimony, but it means nothing if we don't personally share in the salvation. Then it is like a Christmas carol sung out of tune or a feast around us, but never inside us.

If we want to experience the joy of Christmas in the true sense of the word, Christ has to arrive in and inhabit our hearts with His salvation and peace. Christ's coming to the world is the objective event; His coming to my heart, the subjective. We thank God that His coming can be a subjective reality in the heart and life of everyone who believes in Him.

He came to find and redeem what was lost, and He gave everyone who accepted Him the right to become a child of God (see John 1:12). Do you believe this? Do you believe that He comes to where you stand, worried and overwhelmed by your sin? He comes to you with His hands filled with grace and forgiveness and blessings; He comes to convert your sadness into joy. Christmas is essentially a feast of salvation, because your Savior came!

Jesus, my Savior, thank You that I may relive the all-surpassing joy and happiness of someone who has been redeemed. *Amen.*

Our Fears Allayed by a Child

The angel said to her, "Do not be afraid, Mary, you have found favor with God."

~ LUKE 1:30

With this message, God wants to free Mary – and through her all of humanity – from fear, and replace this fear with exultant joy. That is why the angel said on that first Christmas Eve, "Do not be afraid. I bring you good news of great joy" (Luke 2:10).

This world has become a maze of fear. And it all began with the Fall when Adam said, "I was afraid ... so I hid" (Gen. 3:10). And on the day of judgment sinners will still plead in a last, terrified prayer meeting "They will say to the mountains, 'Fall on us!' and to the hills,' 'Cover us!'" (Luke 23:30).

Fear is not merely a figment of man's imagination. From the cradle to the grave it remains a terrible presence. We fear the unknown as a child fears the dark. We fear for our health, for loneliness, for old age, and then for that fear of all fears: death. Everywhere and in everyone there is a constant fear for thousands of threatening things.

At Christmastime God once again sends His messenger to bring us tidings of great joy: the love of God expels all fear because the source of fear, namely sin, was conquered by Jesus at Bethlehem. In each terrifying storm of life He is with us to tell us, "Don't be afraid. Immanuel, I am with you!"

Shepherd of my life, even though I walk through the valley of the shadow of death, I will not be afraid, because You are with me. *Amen.*

Christmas: Feast of the Child

She gave birth to her firstborn, a Son. She wrapped him in cloths and placed Him in a manger, because there was no room for them in the inn.

~ LUKE 2:7

At Christmastime we all become children once again. In our hearts we relive the timeless adventure of unquestioned faith, where all things are immediately possible and where the child Jesus is in the center of everything.

For a short time, as in a dream, we leave our predictable way of life and walk the path of rich imagination, of amazement and exciting joy, while we freely rejoice in the immeasurable love of God. Even the staunchest spiritual realist experiences stirrings in his heart upon hearing the age-old tale, almost smelling the fragrances of incense and myrrh.

On the other hand, Christmastime is also as real as the gifts that we give and receive; as real as the candles we light and the lights that charm us; as real as the songs that we hear everywhere during this wonderful time. In experiencing the mystery surrounding Christmas, as well as the concrete reality thereof, we are all touched by the wonder of God's love – and all our dreams of peace and joy are rekindled.

If we have forgotten how to experience Christmas like a child, with joyful and excited expectation, we have to learn anew to discover the enchantment of Christmas.

I thank You, Lord Jesus, that I may experience the remembrance of Your birth like a child and that I can therefore see the gates of Your kingdom open before me. *Amen.*

Christmas: Feast for the Elderly

Moved by the Spirit, he went into the temple courts. When the parents brought in the child Jesus to do for him what the custom of the Law required, Simeon took Him in his arms and praised God.

~ LUKE 2:27-28

The pious and just Simeon was already an old man when he held the Messiah in his arms. God blessed him with the sight of the Messiah because he had been faithful in his meetings with God. Because he was present in the temple, he could take the Christ-child in his arms. In so doing Simeon received God's wonderful gift and by implication also accepted Christ as his Savior and Redeemer.

In old age you and I should also learn to wait for God, to listen to His voice, so that we too can receive His wonderful gifts. You must know that Christ was also born for you. That is what faith is – to see the invisible every Christmas. This is the type of faith that will compel you, like Simeon, to proclaim the message of Christ with jubilation in your old age, "A light for revelation to the Gentiles" (Luke 2:32).

This is the miracle that God works with Christmas: He puts the Child of His love in your arms. And with this you receive His love, His salvation, His blood, His body, everything that is necessary for your redemption. What an incomprehensible gift this is. But with Christmas we also have to do something from our side. We must embrace Jesus and accept Him, just as Simeon took the Child in His arms.

Help me, O Child of Bethlehem, to take You in my arms and heart as Simeon did, so that Christmas can become a Christ-feast to me. *Amen.*

Advent-Time

"Behold, I am coming soon!"

~ REVELATION 22:7

The first Advent was when Jesus came to the earth in the flesh as mankind's Savior. He descended from the glory of heaven to the indignity of the manger and the cross. His earthly path would pass through great depths so that He could elevate a lost humanity to the heights of salvation as His glorified children.

His work, which began in humility during the first Christmas Eve, will be completed with His glorious Second Coming to harvest the crop. It will be a triumphant coming in majesty and honor. It will be the day of all days, the great Advent awaited in supplication by the true congregation of Christ. At Christmastime we hear His voice saying, "Yes, I am coming soon." To which we answer with a deep yearning, "Amen. Come, Lord Jesus" (Rev. 22:20).

There are four Advent-times in your life: the coming of Christ in the flesh to earn redemption for you; a coming in the Spirit to give you a personal share in His redemption; a coming in your death to transfer you from the sphere of time into eternity; and finally Christ's Second Coming in glory to conclude the history of mankind, which will be followed by eternal life.

Hence, Christmastime is rich in divine consolation. We see Christ always and everywhere: in His struggle to save you; in your heart where His grace worked; in your hour of dying that gives you victory in Christ; and any moment in the Second Coming of the Savior in glory and majesty.

I praise and thank You, holy Master, for the great blessing of Advent. Make me ever ready for Your Second Coming. *Amen.*

Don't Stop at the Stars

After Jesus was born in Bethlehem ... Magi from the east came to Jerusalem.

~ MATTHEW 2:1

The Magi persevered in their search for the King whose star they saw. God called them in a special way and in terms of what they knew: through the appearance of a star. They were, after all, astrologers, magi, learned priests of their people. Their fatherland was Mesopotamia, situated between the Euphrates and the Tigris; the old land of paradise from which Adam and Eve were expelled. Now they are following the star to worship and bring homage to the second Adam, Jesus the Messiah.

To them the star was the beginning of the light, because they were still children of darkness. In obedience they followed the star and God prepared for them a vision of what was previously unseen by human eyes, unheard by human ears and unknown to the heart of man.

The star enchanted them so that they could find the Child. God indeed calls and searches in many ways: He calls the wise men with a star; He calls the shepherds with heavenly choirs. God's love for sinners gives us stars to guide us and we thank God for these stars.

But we may not remain standing in amazement before these stars. They are only the beginning of the path of salvation. We must proceed from the star to the Word; from the word of God in nature to the Word of God in Scripture.

Bethlehem star, please guide me also to the Jesus-child! *Amen.*

From the Star to the Word

Your word is a lamp to my feet and a light for my path.

~ PSALM 119:105

The wise men were initially guided by a star, but when they arrived in Jerusalem, the Word of God lighted their path to Christ. In Jerusalem everyone was expecting a King, but they did not know where to find Him. The teachers of the law were reflecting on the meaning of the Word of God.

We find the wise men with their star but without a Book, and the people of Israel with the Word but without their King – a King without an address. So they returned to the Word with its irrefutable authority. In Micah 5:2 this particular prophecy is presented, "But you, Bethlehem Ephrathah, though you are small among the clans of Judah, out of you will come for Me One who will be ruler over Israel." To Bethlehem then – to the small city of great things.

The star is therefore subservient to the Word. When the gilt is gone; the truth and reality is still there in the Word. Hence the final journey to Bethlehem is always a journey based on the Word of God. We love the stars and it is hard to part with them – but we must! We need the Scriptures: the, at times, disillusioning, provocative, tormenting, but always purely prophetic Scriptures.

The stars without the Scriptures leave us with an insatiable longing for eternity *and* without the correct address of our King. The Word guides us to the true gold-reef, to Bethlehem, to the stable, the manger and the King.

Jesus of Bethlehem, keep me from becoming so enchanted by the stars that I lose the address of the Child. *Amen.*

Give this Christmas

Then they opened their treasures and presented Him with gifts of gold and of incense and of myrrh.

~ MATTHEW 2:11

The Magi from the east finally understood the true meaning of Christmas: to give. God gave with Christmas: He gave His best, His most valuable, His Son. He gave out of love (see John 3:16). And the Child of Bethlehem also gave: He gave Himself; He continued giving even in His death on the cross.

You must first learn to forget what you did for others in order to remember what others did for you out of love. You must learn to forget what you expect from others and rather ask what you can do for them. For once you have to rid yourself of the idea that the world owes you something, and start to think about what you owe the world. You must be able to relegate your demands to the background and to place your responsibilities prominently on the foreground.

You must discover that your fellow man is as sincere as you are and be able to see the heart hidden behind the exterior – a heart that yearns for love, friendship and compassion. You must be able to close your book of charges and complaints against life and look around you to find places where you can sow seeds of happiness and love.

If you are willing to do these things, even if only for one day, then you have brought *your* gold, incense and myrrh. Only then can you truly celebrate the Christ-feast.

Loving Master, I begin this Advent-time by renewing my commitment to You, so that You can use me as and when You please. *Amen.*

Attitudes of the Christ-Feast

Then Herod called the Magi secretly and found out from them the exact time the star had appeared.

~ Matthew 2:7

Christmas is first and foremost an attitude of the heart. There are many people who share in Herod's attitude. He is the prototype of those people who live in sin and in enmity with God; who want to banish Christ from their lives. They hide their disapproval behind a mask of hypocrisy.

They also want to go to worship the Child. They also celebrate the Christ-feast, but in reality their hearts do not belong to Him. Their motives are impure as they search for the Child. They want to use religion to advance their careers and to keep the crown on their own heads.

Advent proclaims the following message: Christ can be found in Bethlehem, but only by those who have the right attitude in their hearts and whose worship is true in spirit.

This is the attitude of the wise men. They came from a distant land, in the same way that we have to come from the distant land of sin as lost sons and daughters. They persisted in their search and did not allow anything to distract them from their purpose.

Jesus Himself promised that those who seek Him will find Him. The wise men stipulated no conditions. They expected a palace and a golden cradle – what they found was a stable and a manger. Like them, everyone who seeks can experience the joy of finding what God intended for each of us during this Christmastime.

I thank You, O Holy Spirit, that I found the Child of Bethlehem, my Savior and Redeemer. *Amen.*

Christmas and Children

"I tell you the truth, unless you change and become like little children, you will never enter the kingdom of heaven."

~ MATTHEW 18:3

Christmas is the pre-eminent feast of the family and the child. It is difficult to express the excitement and expectations in the heart of a child during Christmas. Grown-ups are different: we are mostly negative – we expect to fail, and then we do fail; we expect to be unhappy, and then we are; we always anticipate the worst, and then it happens.

Advent is a time for recovering the lost glory of our faith in life and eternity. It is a time to believe that God can work the miracle once again: that Christ can be born again in our lives and thoughts. It is a time to devote ourselves anew to God and to rejoice in the fact that His Spirit wants to live in us.

Christmas allows us to obtain new insights into the place of the child in the family. On that first Christmas Eve a Child was at the center of that holy tableau. Similarly, Jesus taught us that the child is at the core of the family. We are not allowed to remove the child from the center simply because we have other interests and responsibilities.

The Christ-feast repeatedly brings us back to the secret of true happiness and joy: mother, father, child – and God! May Christmas lead us to a renewed resolution to maintain the sanctity of the family. Then Christmas will bring you the happiness and peace of family bliss.

We praise You, Lord Jesus, for bestowing a new and particular significance on family. *Amen.*

How Will You Prepare for the Feast?

To us a Child is born, to us a Son is given, and the government will be on His shoulders. And He will be called Wonderful Counselor, Mighty God, Everlasting Father, Prince of Peace.

~ ISAIAH 9:6

During this time of the year, especially in the Western world, people are preparing for the "holiday season". It is a time when things in the academic and business world are gradually coming to a standstill. Christmas is approaching. Families get involved in spending sprees and there is the prospect of pleasure, joy and merry-making on a large scale.

We do not want to condemn such activities at all. We must just not forget that it is also the blessed time of Advent. It is a time in which to prepare ourselves, not for parties or last-minute shopping expeditions, but to celebrate. Because the Savior of the world was born and we want to celebrate it with joy, and with holy zeal.

We must reflect on the reason of His coming to this sin-drenched world. We must once again examine our spiritual lives, humbly standing before God, asking Him to make us worthy, through the work of His Holy Spirit, to celebrate this feast.

It is an overwhelming thought that God bent down and took it upon Himself to come and live amongst us as a Man. May it be the foremost thought in your heart and in your celebrations during the days of Advent.

Holy Jesus, prepare our hearts so that we may celebrate Christmas in a worthy manner. *Amen.*

The Sun Shines, but I Am Blind

"For you who revere My name, the sun of righteousness will rise with healing in its wings."

~ MALACHI 4:2

The sun shines in glory and majesty, high in the firmament, far and inaccessible in its reign. The eye cannot look at it directly without being blinded. As the sun is, so is our God. Elevated high above the earthly turmoil, He reigns over the entire world.

Even though I try to shield my eyes from His splendor, He remains there. Like the sun that brings light, warmth and growth with its comforting rays, God also comes to us in the Advent-time. But unlike the sun, God is also still close to us in spite of His untouchable splendor.

We cannot go to the sun, but the sun can reach down to us. God sends His light to illuminate our dark minds, warm our cold hearts and turn the night of our sins into the day of His grace. In Jesus Christ the Sun of justice descends upon us. God from God, Light from Light.

Zechariah sings the praise of the Child of Bethlehem by describing Him as the rising light that visits us to shine on those who are overwhelmed by darkness and the shadow of death. So many are lost in the dark maze of sin. The sun shines, but they are blind. But, says Malachi, there is healing in His rays. He takes our ailments upon Him and carries the burden of our grief.

After Christmas, we have to return to everyday life and we must continue to carry the light we receive from Him into a dark world.

Sun of Justice, thank You for reminding us in this Advent-time that we have a calling to be the bearers of light in this world. *Amen.*

The Core Truth of the Christ-Feast

This is how God showed His love among us: He sent His one and only Son into the world that we might live through Him.

~ 1 John 4:9

The most astonishing truth about Christmas is that God loves us. God is love and He loves us with a love that gives only the best and most valuable – as with Christmas when He gave us His Son. He also loves us with a love that forgives and cares. We dare not leave such love unanswered.

"Since God so loved us, we also ought to love one another," says the apostle John (1 John 4:11). Love must triumph in our everyday lives: in our marriages, in our homes and in our relationships – not only with words, but with deeds of love.

However, it is also true that Christ did not remain in the manger; He grew to become a Man of sorrow in Gethsemane and at Golgotha. Therefore we, as His followers, may not remain infants in faith or become stuck in a faith centered only on the stable. We must grow to spiritual maturity.

Like the shepherds, we must also be loving witnesses and praise God for everything we have heard and seen. We must proclaim the wonder of love: redemption, grace and peace.

The gate is always open to everyone who wants to enter – this is the love-truth of Christmas.

Loving Father, thank You for revealing Yourself and the fullness of Your love to sinners like us at Christmastime. *Amen.*

Meditation for Christmas

The Word became flesh and made His dwelling among us. We have seen His glory, the glory of the One and Only, who came from the Father, full of grace and truth.

~ JOHN 1:14

It is every Christian's calling and duty to approach Christmas with the right attitude. Commit to placing Christ at the center of your celebrations. Commit to giving Him the place of honor in your heart during this time.

Refuse to be a part of the mad rush and the excessive wastage that occurs close to Christmas. Do not become so absorbed in Christmas decorations that the stable, the crib, and especially the Child, are lost. Let us pray for the simplicity of the shepherds so that we can arrive at the core of Christmas: the Christ Child.

Ensure that Christmas remains a family celebration. Do not go and search for Christmas joy in the world outside, but find it in the warmth and intimacy of the family: father, mother and children, as it was on the first night around the manger. Ensure that Christ is always welcome in your home during Christmas by avoiding superficial pleasure, worldly fun and worldly parties.

Remember that death lurks on the roads, especially at this time of the year. Christ came to bring life – let us drive responsibly like His children would.

Do everything in your power to instill the right approach to Christmas in your children. When you are no longer here, these will be their most precious memories.

Jesus of Bethlehem, help me approach Christmas in a pure way, through the work of the Holy Spirit in my life. *Amen.*

Come, Lord Jesus!

She gave birth to her firstborn, a Son. She wrapped Him in cloths and placed Him in a manger, because there was no room for them in the inn.

~ LUKE 2:7

The wonder and mystery of Christmas has a profound influence on Christians around the world.

For many people, however, Christmas has no spiritual meaning. The entertainment world emphasizes pleasure and superficial enjoyment so much that the deeper meaning of this sacred time is largely overshadowed. To a large percentage of people Father Christmas is of greater importance than the Christ Child.

When Jesus was born in Bethlehem, He came to a world that was similar to the world we live in today. People were obsessed with themselves and their own interests. There was no room in their lives for Jesus Christ.

Yet history has shown what an enormous impression Christ has made on the world and on the lives of millions of people. When you enjoy the celebrations and festivities on Christmas day, do not refuse the living Christ access to your life. Open your heart and life to Him and you will experience the fullness and joy which Christmas holds.

Not making room for Christ at this time, is to make a mockery of what God intended Christmas to be.

Child of Bethlehem, Redeemer and Savior, I open my entire life to You once again and I invite You to move into my life permanently. *Amen.*

Tender Comfort at Advent-Time

When anxiety was great within me, Your consolation brought joy to my soul.

~ PSALM 94:19

There is unfortunately a lot of sorrow surrounding Christmas-time: some people are gravely ill; others have to come to terms with the effects of old age; for others Christmas will never be the same again because the family circle has disintegrated irreparably through separation or death. There is much grief because death performs its grim task mercilessly on our roads – particularly during this period.

There are parents who long painfully for their children who will not be home for Christmas because they have emigrated, or live too far away to be able to be home for Christmas, or because estrangement has set in, threatening to break the hearts of parents.

There are countless reasons why these days hold little joy for many. One of the most terrible is the loneliness of those who will miss a loved one this Christmas due to death. Who can truly express or comprehend this longing?

The Child of Bethlehem had to travel these dark roads Himself as a man on earth, and therefore He is one with us in our grief and pain. He too had to sob for His loneliness at one time. He cares for you and He understands. He is mighty to touch your heart with consolation. Remain close to Him and you will experience the joy of victory, because His love will pull you through.

God of the lonely and sorrowful, thank You for comforting us. *Amen.*

The Sign of God's Love

"This will be a sign to you: You will find a Baby wrapped in cloths and lying in a manger."

~ LUKE 2:12

As with the arrival of a baby in a family, thousands of people yearned for the coming of the Child of Bethlehem: the prophets and the Old Testament believers; His parents and the devout people of His time – Simeon and Anna; Zechariah and Elizabeth. Similarly we look forward to the annual commemoration of His coming with the honest prayer, "Grant us in these days a true Christ-feast!"

God speaks to man in a thousand voices: on Sinai the thunder roars; in Sodom and Gomorrah God speaks with fire and brimstone; in the life of Job God speaks through loss, illness and tribulations. But at Christmas God speaks through a Child who beckons us back to the heart of God from a mother's arms and from a manger. God becomes a child and speaks to us in a language everyone can understand.

The Child of Bethlehem speaks to us about God's immeasurable love, and tells us exactly how much God loves the world! Will this love not compel us to love our children more and to desire their salvation? Having children always places before us a choice: to love and comfort them, or to neglect and sadden them. The Child of Bethlehem puts before us the same choice: will we love Him or will we sadden Him?

Holy Father, I gratefully accept Your miracle and my heart chooses You as King for all eternity! *Amen.*

The World's Need

Now these three remain: faith, hope and love. But the greatest of these is love.

~ 1 Corinthians 13:13

The state of the world is a cause for concern. Constant strife, war, terrorism and hatred amongst people are flooding the world like an ominous wave. Many plans are made to ensure people's safety, although these can cause more distrust and disunity.

God's solution, although deemed impractical, idealistic and simplistic, is clear: you must love God above all and love your fellow man as you love yourself. There is no command from God that is more important than this.

If humankind could just learn to love, the adversity of the world would start disappearing and a solution to problems would be closer. Most people accept this truth, yet they refuse to use it in practice because it demands faith, courage and sacrifice. If contemporary Christians would live and preach the gospel, it would be the biggest single contribution to peace on earth.

Love is not only an emotional or sentimental approach to problems. To really love means to impress God's stamp on every situation where injustice, hatred, bitterness and other negative and sinful powers fester unchecked.

Christmas is the ideal time to start flooding the world with love. Let love be your inspiration and guide and you will find yourself a co-worker of God in healing and uplifting the community where God has placed you.

God of love, through Jesus Christ I put myself under Your command as an instrument of Your love in the world. *Amen.*

The Glory of God

The Word became flesh and made His dwelling among us. We have seen His glory, the glory of the One and Only, who came from the Father, full of grace and truth.

~ JOHN 1:14

While preparations to celebrate Christmas are in full swing across the whole world, we are reminded of the fact that Jesus took on the form of man. Through this, God revealed the highest meaning of love to mankind.

In a cruel world, where there was so little compassion, so much indifference and contempt for human rights and truth, God realized that the only way to bring His message to mankind was by doing it personally. The Son of God was thus born and came to live amongst us.

The world in which we live desperately needs love, compassion and caring. There is overwhelming evidence of violence, lack of involvement, cases of unconcealed cruelty. In many areas moral standards have declined, with the result that there is a fierce battle for survival, while people show little respect for Christian principles.

In this time of Advent, you have the opportunity to help and restore love, peace and stability in an unsettled world. You may puzzle about what you can do, but in the power of the Holy Spirit you can reflect the glory of God by allowing His love to flow through you, helping to lighten the burden of others. Do this and you will know the true meaning of Christmas.

Incarnate Word, help me to spread love, caring and compassion like You demonstrated to me. *Amen.*

Immanuel – God with Us

"The virgin will be with child and will give birth to a Son, and they will call Him Immanuel – which means 'God with us."

~ MATTHEW 1:23

Before Jesus came to earth, man was wasting away in the loneliness of sin. His greatest need was for the Divine touch. Christmas declares that God, through Jesus Christ, came to take us in His arms – never to let us go again.

Immanuel: God is with us to replace fear with exuberant joy! This world has become a maze of fear. Our anxiety complex is the fruit of sin. Since Adam fearfully hid from God in paradise, man has been experiencing countless uneasy fears. God's message at Christmas is, "Do not be afraid; I am with you."

Immanuel: God is with us to drive away the darkness with radiant light. Zechariah calls the Child of Bethlehem the Rising Sun "to shine on those living in darkness and in the shadow of death" (Luke 1:79). He comes to put an end to sin and to guide us into the wonderful light of God. Christmas gives us the right to pray, "Lead, kindly Light, amid the encircling gloom, lead Thou me on!"

Immanuel: God is with us to replace destructive hatred with self-sacrificing love. He came to teach us that hate can be conquered only by love. That love always triumphs. That if God loved us so much that He gave His Son for our sins, we too should love one another and forgive one another. In this way the Jesus Child is not just born in Bethlehem – but in our hearts. Not only is God with us, but we are with God!

Gloria in Excelsis Deo! Praise, praise the Lord! *Amen.*

Have You Accepted Him?

Today in the town of David a Savior has been born to you; He is Christ the Lord.

~ LUKE 2:11

Christmas prompts us once again to face the relentless demand to either accept or reject Christ as God's gift. Our choice determines our temporary and eternal well-being.

Many people are overwhelmed by the idea of giving themselves unconditionally to Christ. For some reason they are afraid to accept God's gift unconditionally.

They fear their own unworthiness or incompetence; they fear complete surrender; they are even convinced that their sins from the past make it impossible for them to accept God's gift. The good news of Christmas, declared by the angel, is that God gave His Son to be the Redeemer and Savior of humankind on the basis of God's love that encompasses and forgives all.

The angel made this announcement, not to a king or to the spiritual leaders of that time, but to simple and humble shepherds. This in itself should be an indication that God's Christmas gift, His Son, is for the whole world, also for you with your particular fears and needs.

If you hesitate to become a disciple of the living Redeemer, or if you feel undeserving, incompetent and afraid, just allow God's perfect love to fill your life. Christmas has come to deliver you from all guilt and fear. Accept Christ as your Savior – He is God's gift to you. Allow Him to guide you and to control your life.

Glory to God in the highest, and on earth, peace to men on whom His favor rests (Luke 2:14). *Amen.*

Never the Same Again

The shepherds returned, glorifying and praising God for all the things they had heard and seen, which were just as they had been told.

~ Luke 2:20

There are some experiences in life which are soon forgotten, and others which will be remembered for a long time. The events of that unforgettable night when the angel of the Lord visited them, were captured in the memories of the shepherds forever. They would undoubtedly speak about it for the rest of their lives.

One wonders if they ever met the Man whom they worshiped as a child in Bethlehem. We will never know. However, we can safely assume that the lives of these humble shepherds could never be the same after worshiping Him in the manger on that first Christmas night.

If you have had the enriching experience of true worship; if you have been spiritually inspired while you lifted your heart in worship and praise, it is something which will remain with you forever.

There may be dark moments of doubt and you may long to relive the glory of that worship. Once you have experienced it, however, it becomes an inextricable part of your life. It simply means identification with Christ and a renewal of your spiritual strength.

Lord Jesus, I worship You and identify with You. I thank You for the glorious new life that I have gained through Your birth, life, death and resurrection. *Amen.*

Christmas in Practice

May the God of hope fill you with all joy and peace as you trust in Him, so that you may overflow with hope by the power of the Holy Spirit.

~ ROMANS 15:13

Christ should not just remain in the manger for the Christian. He wants to bring us and, through His salvation, fill our hearts with pure joy and peace. That is the obvious meaning of Christmas.

Christmas is not done yet. It is not the last word about Christmas at all. Our spiritual laziness and self-centeredness lead us to delight in what Christmas holds for us personally. The Christmas message, however, is for "all people". Christmas should teach us to be light and salt to the world.

Our hearts should become a station for transmitting God's peace and joy to the world. We may not keep it to ourselves. God does not ask the impossible of us; "But you will receive power when the Holy Spirit comes on you; and you will be My witnesses" (Acts 1:8).

Give a small piece of the joy and peace of Christmas to those around you. Let them realize that you stood at the manger, and that the joy and peace emanating from it touched your heart and warmed it.

In this way your faith will grow and your joy and peace will not be limited to Christmas, but will break forth to enrich and elevate every day of the year.

Christ of every day and every night, let the peace of Christmas make the world a better place throughout the whole year. *Amen.*

Deal with Your Feelings of Guilt

You crown the year with Your bounty, and Your carts overflow with abundance.

~ PSALM 65:11

We are inclined to think that, because the year is almost over, its hold on our lives has lessened. The discouragement, failures and frustration suddenly do not seem so formidable when we look in expectation to the new year. The coming days are vivid with promises waiting to be fulfilled.

In spite of that, however, the influence of the past is still with us. Regardless of how noble our hopes for the coming year may be, we basically remain that which we have been over the past year, and no amount of wishful thinking can change this truth.

It could be discouraging were it not for the fact that Jesus demonstrated to His disciples how to deal with the past. In reviewing the past year under the guidance of the Holy Spirit, you will see the dark valleys of disappointment and dejection, but also the summits of inspiration. You can learn from both these experiences.

When you have evaluated the past year, rejoice in it and find further inspiration in everything that is Christian, true and noble. When the ghosts of your failures and sins torment you, ask God's forgiveness for the times when you were disobedient to Him.

Then you must forgive yourself and not enter the new year with feelings of guilt. Do not allow thoughts of the past to cast a shadow over the beauty and happiness of the present and the future.

Holy Spirit of God, let me review the past year with equilibrium, and let me take the good from it and build on it in the new year. *Amen.*

Peace Until the End

"I am the Alpha and the Omega," says the Lord God, "who is, and who was, and who is to come, the Almighty."

~ REVELATION 1:8

And so we near the end of the old year. There are many things we are ashamed of, but many that we are thankful for. There are regrets for missed opportunities, but we have received so much grace from God. The year brought grief, but also joy; defeat, but also victory; storms, but also sunshine.

God is still our Father, a privilege beyond compare. Let us, therefore, count our blessings today, knowing that He remains constant – yesterday, today, and forever.

You are richer today than you were yesterday if you smiled often; gave something of yourself to others; forgave your enemies; made new friends; turned problems into opportunities.

You are richer today than you were yesterday if you noticed God's handiwork; if you learned what is really important in life; if you have a little more patience with others' faults.

You are richer today if a child smiled at you, a dog licked your hand, if you looked for the best in others, and if you gave the best of yourself to others and to God. Then you can enter the new year secure in His love.

Eternal God, I thank You for guiding me through another year and for assuring me that You will never abandon or forsake me. *Amen.*

Year-End Meditation

"So do not fear, for I am with you; do not be dismayed, for I am your God. I will strengthen you and help you; I will uphold you with My righteous right hand."

~ Isaiah 41:10

When the year draws to a close, one needs to look back and review the past year. Unfortunately, for many people this means concentrating on failures, disappointments and other setbacks. This causes them to face the future with fear and hesitation.

Meditating on the past definitely has its place in your life, but it must be done constructively. You should develop the ability to learn from your mistakes, without groaning under their burden when you open up feelings of guilt. Similarly, when you think about the successes of the past, it is no excuse to rest on your laurels. It should serve as inspiration to take you to even greater heights.

After you have reviewed the events of the past year, it is essential for you to decide to meet the new year in the intimate company of the living Christ. Allow Him to be your Counselor and Guide. Let your mind be sensitive to the whisperings of the Holy Spirit and resolve to be unconditionally obedient to Him.

In so doing, you can rest assured that, regardless of what happens in your life, you can face the future with confidence, assured of the peace that comes from God alone.

Eternal God, thank You for the assurance at the end of this year, that You are always with us and that You will hold us in Your hand. *Amen.*

All's Well that Ends Well

Give thanks to the LORD, for He is good, His love endures forever.

~ PSALM 106:1

I know to Whom I have entrusted myself, even when my light turns to darkness. I know the Rock on Whom I have built, He is the One Who is my salvation.

With these words we leave the old year behind and enter into the new year. Now, in the last moments of this year, we can see the complete journey God mapped out for us this past year. We praise Him for every step of our pilgrimage, because He loved us all the way.

There is much for which we have to beg forgiveness: precious hours that we wasted, love we withheld, prayers we never prayed, opportunities we neglected. There are also innumerable reasons why we can thank our Lord: for protection; for healing; for support; for our daily bread.

May we find inspiration in the words of Marie Louise Haskins, "Put your weak hand in the mighty hand of God, then step out into the dark with courage. It will be far better for you than a light, and safer than a familiar road."

We bring You our abundant praise for the good year that we had, Lord. We enter the future holding Your powerful yet loving hand. *Amen.*